A49 an asian spirit in contemporary design

A49 an asian spirit in contemporary design

Architects 49

Publishing

Published in Australia in 2009 by
The Images Publishing Group Pty Ltd
ABN 89 059 734 431
6 Bastow Place, Mulgrave, Victoria 3170, Australia
Tel: +61 3 9561 5544 Fax: +61 3 9561 4860
books@imagespublishing.com
www.imagespublishing.com

Copyright © The Images Publishing Group Pty Ltd 2009
The Images Publishing Group Reference Number: 816

All rights reserved. Apart from any fair dealing for the purposes
of private study, research, criticism or review as permitted under
the Copyright Act, no part of this publication may be reproduced,
stored in a retrieval system or transmitted in any form by any means,
electronic, mechanical, photocopying, recording or otherwise, without
the written permission of the publisher.

A Cataloguing-in-Publication record for this title is available from
the National Library of Australia

ISBN: 978 1 86470 322 1

Edited by Robyn Beaver and Beth Browne

Designed by The Graphic Image Studio Pty Ltd, Mulgrave, Australia
www.tgis.com.au

Pre-publishing services by Splitting Image Colour Studio Pty Ltd, Australia
Printed on 150gsm Hannoart Silk Matt paper by Everbest Printing Co. Ltd.,
in Hong Kong/China

IMAGES has included on its website a page for special notices
in relation to this and our other publications.
Please visit www.imagespublishing.com.

Contents

Foreword	9
by Craig W. Hartman	
Preface	10
by Nithi Sthapitanonda	
Introduction	11
by Prabhakorn Vadanyakul	
Architecture in Context II: The Work of Architects 49 from 2002 to 2007	12
by Chaiyosh Isavorapant	

Architects 49

Honda Showroom	18
The 49 Terrace	22
Subaru 3S Center	26
Hua Hin Boulevard	30
Central World	32
Central Plaza Khon Kaen	38
The Gateway Ekamai	40
IMAGIMAX	42
T.C. Pharmaceutical Office	44
Siam Winery Trading Plus Office & Warehouse	50
K1 Computer Center	52
S1 Data Center	54
Bangkok Airways New Office	56
The Embassy of The Kingdom of The Netherlands	58
MCOT Operation Building	62
MCOT Complex	64
NIKS (Thailand) Head Office	71
Poh Teck Tung Foundation	72
Ocean Newline Office & Residence	74
I.P. Trading	76
SET Multipurpose Building	78
Royal Archive	80
Pipattanasin Office Building	82
Energy Complex	86
The Thai Red Cross Society Museum	92
Thailand Cultural Center	94
Cementhai Building Products Gallery	98
SCG Experience	102
Mae Fah Luang University	104
The Bhumirak Dhamachart, The Royal Nature Conservation Center	108
Surat Osathanugrah Library	110
Southeast Asian Ceramics Museum	114
Pongthip Osathanugrah Communication Arts Complex	118
Rajini School	122
Bangkok University Landmark Complex	124
Mahidol University Technology Innovation Center & Main Auditorium	128
Faculty of Arts, Mahidol University	134
Pine Valley Golf Resort & Country Club	136
The Royal Bangkok Sports Club	138

The Tubkaak Krabi Boutique Resort	140
Mission Hills Phuket Golf Resort & Spa	146
Sofitel Patong	150
Maldives Resort & Spa	152
The Funama Resort & Spa	153
The Lonudhua Resort & Spa	154
The Maavela Resort & Spa	155
Koh Kood Resort	156
Phuket Renaissance	158
Jumeirah Phuket Private Island	162
Pullman Bangkok King Power	166
Holiday Inn Express	172
Red Mountain	174
Oasis at Mulberry	178
Bukit Gita Bayu	180
Samui Pavilion	182
Cocoon Life Style	184
Cheras Residential Development	186
The Peak	188
The Clover	190
Jumeirah Park Apartments	192
Urbana Langsuan	194
The Fraser Suites Urbana Sathorn	196
SK41 Condominium	198
Athenee Place	200
The Emporio	202
Wireless Road Project	204
King Power Complex	208
Siam Square Commercial Development	220
Waterfront Development at Khlong Toei	222
Land & Houses Urban Development at Chiang Mai	224
The Danet Gateway	226
Thu Thiem New Urban Area	230
Wat Pa Sunantawanaram	232
Maharattanaviharnkot Wat Pra Dhammakaya	234
World Peace Valley	236
Guan Yin Shrine	238
Wat Pa Sunantawanaram Pagoda	240
Pra Bhothiyanathera Pagoda	240
Wat Pah Nikhotharam Pagoda	241
Mahavihard Pramongkol Thepmunee Memorial	241
Baan Sukhumvit 38	244
Baan Lat Phrao	248
Baan Muang Thong 3	252
Baan Windmill	256
Baan Hua Hin	260

Interior Architects 49

Central World	266
Ramayana Restaurant	270

King Power Headquarters	272
Bangkok University Landmark Complex	274
Dholhiyadhoo Resort & Spa	276
Pullman Bangkok King Power Hotel	278
So Bangkok	280
Seri Tanjung Penang Condominium	282
Aksra Theatre	284
House Design	286

Landscape Architects 49

Central World	292
King Power Complex	296
MCOT Complex	300
TALA 2007	302
The Tubkaak Krabi Boutique Resort	304
Domus	308
Prime Nature Villa Hua Hin	312
Prime Nature Villa On Nuch	316
Residential Compound at Sukumvit 16	318
Garden Design for Private Residences	322
Master Planning	328

Graphic 49

Logo Design	334
Devarana Spa	336
Suvarnabhumi Museum Shop	337
Savoury Gastrocafe	338
Alila	339
Bank of Ayudhya	340
TMB Bank	342
Government Housing Bank	344
MCOT Complex	346
CP Lotus Superstore, Super Brand Mall, Shanghai	347
Central World Office Tower and Shopping Complex	348
Thailand Creative and Design Center (TCDC)	352
King Power Complex: Headquarters, Duty Free Shops, Joe Louis Puppet Show, Ramayana Restaurants, and Pullman Hotel	354

49 Lighting Design Consultants 356

Appendix

Project Chronology	364
Project Data	378
Honors and Awards	392
Bibliography	393
Firm Profile	395
Principals' Biographies	396
49Group	400
Photography Credits	418
Acknowledgments	419
Index	420

Foreword

For nearly twenty years, Architects 49 and Skidmore, Owings & Merrill have exchanged staff members and shared ideas ranging from culture to architecture and technology. Without hesitation, I refer to Nithi Sthapitanonda, President of A49, as the most important architect in Thailand. Along with his partners, he has earned the respect of—and worked with—individuals at the highest level of government and industry, while simultaneously cultivating a team that is very much like a family. Equipped with the latest and most sophisticated computer-aided design and information technology, A49 has set a benchmark for design innovation. The firm's talented staff is uniformly passionate about architecture, the environment, and urban design.

A49's office, which Nithi himself designed, expresses the firm's ethos perhaps better than words. It is a beautiful, light-filled three-story building constructed of modest materials—concrete, wood, and glass—located on an intimate Bangkok soi, a small street. The building is punctuated by light courts and gardens, which serve as gathering places for the employees. No doubt this stimulating environment provides them with the inspiration to create such award-winning work as Chiang Mai's Rimtai Saitarn housing project and the Ministry of Foreign Affairs in Bangkok, both distinctive contributions to contemporary Thai architecture.

Nithi and his partners have modeled A49 after modern American architectural firms, including SOM, that bring together the disciplines of architecture, urban planning, interior design, and engineering under one roof. Steadfast believers in multi-disciplinary, collaborative design, the A49 partners work through a studio approach. The result is the highest level of sensitivity given to every detail from a project's conception through documentation.

Undoubtedly, Nithi Sthapitanonda and his Architects 49 will continue to bring pride to Thailand and the discipline of architecture for many years to come. It is with the greatest pleasure and privilege that I introduce this monograph—a comprehensive survey of quality, creativity, and innovation.

Craig W. Hartman, FAIA
Partner in Charge of Design
Skidmore, Owings & Merrill LLP, San Francisco

Preface

In 2008, Architects 49 and its affiliated firms in the 49 Group celebrate the 25th anniversary of the firm's establishment. On this occasion we have brought together another collection of our works, intended to complement our 2002 volume *Architects 49: the Master Architect Series V*, which was also produced by The Images Publishing Group of Australia.

Since that first book was published, the 49 Group has grown steadily, adding many new affiliated companies. The Group is now one of the largest and most multi-disciplinary architectural and engineering practices in Southeast Asia, with full proficiency in every building-related field. Our projects span a wide range of types—from houses, resorts and hotels, to high-rises, museums, and education facilities.

During the past eight years we have designed many works in Thailand and throughout Asia that we believe are significant and worth introducing to readers. These projects resulted from much determination and effort on the part of our architects and engineers. Through this book we hope to share our design knowledge and philosophy, allowing readers to gain a full understanding of each project.

Today the 49 Group's 12 firms include more than 350 architects, interior designers, landscape architects, graphic designers, lighting design architects, and engineers in building-related fields. We are motivated by a shared philosophy and working standards, which are reflected in the projects in this book.

The fields of architecture and engineering are increasingly borderless. This is resulting in greater international competition as well as many new opportunities. With this in mind, the 49 Group is strengthening its working systems, human resources, and communications. We do more and more work in places such as Singapore, Malaysia, Vietnam, China, Abu Dhabi, and Bhutan. Our service level is geared toward an international clientele.

We hope that this book will help our colleagues and clients overseas to learn more about our projects in Thailand, while giving readers here the opportunity to see more of our work abroad. We especially hope that this book will benefit students, inspire greater collaboration between the architectural and engineering communities, and contribute to the development of these professions in Thailand.

I would like to express my gratitude to all those who have contributed to making this book, particularly to the clients, without whom these projects could not have been accomplished.

Nithi Sthapitanonda
President
Hon. FAIA, Hon. FJIA

Introduction – Architects 49

Beyond making people aware of Architects 49's works, this volume has the additional purpose of fostering an understanding of A49's principles, purposes, and evolution in architectural design concepts since its beginnings 25 years ago.

The works presented here reflect how architectural design in Thailand has changed generally through various eras and with particular kinds of projects.

This volume follows our first monograph, published more than a decade ago. The reader will note how the evolution of technology has improved the clarity and sharpness of architectural design presentations to clients, giving a highly realistic idea of how a structure and its elements will look on completion, thereby facilitating client decisions. But, ultimately, it is the architect's concepts that drive developments in architectural design.

This second volume includes a wide variety of projects in type and size. However, A49 gives the same degree of importance to design with all projects, regardless of size or type. This is the case because, according to our philosophy, ideas cannot be measured in size, nor can architectural projects. Nor does size define the value of a structure.

To demonstrate to readers how A49 actually works, this volume shows the complete design process followed by A49's architects from beginning to end, from concept to blueprints, including the various media used in presenting proposals to clients, as well as the finished results.

A49 intends to publish future monographs to record the changes in architecture through future eras and to show that architecture is compatible with nature—neither a danger, nor a risk, and nor does it consume excess resources. Everyone must stop and think about this.

A49 will continue to be an organization governed by a commitment to the principle of preeminent quality.

Prabhakorn Vadanyakul
Managing Director

Architecture in Context II: The Work of Architects 49 from 2002 to 2007

To fully understand the role of Architects 49 within Thailand's architectural scene in the past five years, reviewing some social and economic conditions is inevitable. Although political instability is still one of the country's salient problems, the amount of investment by business in some areas is surprisingly on the rise. Foreign investments in various sectors show substantial growth and have had a strong impact on the overall economic system. For example, real estate at the center of Bangkok became a focus point in the eyes of foreign investors.

Another area of business that is gradually growing and becoming one of the most important sources of national income is tourism. Thailand has been among the world's top tourist destinations for decades. Reports from the government National Economic and Social Development Board have shown that Thailand's gross domestic product (GDP) in 2007 grew by 5.1 percent, improving from 4.5 percent in the previous year. The consumption rate in various sectors such as hotels, restaurants, and real estate is expanding at a satisfactory rate. These areas of business are of vital importance to the architecture and construction sectors. Along with foreign investments, the influx of production and construction technology from foreign sources has enhanced the potential of how architectural spaces could be articulated. The qualitative limitations imposed by materials and construction techniques, which have been serious constraints for architects for many years, seemed to be decreasing.

Since its founding in 1983, Architects 49 has been working in a vibrant and volatile economic environment, especially in the period between 2002 and 2007, which covers most of the projects shown in this monograph. The group's additional companies such as IA49, focusing on interior design, and AE49 with ME49 responsible for engineering design, add to the strength of the group that has been building over the years. The group is now capable of undertaking architectural projects from master planning, architectural and landscape design, and construction management through to corporate graphics. The emergence of Architects 49 International in 2006 is the group's effort to expand its activities to the world scene. In addition, as the largest architectural design office in Thailand, the firm is undertaking important projects in the kingdom in all areas. From a residence for a single family to resorts with high-end amenities, from cultural centers and museums to business offices and condominiums, Architects 49's design is proven by many successful projects in a variety of scales in and outside the country. Seen in this light, a review of the role of Architects 49 is also an examination of the development of contemporary Thai architecture and the international role of Thai architects.

The first substantial area of focus for Architects 49 was the residential sector. The firm has been responsible for residential projects that continue to pioneer not only in terms of architectural form, but also in ways of living. A series of recently built houses illustrate a way of life that is the outcome of the established opposition of nature and the urban realm. At one of these houses, Baan Lat Phrao in the midst of Bangkok, the opposition was interpreted into courtyard gardens applied in various dimensions and positions. These spaces generate a mediated transition between each function and between each unit through the light glass walls. Separated from structural columns, the glass's translucency allows a clear view while reflecting spaces all around.

At Baan Sukhumvit 38 and Baan Windmill, also in Bangkok, the intersection of nature and the city was planned as a mediated space that evolved into a courtyard adjacent to a veranda. The courtyard and veranda accentuate the meaning of transitional spaces and activate possibilities for interaction among the residents. Moreover, the concept of interplay between courtyards and verandas is derived directly from indigenous Thai architecture that signifies the family value of living together closely. This blurs the concept of clearly defined functional areas, which has occupied residential design in Thailand for many years. The idea is further emphasized at Baan Patong in Phuket, an island in the south of Thailand. In this house, courtyards and verandas play a vital role in space articulation because of their semi-open characteristic that allows most of the living areas to be utilized. These spaces suggest a way of living with less specific functions in certain areas while profiting from Phuket's surrounding. The island has been acknowledged on the international scene for its beautiful beaches and islands that are scattered with luxurious hotels and restaurants—a haven for activities such as diving, surfing, or yachting. The house, owned by a German and Bangladeshi couple, combines programs of residential areas with guest houses for friends. Architects 49 encouraged a binary program that utilized the familiar elements of courtyard and veranda in a distinctive way.

As one of the largest sources of national income for several decades, the expansion of the tourist sector has been well observed. The activities related directly to tourism—the hotel and restaurant sector—expanded 11.2 percent in 2008 over the year before. One of Architects 49's most interesting projects within this sector is the much-praised Tubkaak Boutique Resort in Krabi, a beach province in the south of Thailand. In this small-scale resort (44 rooms), preservation of the existing landscape, including beautiful trees, was a prerequisite for the overall planning and landscape design. Most of the buildings face toward the beach with a picturesque row of 13 islands, which becomes a vantage point for each unit. A densely forested mountain, designated as a national park, at the rear of the site provides fresh air, while fresh water from the existing creek is used as water supply. The building form is related to vernacular architecture and local fishing boats with its large gable roof covering most of the interior space. The overall planning, through subtle bushes and rows of trees, veils each building to create its own private area with a calm and serene surrounding.

Beside resorts, another type of building related to tourism is a relatively recent creation: the duty-free shop outside an airport. The King Power Duty Free Shop is a distinctive project in this category. Architects 49 interpreted the program as a gateway embracing customers with an impressive glass and steel dome. The interior space beneath the dome activates the visitor's activities with an almost weightless appearance with glittering clear light. After a warm welcome, customers ascend through glass elevators or escalators to the duty-free retail spaces, restaurants, and theater at the second, third, and fourth floors respectively. The entrance dome's brightness and the gleaming interior spaces enhance the experience of shopping that is part of the new tourist culture. This "brand culture" phenomenon, spread throughout the world, means that for some tourists, traveling is merely the means to an end—the enjoyment of brand-name merchandise shopping.

In the realm of education and cultural activities, an important concept has emerged that has redefined the meaning of knowledge. The effect of internet communications and websites such as Wikipedia, where any text can be written and rewritten at will, shakes the roots of knowledge as a whole. Rather than respecting a higher truth, knowledge is based more and more on certain points of view and thus can be varied accordingly. This idea could be well illustrated in Thailand by the emergence of various kinds of personal museums as an "alternative" version of knowledge in competing with the "official" or governmental one.

Within this context, the Southeast Asian Ceramics Museum is such an institution with an "alternative" point of view. As the museum's name suggests, this is a museum covering an area with a diversity of culture and a wide historical span. Architects 49 buried most of this small building underground and covered the crescendo concrete roof with lawns of green grass. To enter the building, the visitor has to step down from the pedestrian level to an area similar to a natural cave with a wall of waterfall. An experience of walking through this area signifies man returning from hunting and gathering in an early stage of human civilization. The interior space is dimly lit under a low ceiling.

This metaphoric cave space lets natural light penetrate through rhythmically placed ceiling openings on the uneven roof structure. The ensuing contrast between exterior and interior spaces defines an experience of living with nature in which man gains his self-orientation within the earth and sky while constructing his own identity. One of the very first outcomes was ceramics, evidence of human civilization. By this metaphor, the architecture encourages viewers to contemplate their own version of understanding the subject rather than trying to pursue any established ideas.

Interestingly, this museum is situated adjacent to the central library of the privately owned Bangkok University. In contrast to the museum, the library stands up high with a main entrance brightly lit under a glass dome. This dome accommodates a connecting ramp approach to each floor, which functions as the main circulation and signifies the meaning of the building: the ascent of man. The significance of the library and the connecting museum is clear: man gained his knowledge from the past and ascended to a higher intellect. And vice versa, one has to learn from the past to understand oneself. This interpretation of human knowledge was so successful that a number of educational projects completed subsequently around the country revealed the success of Architects 49's design strategy within this field.

The interplay between the concept of the man-made environment and its context is often confused when considering the situation of urban life. As a well-established notion, physical and intangible factors are both necessary in the understanding of any urban area. In the case of The 49 Terrace, a small shopping complex at the center of Bangkok, the relationship of these two factors was explored in terms of "lifestyle." The program was to provide a shelter for the "lifestyle" aspects: café, fusion food restaurants, boutique spas, pet shops, paper craft merchandising, and so on. Architects 49 responded to this program by creating retail spaces and common spaces in terms of the interplay between interior and exterior spaces. The interior spaces are equalized but further differentiated from mediated spaces such as terraces, bridges, and stairs. These open and semi-covered transition areas are produced to resolve and enrich the overlay of interacting programs. The result is a complex space calibrated to accentuate the subtle relationships between inside and outside. And surprisingly, the open space also embraced the sky at its most beautiful, despite the context of high-rise buildings.

Another area that belongs to the urban context and is a substantial part of the work of Architects 49 is office buildings. For example, the Mass Communication Organization of Thailand (MCOT) complex evolved from the renovation of existing buildings to the design of new buildings. The master plan accommodated all evolving phases so that the buildings work together as a whole and respond to each other's presence. The composition of shining white brise soleils and metal cladding on each façade clearly defines exterior and interior spaces while suggesting various kinds of working areas inside. In relation to practical problems such as energy conservation, climatic response, and even material scales and construction methods, the buildings suggest the efficiency of the working experiences inside.

Besides office buildings, high-rise condominiums, and hotels are projects that allowed Architects 49 to develop their skills. Projects such as the Energy Complex office building, the Emporio Place condominium, and the Holiday Inn Express are among several buildings being undertaken. The urban contexts and building programs are synthesized into a variety of forms.

In recent years, Architects 49 has developed an interest in the area of non-commercial projects, especially religious buildings. The movement toward a re-thinking of Buddhist philosophy in Thailand has led to new kinds of ritual and habitation in religious life. It should not be surprising that new styles of architecture are integral to this movement. This difficult but successful interpretation is most notably illustrated in the hall of Wat Pa Sunanthawanaram at Kanchanaburi province, west of Bangkok. Situated at the foot of a small hill in the forest, the interior and exterior spaces of the hall are almost at the same scale. They are in balance and connected to each other by the open wooden façade. The space articulation allows both areas to function as a place of gathering and meditation, to heighten spiritual value, and be able to connect to each other during a service with a large number of attendants. The scale of building and its construction details thus provided a calm atmosphere, emphasizing the idea of the Buddhist philosophy of simplicity.

This introduction concludes with the emergence of the newly formed Architects 49 International on the world stage. Buildings designed by this firm have gradually appeared during the past five years. Fine examples among the projects undertaken are the master plan of The Danet Gateway in Abu Dhabi, and Jumeirah Park Apartments in Dubai, United Arab Emirates. Projects developing in Malaysia, Singapore, China, and the Maldives should be considered as an effort by the firm to cope with new kind of challenges.

Architects 49 is intentionally diverse in its abilities. Each design, embedded under specific circumstances, emerges into distinctive architectural forms and endless possibilities. Architects 49's interest in the context of each building differs and departs from any pre-existing ideas. The architectural practices are becoming more problem- and context-based, not only in terms of the appearance of buildings as a whole but also in terms of how they are perceived within their own environments.

Chaiyosh Isavorapant
Master of Fine Arts, Program in Design
Faculty of Art and Design, Rangsit University

A49

Architects 49

Honda Showroom

Location: Ekamai, Bangkok, Thailand
Client: Sukhumvit Honda Automobile
Area: 10,000 square meters
Year: 2003–2005

The Honda Showroom in Ekamai is situated on one of the busiest junctions in Bangkok. Parallel with an old office building to the east and a proposed park to the west, it is close to the Bangkok mass transit sky train station and a major bus terminal.

The architectural vision was to assist in bringing order to the highly complicated urban structure of this area of Bangkok.

The district is extremely congested due to road traffic, the bus terminal, and sky trains. The building's design emphasizes a visual connection with these other local functions.

The four-story building, with around 10,000 square meters of floor space, is divided into three main components: showroom, customer service, and parking lot and other services. The showroom, which features a curved curtain wall, is at the front of the building on the second floor, while customer service is on the first floor. The parking lot and other services are located behind the building.

Special attention was paid to the glazed connection system and vertical structures that are offset 30 millimeters from the glass. The design intent was to create a strong relationship between the building and its context, both visually and physically. The flow of pedestrian traffic is subtly diverted into the building, linking pedestrians to the park via the curved outline of the building. The showroom interior contains a large ceiling volume that appears to float at night, lending the building a strong character. The first level's 2.2-meter height offers a sense of intimacy in contrast to the double-height space on the second floor. The intention was to provide a comfortable human scale for both the building's users and passersby. Materials were chosen within the given project parameters and according to the needs for each space, with a view to reducing energy consumption in order to actively improve the urban community.

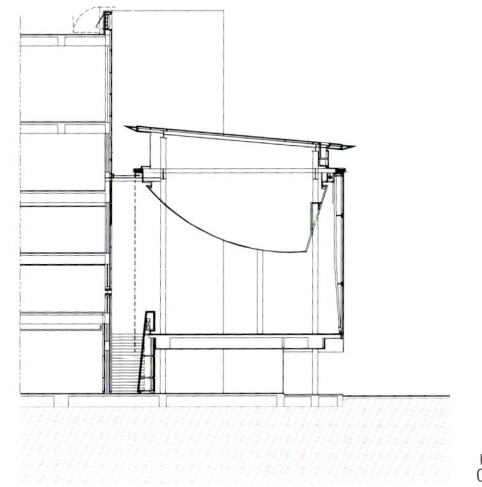

21

The 49 Terrace

Location: Sukhumvit 49, Bangkok, Thailand
Client: The 49 Terrace
Area: 1,885 square meters
Year: 2003–2005

A small neighborhood retail facility serving an upscale residential area, The 49 Terrace is a gathering place with a pleasant environment where people can meet and spend time shopping.

Three levels of retail shops and outdoor terraces surround a treed central opening court. Visual connection with the half-level connecting stairs provides unimpeded customer access to the retail outlets on the higher floor—all shops are clearly seen from the central courtyard space.

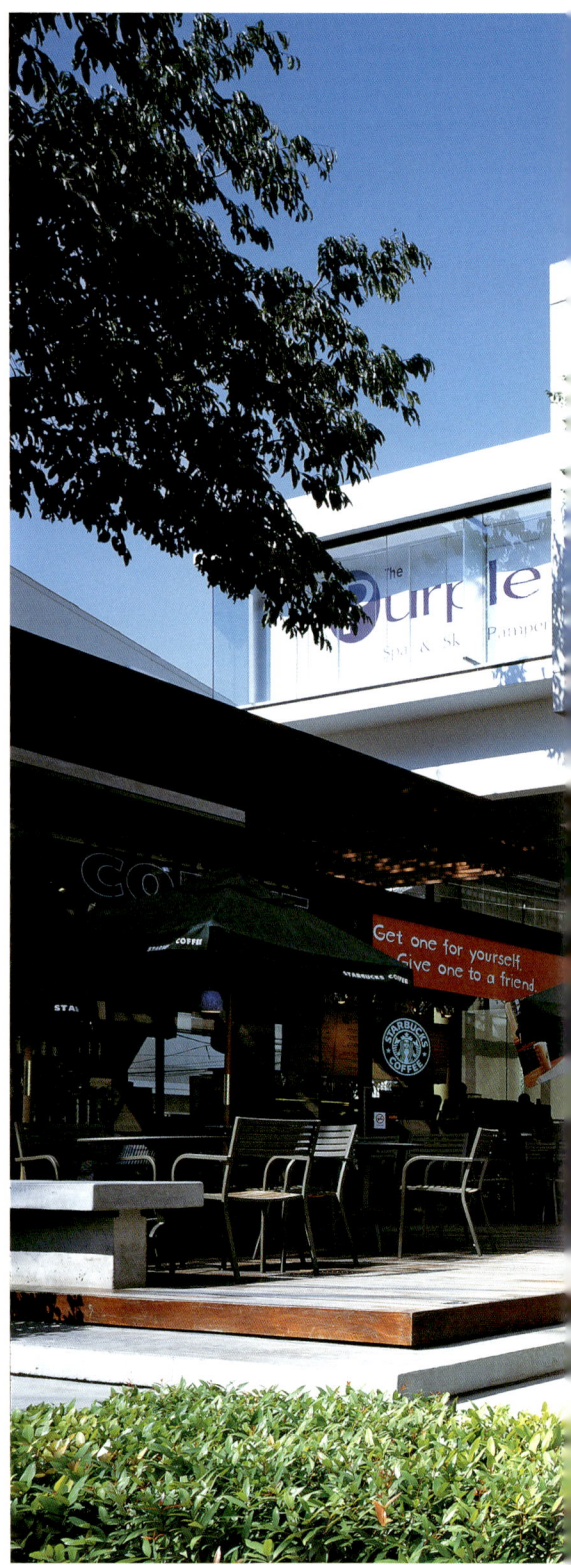

Multiple open spaces integrate with simple yet well-proportioned architecture.

Existing and newly planted trees are integrated into the design to preserve a degree of transparency while creating a screen-like quality from the street.

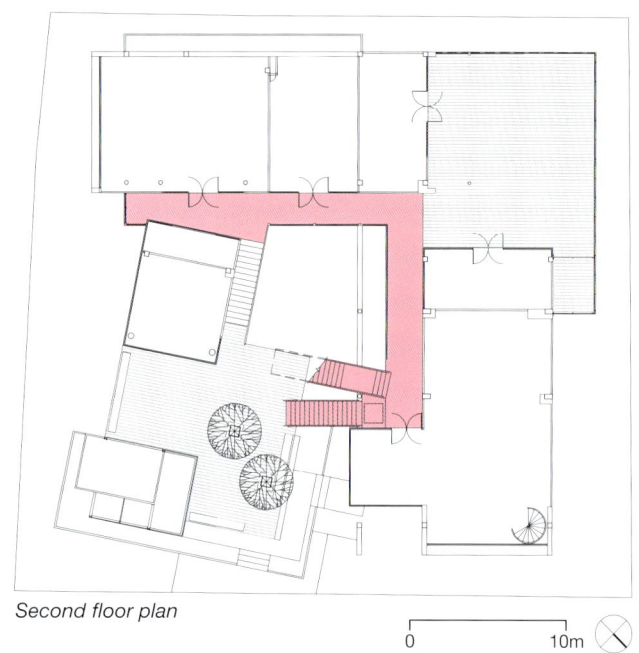

Second floor plan

0   10m

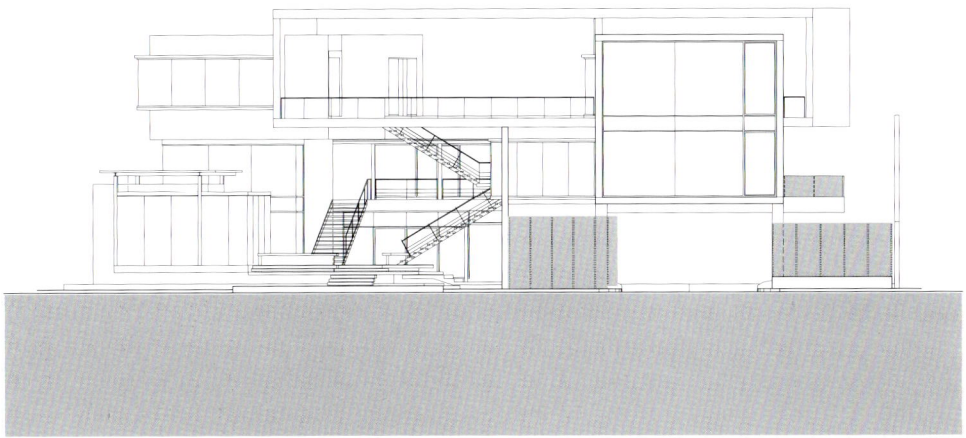

Subaru 3S Center

Location: Sukhaphiban Road, Bangkok, Thailand
Client: Motor Image Subaru (Thailand)
Area: 4,390 square meters
Year: 2005–2006

Motor Image Subaru Thailand has achieved a milestone in Thailand with its first 3S Center, aimed at enhancing market appreciation via an integrated combination of showroom/service/spare parts (3S). The center is a world-class car facility offering not only a showroom, but additional functions such as a delivery room, demonstration area, and test track.

The center benefits from the rather narrow and long site. The test track takes advantage of the entire length of the site, allowing slalom and speed driving to be efficiently tested. Following the city planning requirement, the center is split into two buildings. The three-story front building occupies most of the site's width. Housed in the first floor are the reception counter, the hexagonal special car gallery, the technological and accessory showcase, and a connection to the service center at the rear building. The second floor contains the main showroom, where 12 cars can be comfortably displayed, the training room, and the customer lounge area that overlooks the test track at the back of the site, allowing visitors to see the performance of the cars and to hear the roar of the engines. The second floor is connected by the void and continuous staircase to the third floor, where administration and sales offices are located with visual access to the main showroom area. While the rear building occupies less than half of the width, it stretches more than 100 meters along the length of the site, leaving the rest of the land for the test track. Accessed through the driveway underneath the front building, this long building houses the service counter, spare parts warehouse, and 12 service bays.

The design of the center originated from the hexagonal model often found in nature—a most efficient and physically powerful form that is also often found in many mechanical components, especially in automobiles.

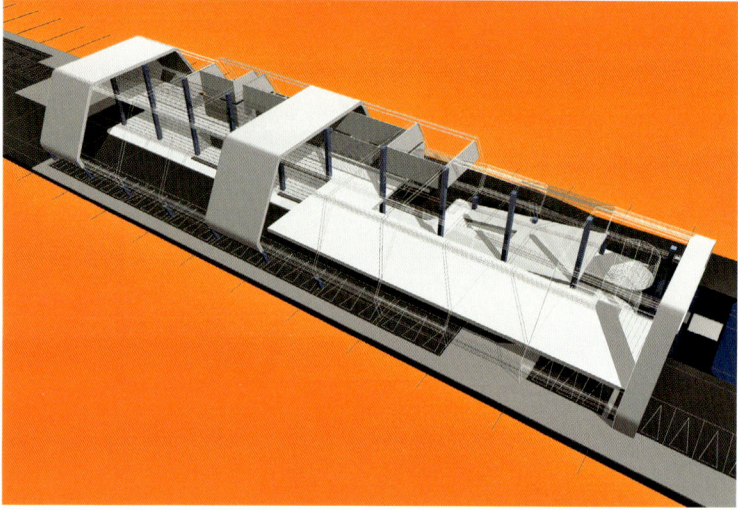

Coincidently echoing Subaru's 'Six Stars' trademark, the center's design bridges architecture and engineering and promotes a future vision where science and art are aesthetically balanced.

Hua Hin Boulevard

Location: Hua Hin, Prachuap Khiri Khan, Thailand
Area: 14,000 square meters
Year: 2005–2008

Located in the commercial area of Hua Hin, where every major attraction—including the legendary Hua Hin market—is within walking distance, Hua Hin Plaza offers a scale appropriate for its visitors.

The mid-size lifestyle shopping center, with a relaxing atmosphere and modern open-air retail spaces, devotes an outdoor area to a multipurpose plaza that serves various events both day and night. Along with these well-planned retail spaces, the center contains a restaurant, food court, supermarket, beer garden, coffee terrace, spa, and fitness facilities.

The architecture celebrates a connection to the sea, with wooden details and the simplicity of white concrete offering a welcoming feel.

The same architectural principles are applied to the seven-story condominium at the rear of the project. It has an L-shaped slab with a swimming pool on the second floor and space for parking on the basement and ground-floor levels.

Central World

Location: Ratchadamri Road, Bangkok, Thailand
Client: Central Pattana
Area: 440,000 square meters
Year: 2003–2006

Central World Plaza has re-emerged as a result of a renovation and addition to the former Bangkok World Trade Center, which has stood for almost 20 years. It is now the largest shopping center in Bangkok's best location.

Additions were made to various parts of the complex, including zone D (nine stories with a two-story basement), zone E (three stories with a two-story basement), and zone F (11 stories with a two-story basement). With an average of seven stories, it is a massive building with large and deep floor plates. The center can be accessed from many directions including the skywalk to the Bangkok mass transit system.

The design offers a variety of spatial experiences including unique multiple atriums, which provide a sense of direction while also allowing in natural daylight and promoting a feeling of openness.

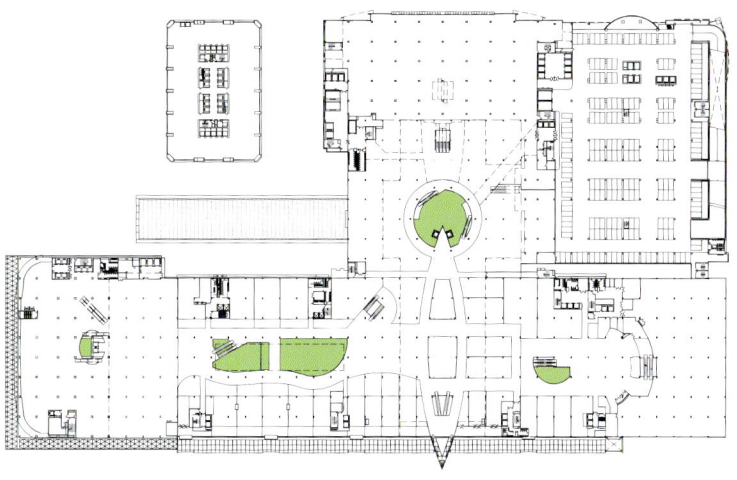

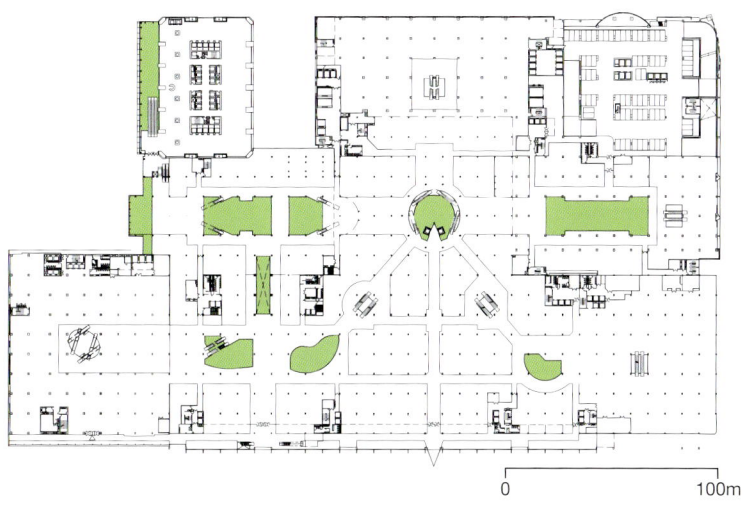

0 100m

To transform the large solid box, the new second-skin façade was wrapped around the lengthy elevation, which includes an escalator and space in between. The façade glitters and encourages movement toward the front plaza. This remarkable façade is the longest curtain wall in Thailand and fittingly introduces one of the world's finest multipurpose commercial complexes.

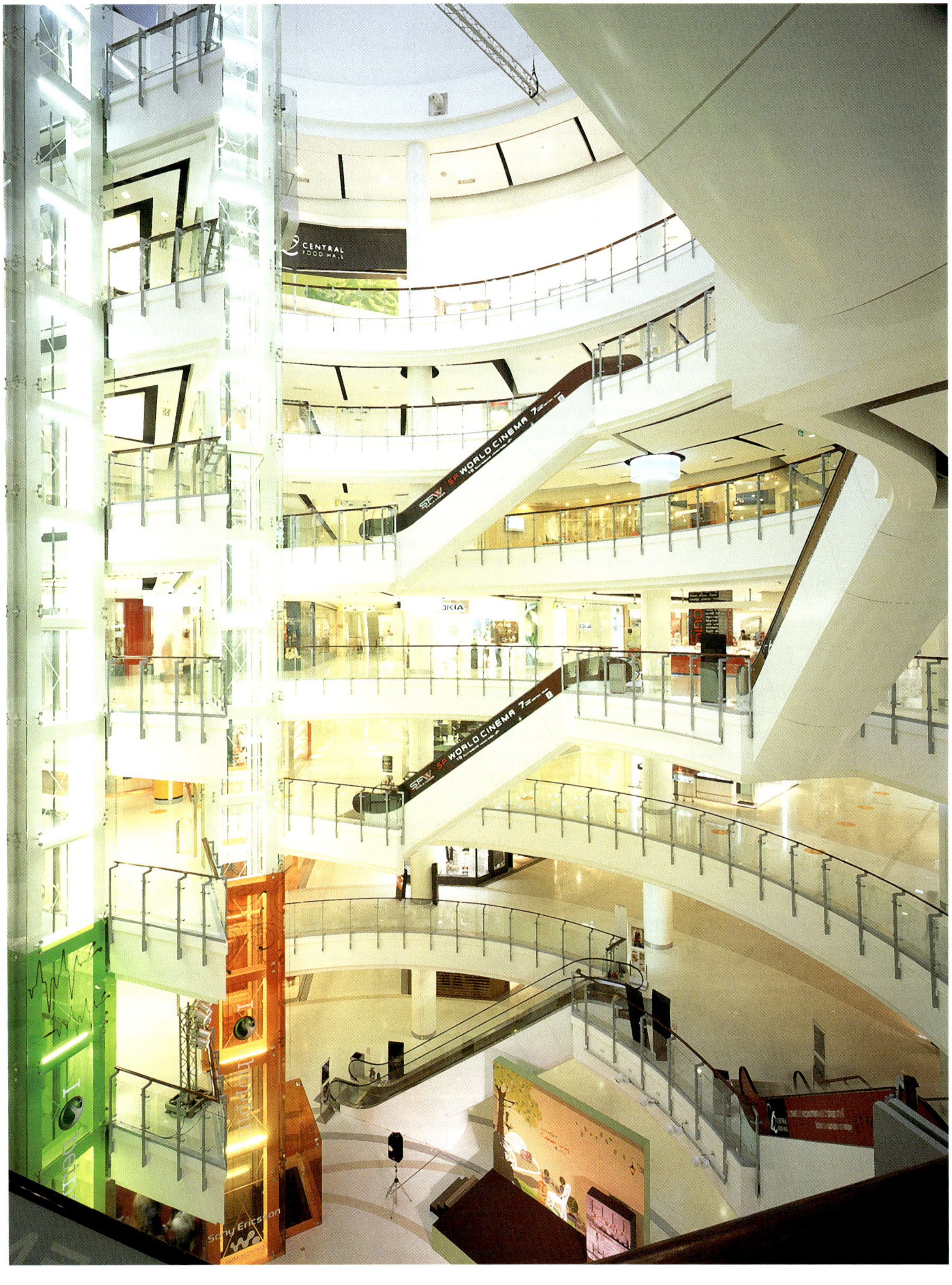
CENTRAL FOOD HALL
SF WORLD CINEMA
SF WORLD CINEMA
Sony Ericsson

Chinese New Year
mad about

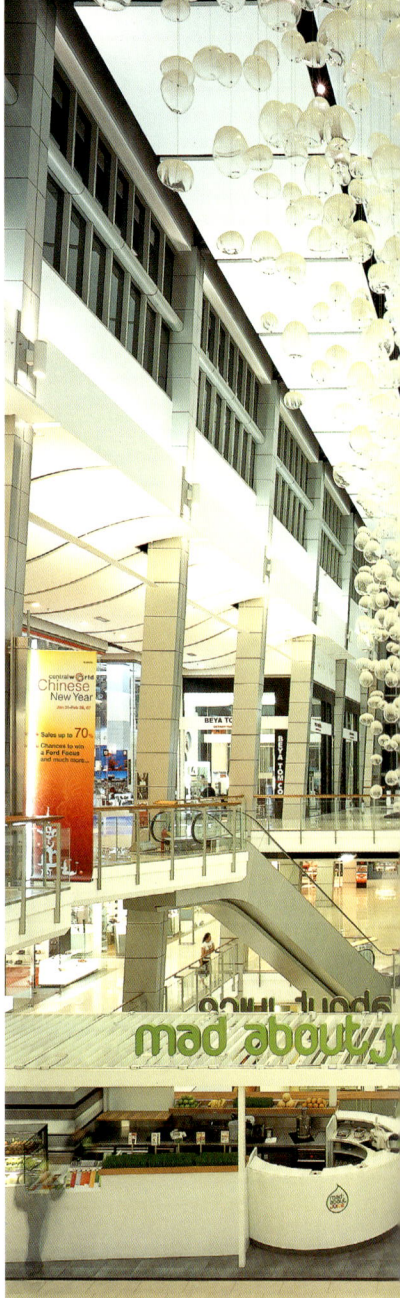

Chinese
New Year
Sales up to 70
Chances to win
a Ford Focus
and much more...

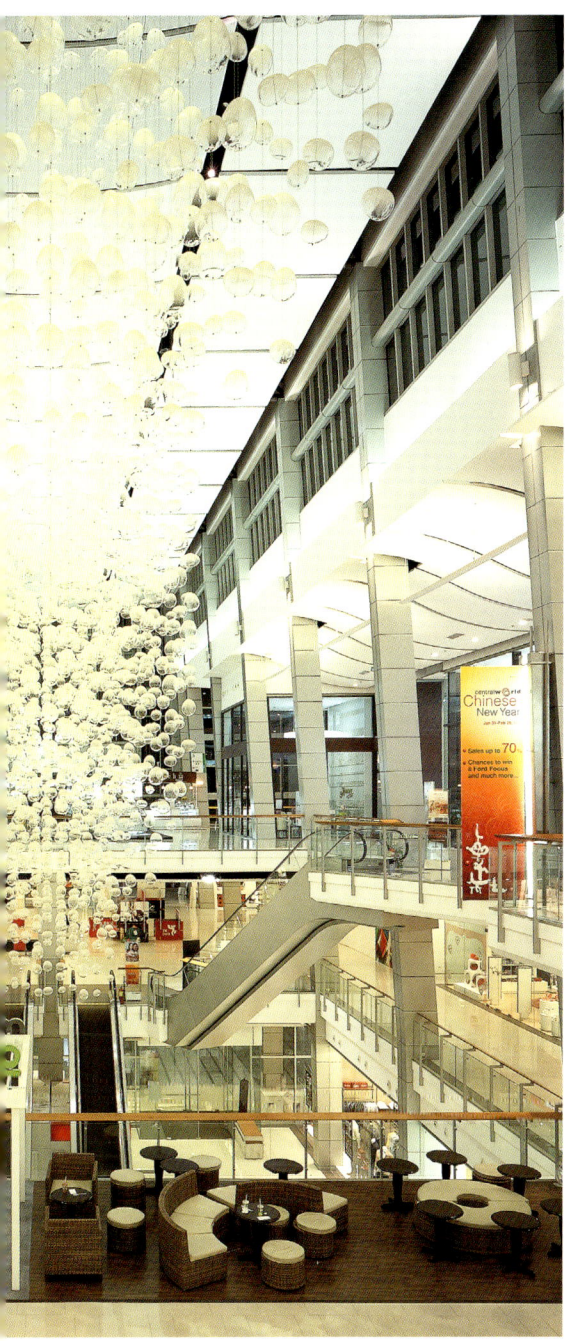

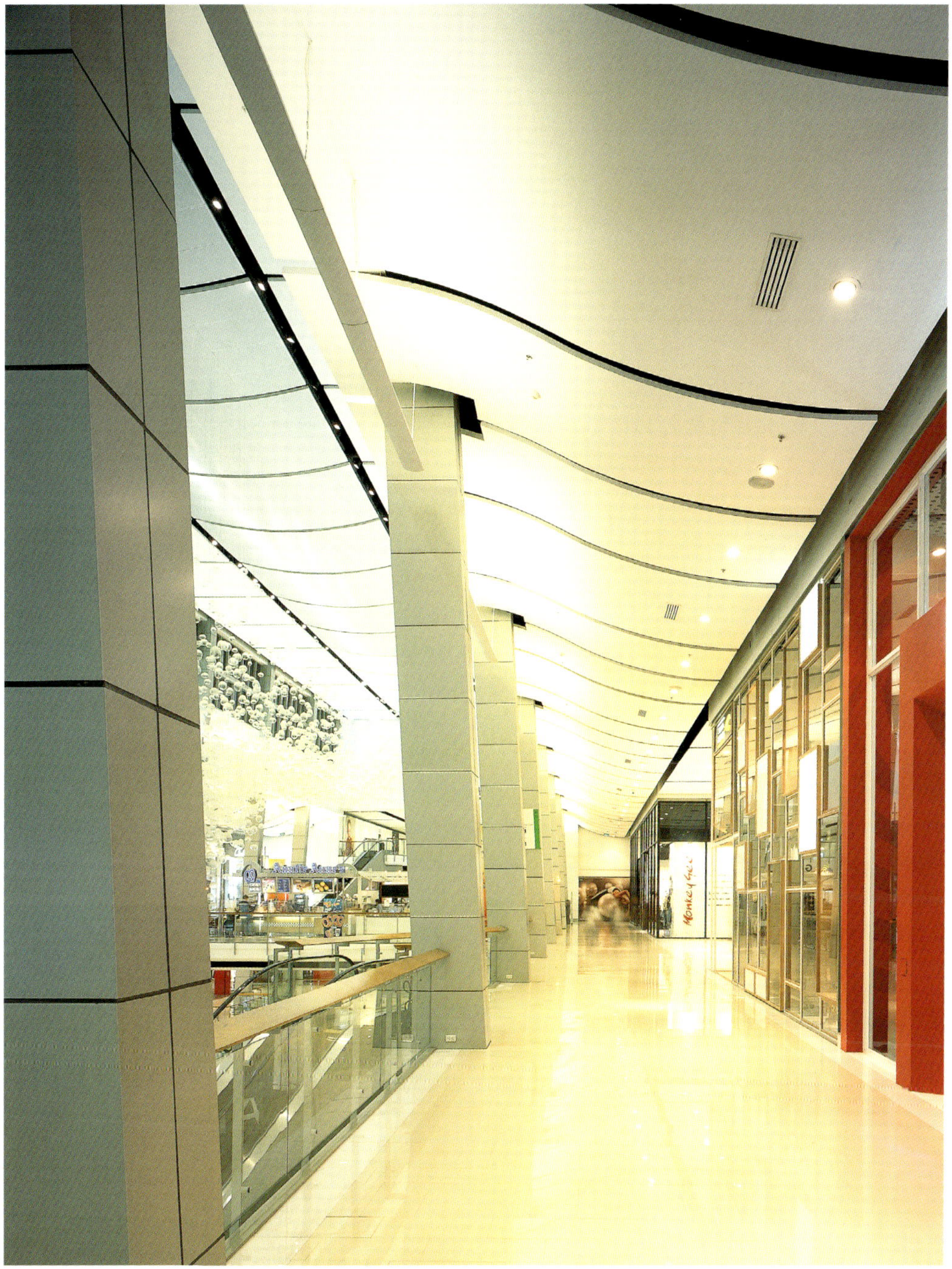

Central Plaza Khon Kaen

Location: Khon Kaen, Thailand
Client: Central Pattana
Area: 72,500 square meters
Year: 2008

This project is situated at the gateway of Khon Kaen, the portal city to Thailand's northeastern business district. The 80-hectare compound is located opposite a public park.

The 160,000-square-meter building is split into two functional structures. The front structure accommodates retail functions. The rear serves mainly as parking for 800 cars. Specialty functions, such as a fitness club and convention center, are located above the parking structure, leaving the lower parking area conveniently connected to the commercial floors. The commercial floors are organized by the classic "dumbbell" system where the anchor stores, such as B2S, Super Sport, Power Buy, and the food court, are placed at the end of the circulation trajectory. This arrangement attracts visitors and is an efficient use of the 80,000 square meters of sales space. The precise dimensions for the floor-to-floor space were determined following a workshop. The first floor is 5.2 meters high while the upper floors are 4.8 meters high; the average corridor width is 3 meters.

The project embraces the Isaan culture of northeast Thailand, which is evident in the articulation of intersecting corners. The woven pattern of handcrafted projects is distilled, enlarged, and dematerialized by details such as wire mesh and steel patterns. The woven details wrap around the anchor space with some areas exposed as outdoor space. The woven pattern then unfolds to become expressed elements of other parts of the project such as the entrance canopy and advertising banners.

The Gateway Ekamai

Location: Sukhumvit 42, Bangkok, Thailand
Client: Thai Red Cross Society
Area: 113,500 square meters
Year: 2008

The Gateway Ekamai is located at the heart of the Ekamai district, an area of increasing prominence on the eastern side of central Bangkok and home to condominiums, commercial buildings, and community malls.

The goals of this project were to create a one-stop shopping mall at the gateway to downtown Bangkok, to achieve the full income potential of the project to support the Thai Red Cross Society, and to fulfill the mission of promoting the welfare of Thai society. The center includes stores and two types of service facilities: a family and education center with a family and education convention hall, and an IT center.

The design reflects the unity and artistry of Thai culture. The exteriors and interiors blend harmoniously with the landscape, using textures from traditional woven handcrafts.

The concept of "Green is Life" is embodied in the shrubbery, trees, and other plants that complement the activities staged at the center and the stores in the mall. The greenery promotes a pleasing rustic environment for the center in its urban setting. The design of the open plaza provides access to the Sky Train and the center from adjacent areas. The project applies the green building concept through energy conservation, water management, using the maximum amount of natural energy sources, careful selection of building materials, ensuring an appropriate proportion of openings, and recycling waste and used materials.

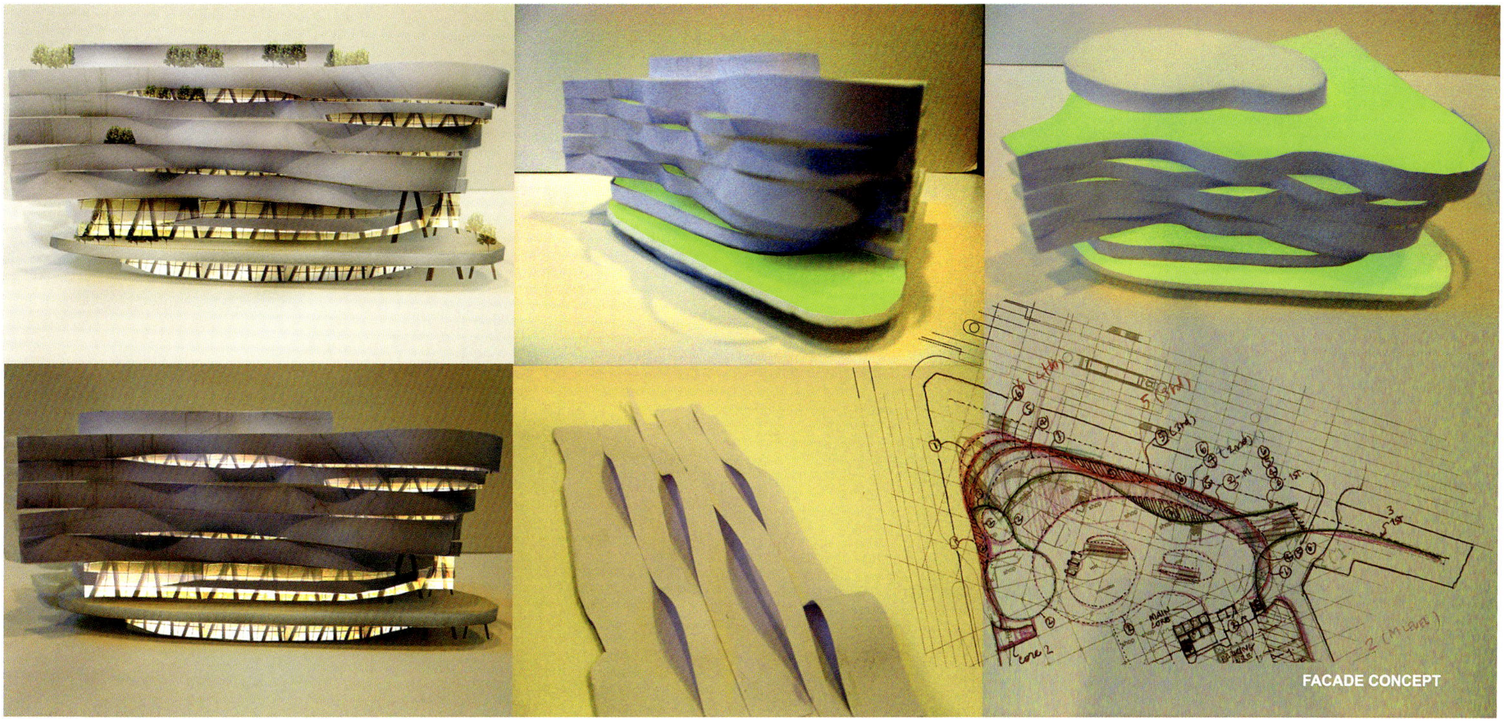

FACADE DESIGN CONCEPT
KEY WORD : **THAI SURFACE AND GREEN**

M (SECOND LEVEL / BTS LINKAGE)

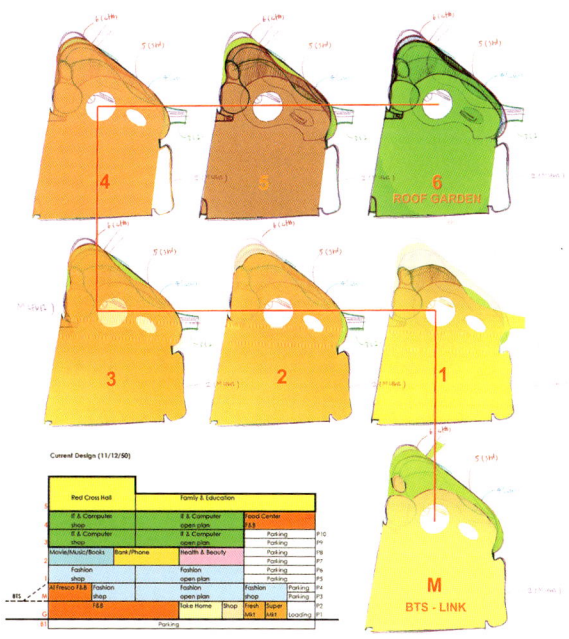

IMAGIMAX

Location: Narathiwas Rajanakarindra Road, Bangkok, Thailand
Client: Saksiri Koshapasharin
Area: 11,179 square meters
Year: 2003–2006

Located on a rather wide site on the Narathiwas Rajanakarindra Road, this project benefits from the site's geography in combination with a number of established trees.

The building is fully equipped for the business and study of animation. Its three- to five-story volumes with modern, simple, and calm façades express the technology inherent in the business.

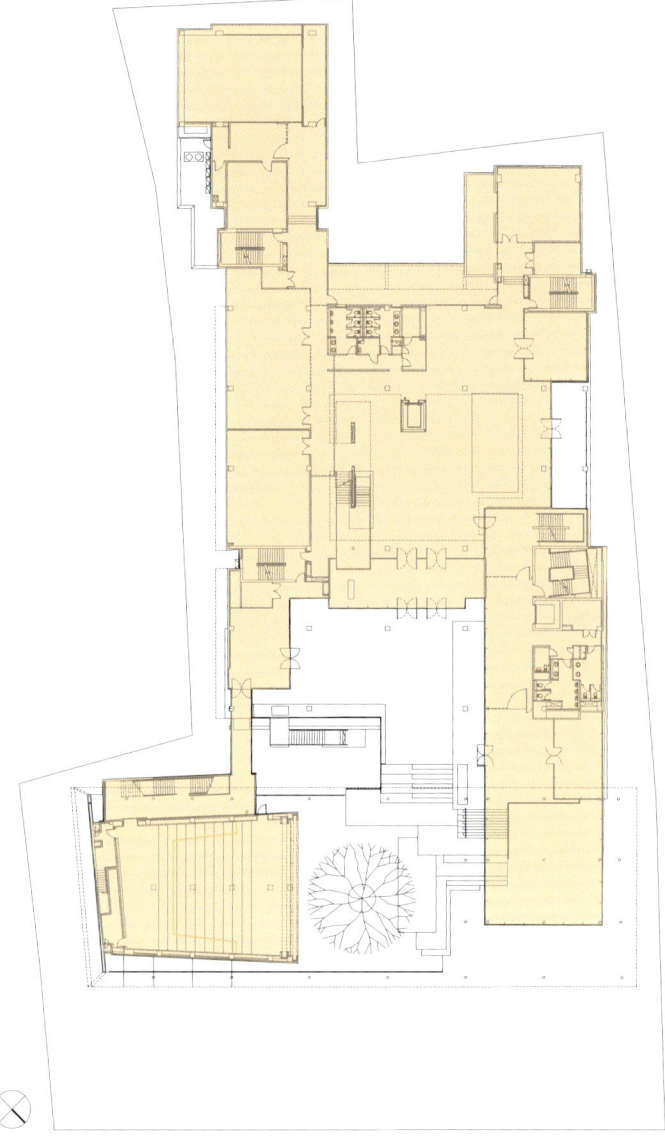

By placing the animation auditorium at the front and through the use of privacy glass, the animation can be viewed from both inside and outside the building, providing a positive and attractive approach to the project. The offices, research area, and studio are located at the rear of the site to provide a peaceful working environment as well as service access from the rear.

The idea of the outdoor and courtyard areas originated from a single, picturesque mature tree. An area around the tree was created for shaded activities and also acts as a connection node to the other function area.

The frame and skin of the building are composed of natural materials including wooden flooring, granite walls, and exposed concrete.

These materials offer a sense of the dignity and truth of nature, which frames the colorful and glittering art of animation—the technology of the privacy-glass façade acts as a screen to attract the attention of passersby.

T.C. Pharmaceutical Office

Location: Prachin Buri, Thailand
Client: T.C Pharmaceutical Industrial
Area: 13,570 square meters
Year: 2002–2004

The office for T.C. Pharmaceutical Industrial at Prachin Buri was designed as a group of one- and two-story buildings amid a 4.8-hectare green plot. The landscape was designed as natural forest: vegetation complements an enormous pond that refreshes and offers a reflection of the building and its surroundings with great aesthetic effect.

The landscape and wooden bridge across the pond attract visitors from the main street where only a glimpse of the buildings can be seen. The drop-off area welcomes visitors to the front pavilion (*sala*), and the colonnade (*rabiang kot*) aids circulation while offering scenic views of the buildings on either side. The view to the left is of the detached multipurpose hall, while the double-height lobby for the offices is to the right. The lobby also enables views of the

surrounding gardens. The offices are clustered around a central courtyard, which floods the colonnade with sunlight and offers an enchanting recreation space for the building's users. The building to the right opens onto another natural shaped pond and water pavilion. While most of the second floor is occupied by administration, it is designed with a wrap-around terrace, allowing staff to appreciate the surrounding nature and protecting the first floor from sunlight and rain.

The contemporary Thai roof forms are tiled with glazed terracotta and have a lengthy overhang with wooden bracing applied at intervals, reflecting the customary and intelligent Thai solution for climatic effects. Other positive elements include reduced energy consumption on air conditioning and a track to encourage bicycle use.

Siam Winery Trading Plus Office & Warehouse

Location: Pathum Thani, Thailand
Client: Trading Plus
Area: 8,900 square meters
Year: 2002–2006

Situated in a former rice field beside a freeway, the Siam Winery distribution warehouse was initiated by a requirement for a headquarters and warehouse to distribute the winery's product to the entire country. However, a restructuring of the organization postponed the need and split the project into two phases.

The design of the warehouse is heavily influenced by the modular system: all elements, from the sizing of the product to the rack and the palette, all are standardized. Even the 6- by 18-meter steel-truss roof structure is modulated to provide maximum storage efficiency and to aid circulation of the forklift in combination with a bay for parking and a control office to fully manipulate traffic inside the warehouse. The single-story warehouse offers an interior height of 10 meters that serves three levels of a shelving system and contains more than 7,000 square meters of storage space, which is equal to six million bottles and one million cans. A canteen and a service office attached to the warehouse were designed according to the same principles.

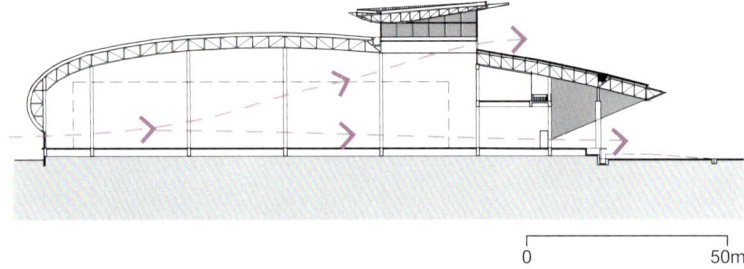

Taken from the core business of the organization—the wine cooler—the project's major design concept began from the grape. The line and color of the green along with the exposed running bond brickwork evoke the sense of being in a vineyard.

K1 Computer Center

Location: Bangkok, Thailand
Area: 6,105 square meters
Year: 2002–2005

Located on a private site, the computer center provides ultimate protection for the digital data at the core of this organization.

The program called for a structure that allowed no single point of failure. It was required to withstand being cut off from the grid for a least one month, no matter what kind of situation might happen, whether flooding, magnetic field shock, or other possible attacks and natural disasters.

Despite the simple box volume and fortress-like design solution, the design offers an enigmatic aesthetic, yet responsive appearance, to the function of the building. Its façade is clad with dark aluminum composite panel in combination with aluminum louvers, an appropriate solution for durability, maintenance, and construction speed. The result placed the project among the most advanced computer centers in the country; as a result, the practice continually receives new commissions for this particular typology.

S1 Data Center

Location: Vibhavadi Rangsit Road, Bangkok, Thailand
Area: 11,600 square meters
Year: 2003–2005

Planning for this project began with the aim of maximizing usage of the site while controlling the size of the building, limiting it to less than 23 meters in height and 10,000 square meters in gross area.

An additional requirement was that the building must be set back 6 meters from the perimeter.

The result was a five-story building with a rather simple structure, 6 and 8 meters wide. The first floor serves as a welcome hall with the mechanical room positioned from the middle of the building to the back. The second, fourth, and fifth floors house the working spaces supported by the double core and double back up between two main risers on the east and west. The core also acts as a heat barrier.

The third floor, the heart of the project, is for information storage. This floor requires extreme security not only from personal access but also from external terrorist acts.

The east and west façades are solid and clad with aluminum composite panel. In contrast, the north façade, with its unitized glazed curtain wall, works with the vertical aluminum fin to offer a sense of security and privacy, as well as reducing verticality to help reduce dust stains while maintaining an elegant appearance.

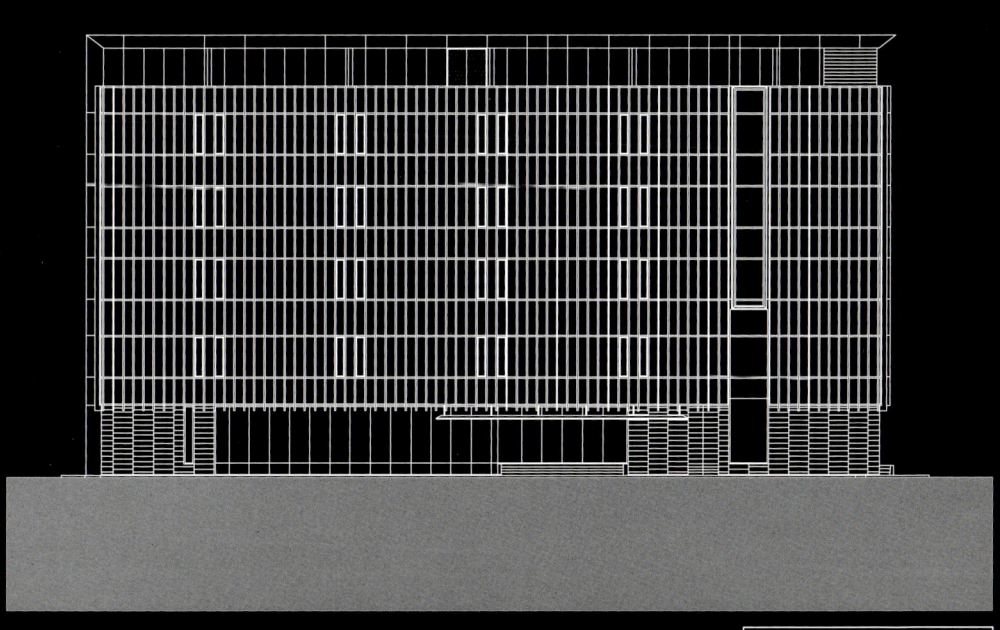

0　　15m

Bangkok Airways New Office

Location: Suvarnabhumi Airport, Samut Prakan, Thailand
Client: Bangkok Airways
Area: 7,500 square meters
Year: 2005–2007

Bangkok Airways required an office building for its own operations, with some additional buildings for rental. The result was 13 buildings on a site to the south of Suvarnabhumi Airport. All buildings were constructed according to the same prototype and the construction phase began with three building units. The site is long and narrow, parallel to the canal, and perpendicular to the airport runway. It is also in a zone where buildings higher than four stories are not permitted.

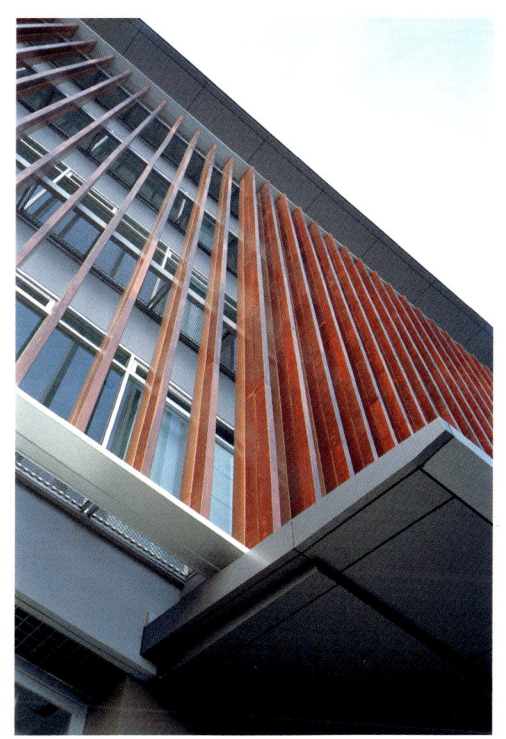 

Preliminary design ideas sought an arrangement of the façade that could reduce the impact of sound waves.

This was followed up with the solution of minimizing repetition of the same 13 units by using façades that look different from various angles, in a technique similar to a hologram. The façade of each building is divided into three different configurations: the south façade is composed of a double-layer skin with a vertical blade outside the tinted glass layer; solidity is applied to the east and the west façades; and the north façade is clad with glazed curtain wall with the same pattern.

The vertical blade—the composite section formed with timber and steel—has proven to be a satisfactory acoustic barrier.

The Embassy of The Kingdom of The Netherlands

Location: Pleon Chit Road, Bangkok, Thailand
Client: The Royal Netherlands Embassy, Thailand
Area: 4,000 square meters
Year: 2003–2005
Principal Architect: Henket & Partners Architecten

Located between the noisy Wireless Road and the peaceful Tonson Lane, close to the sites of the US Embassy and the US ambassador's residence, the existing campus dates from the end of the 19th century. It forms a beautiful park, an exceptional green oasis of trees, space, and tranquility amid the hustle and bustle of Bangkok. To avoid the heavy traffic of Wireless Road and to safeguard privacy and enhance security, the new chancellery opens up from Tonson Lane and is placed on a man-made island.

The main structure consists of two parts: the reinforced concrete building and the double-deck structure supporting a metal deck. As safety was of primary importance, features such as bullet-proof glazing and access control were incorporated. The lightweight Teflon-coated fabric fin attached to the steel supporting structure is an effective sunshade for the office windows, particularly in Thailand's weather conditions.

The ground floor is fully dedicated as general office space. The second floor mostly comprises personal offices, and the third floor is for services and facilities. The main interior features are a long walkway along the building, which connects each floor's main components, and an atrium that functions as a semi-outdoor space connecting the main entrance with the building as well as providing climate protection. The facilities zone includes an elevator, a sculptural fire stairway in transparent glass, pantry, canteen, and bathrooms. All functional space is directed as open plan.

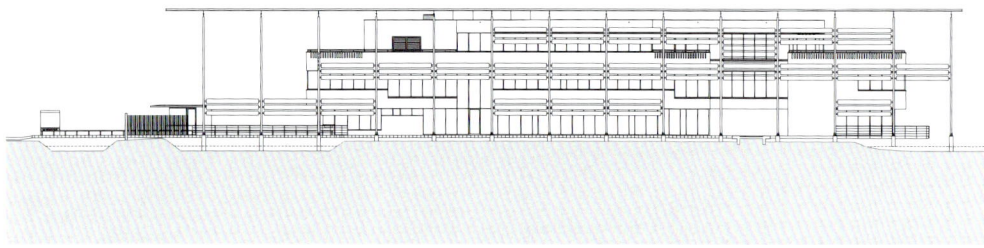

The chancellery reflects the Dutch character traits of openness, transparency, lightness, and functional beauty alongside the Thai traits of tropical lightness and interaction between nature and culture, indoor and outdoor life.

Above the chancellery is an enormous cantilevered roof, which, together with the surrounding trees, offers the required climatic protection.

MCOT Operation Building

Location: Rama IX Road, Bangkok, Thailand
Client: Mass Communication Organization of Thailand
Area: 32,000 square meters
Year: 1994–2001
Contract Winning Design 1994

The Mass Communication Organization of Thailand (MCOT) was in need of a new building to house offices and broadcast studios to accommodate future growth. The building was to be located on a newly available site, which connected to the existing campus from the back. The new building would provide a link between the existing entrance and access from a newly constructed road.

To allow as much open exterior space as possible for future expansion, including the link between buildings, the design was developed as a mid-rise L-shaped building. Views and an attractive appearance were created by grouping similar functions together: new studios connected with existing studios simply via a skywalk passage, while the office occupies the other wing of the L shape. The structure of the new building was built as a "box in a box" from the foundations, pillars, and beams toward the roof, to ensure maximum sound isolation.

A circular canopy was introduced to connect to the office and the broadcasting studio wing; the expression of the dynamic form reflects rapid communication and advanced technology while giving resonance to the existing fabric.

MCOT Complex

Location: Rama IX Road, Bangkok, Thailand
Client: Mass Communication Organization of Thailand
Area: 48,814 square meters
Year: 2003–2007

This project was initiated by MCOT in 2003, along with the re-branding of its television station to become "Modern Nine TV." The 30-year-old campus had opened with two buildings in 1980, and an operations building (also designed by A49 as a result of an award-winning contract) was added in 2003. With the ability to acquire the adjacent plot of land, MCOT has an ambitious determination to become a communication hub for the region. The plan was to revitalize the entire complex, including in the plan a skyscraper that would house the regional office of the international television station.

The 30-year-old, two-story-high broadcasting building was rearticulated by resolving the solid mass as the composition of the plane and enlarging the reception hall with a glazed façade and canopy. The administration building, six stories high and also 30 years old, was reconditioned by changes to space usage. Some of the floor area was eliminated to create additional space for recreating and humanizing the work area by offering outside views and natural light.

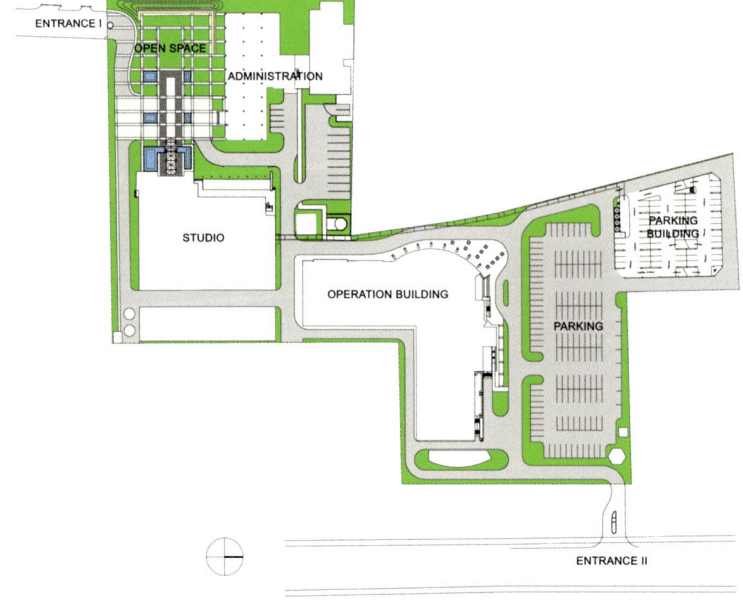

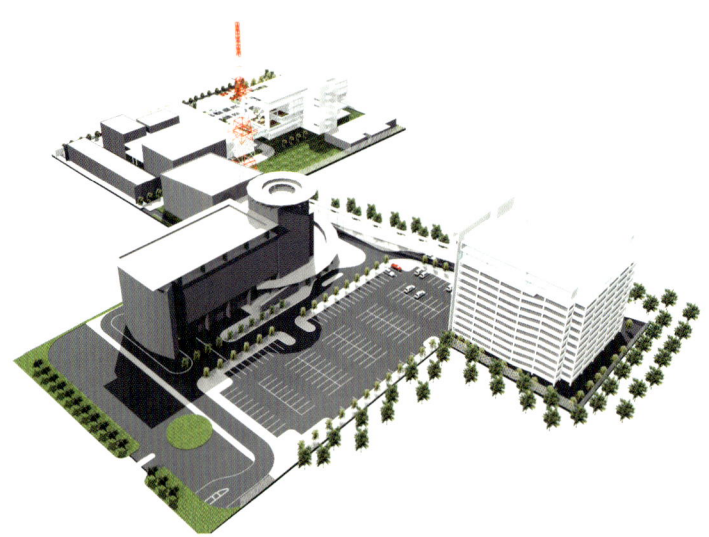

To resolve a critical problem with car parking at the complex, the new 12-story multipurpose building devotes its first 10 floors, and one-and-a-half underground floors, to parking.

To conceal the tedious and rough appearance of the 10-story parking façade, the building turns its solid core to the main area of the complex and is clad with enamel panels that can display graphic signage.

The other parts of the façade are covered with extruded aluminum louvers and precast concrete.

The 11th floor houses the 300-seat canteen, seven activity rooms, and a club room, while the 12th floor houses a fitness center, an 8-meter-high multi-sport court (to enable badminton), an aerobics room, and a locker room. The space in the central area of the 11th and 12th floors is connected by the void, filled with a line of trees and a wooden deck, which leads the circulation up to the rooftop where a jogging track, seating, and plantings are planned.

Phase 1 of the MCOT Complex includes the renovation of the broadcasting and administration buildings, a new 12-story multipurpose building, landscape architecture of the entire complex and graphic signage of the entire complex, all in conjunction with 49 Group. The MCOT identity is expressed by the clean white horizontal lines and precise alignment of the brise soleil, the clarity of the modules, and the proportions where precision and tranquility meet.

NIKS (Thailand) Head Office

Location: Rama III Road, Bangkok, Thailand
Client: NIKS (Thailand)
Area: 12,148 square meters
Year: 2004

The 11-story NIKS building is located on Rama III Road, an area of potential expansion for Bangkok. Surrounded by vast undeveloped land, the elongated site reaches toward the Chaophraya River where the owner's residence is located

The design intent was to create a simple, straightforward but eye-catching building. While maintenance-free and durable materials were chosen, a touch of luxury was provided by the 4.5-meter floor-to-floor height.

To meet the owner's requirements, the building was split into two composite forms: the front office expresses its verticality by the floor-to-ceiling glazing of the exterior wall, which also provides a panoramic view; the solid core was placed on the west side to prevent heat gain from sunlight. The parking space, which occupies the rear of the building and is connected to the office at the first and fourth floors, is topped with storage and event spaces.

The overhanging box at the 9th to 11th floors frames the sky and emphasizes the building's articulation; this is in counterpoint to the folded plane which wraps the working space that ascends to become the roof.

Poh Teck Tung Foundation

Location: Pom Prap Sattru Phai, Bangkok, Thailand
Client: Poh Teck Tung Foundation
Area: 8,632 square meters
Year: 2005
Design Competition Entry

This new extension of the Poh Tek Tung project strongly emphasizes aspects of Chinese culture and tradition. The spiritual walkway of Chinese traditional architecture, a sequential progression to enter a building according to Chinese belief, is adopted.

Having passed through the main dragon gate, a multifunction hall leads the eye to the Chinese garden and connects the spiritual house with the office building. The hall is a shared public space once the door is opened, and it becomes an intimate courtyard when the doors are closed.

In contrast to the traditional style of the new entrance, the simple and minimalist design of the office building acts as a backdrop to the festive spaces near the entrance.

Ocean Newline Office & Residence

Location: Rama IV Road, Bangkok, Thailand
Client: Ocean Newline
Area: 9,957 square meters
Year: 2007–2009

Ocean Newline is a successful construction material supplier. Its headquarters and the owner's family residence are located in seven clusters on a site on the Rama IV Road.

The three-story headquarters building includes a basement level, and forms a composition with the five-story residence, parallel to the congested Rama IV Road.

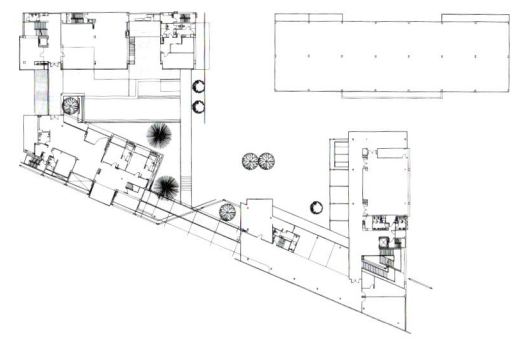

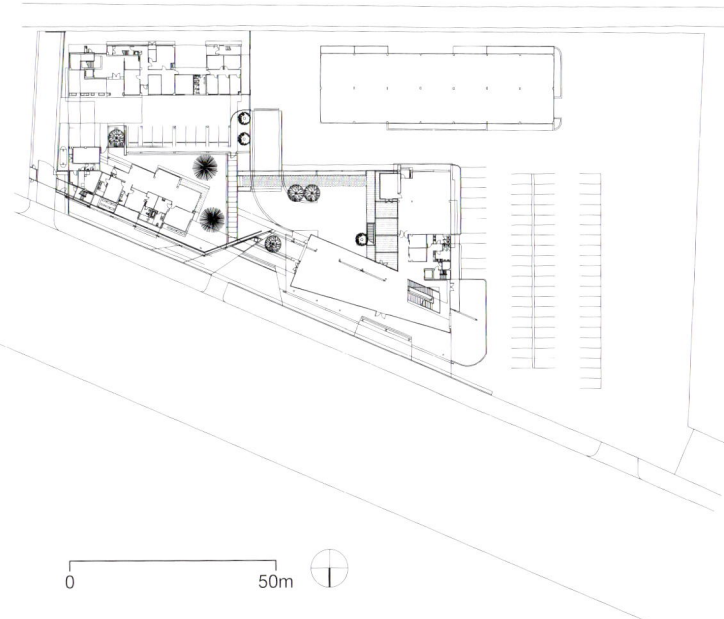

The idea of architecture as showroom was created by highlighting the application of the client's products.

The axis for the adjustable canvas panels creates an eye-catching element from the Rama IV Road to the showroom and the product display area. These panels can also serve as a blind to protect the residential area from visual pollution from the street and to block the harsh west sunlight from entering the office.

I.P. Trading

Location: Saphan Sung, Bangkok, Thailand
Client: I.P. Trading
Area: 4,300 square meters
Year: 2007–2008

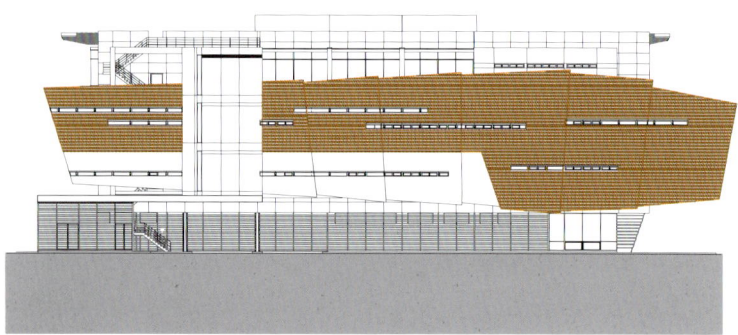

This building, located on a one-hectare site on Sukhaphiban 3 Road, adjacent to Klong Sansab, serves as the headquarters, staff training center, and warehouse for I.P. Trading.

The four-story building is situated toward the rear of the lengthy site, leaving the front area for parking spaces. The west side of the building is articulated by exposed concrete and the curved form of pine wood cladding; the glazed façade is oriented to the east, welcoming the visitor with tall slender columns that enhance the building's elegance.

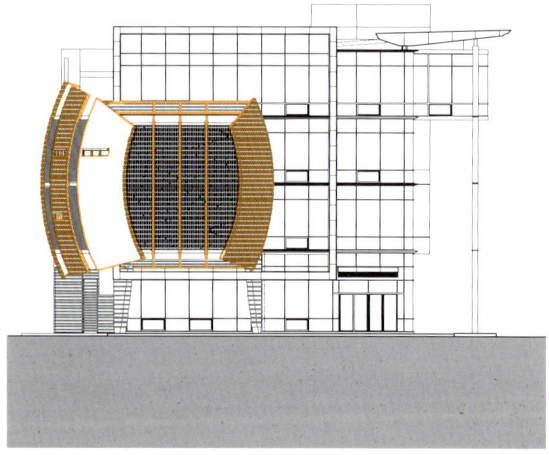

The design concept derives from the core business of I.P. Trading—fruit and vegetable juices—with organic forms and materials that produce a natural, yet exciting appearance.

SET Multipurpose Building

Location: Don Mueang, Bangkok, Thailand
Client: The Stock Exchange of Thailand
Area: 4,800 square meters
Year: 2007–2008
Contract Winning Design

This project involved concerns about context, orientation, and architectural language, with the structure surrounded on three sides.

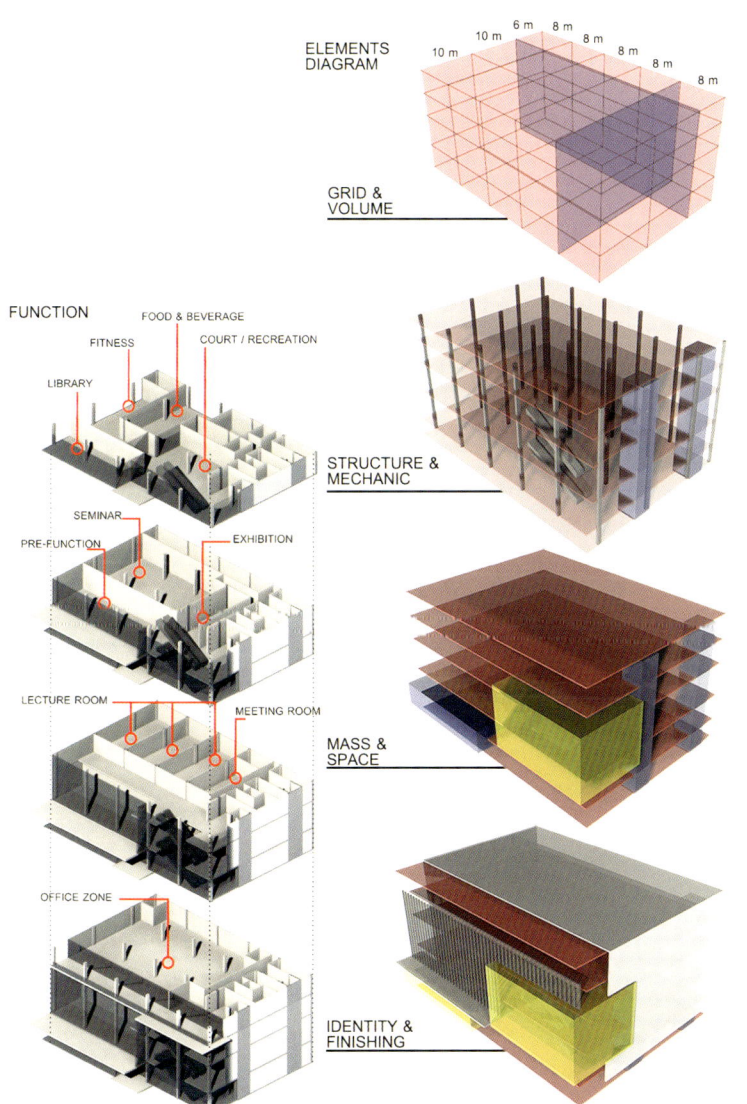

Only the north side faced the vast green lawn. The main requirement was that 70–80 percent of the floor area must be usable in comparison to the gross area.

Building orientation and careful arrangement of internal functions helped to reduce heat absorption and to minimize the use of electric power; the narrow side of the building was oriented to face the trajectory of the sun, and the service and circulation areas placed to the south and the west. The straight circulation is simple and easy to navigate.

A case study into future expansion was initiated by the requirement to build only 2,600 square meters per floor. The study proposed new circulation to connect the old and new structures, ensuring full integration.

The notion of hierarchy was an important consideration in relation to the main building; the aim was to give the new building a sense of resonance to the existing while also respecting and welcoming visitors.

Royal Archive

Location: Nakhon Pathom, Thailand
Client: The Office of His Majesty's Principal Private Secretary
Area: 17,653 square meters
Year: 2006–2009

The Royal Archive is the central collection of invaluable historical information, such as documents, manuscripts, engravings, and photographs of the *Chakri* dynasty. It provides access services to the resource center of the office of His Majesty's principal private secretary.

The center consists of 13,179 square meters of storage area, 1,000 square meters of exhibition space, a library, and additional areas for meetings, an information service center, and archival storage space available for rental.

Clarity of the zoning is the important criteria in the design. The front two-story exhibition hall, with its overhanging roof, serves as an entrance to the project, followed by the three-story library and five-story archive building at the rear. All parking is underground.

The design pursues a contemporary modern architecture, with a sense of Thai culture woven into the details.

Since much of the material and information in the archive is priceless, aspects such as the control of humidity, temperature, and lighting were critical design elements.

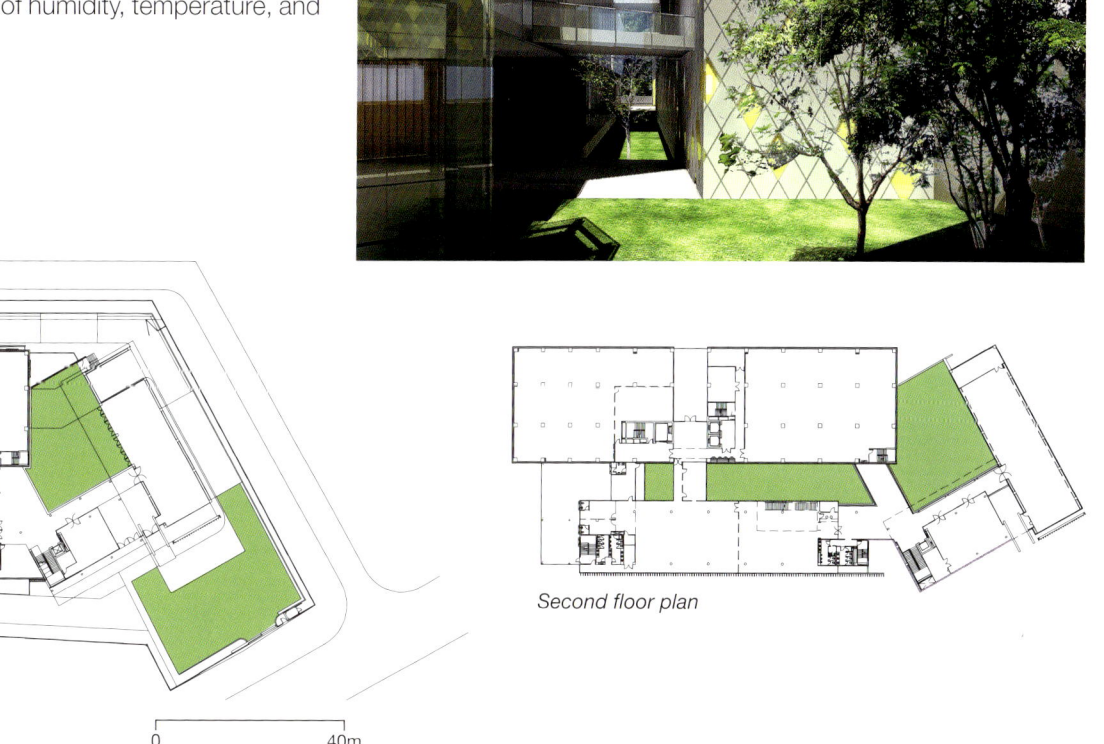

First floor plan

Second floor plan

0   40m

Pipattanasin Office Building

Location: Narathiwas Rajanakarindra Road, Bangkok, Thailand
Client: Pipattanasin
Area: 19,000 square meters
Year: 2003–2006

Following the 1990s economic crisis in Southeast Asia, this building was left abandoned as an unfinished, four-story structure. With the regional economic recovery, a 21-story office building was proposed.

The building form was previously expressed by three articulated stacks, from the base to the shaft and pinnacle. In order to change the appearance of the building, a more monolithic form was pursued. The optimal maximum proportions were restricted by the building codes that required the height of the building to be twice the length from the setback line from the property line plus the width of the road in front.

The façade is clad with tinted glass instead of colored reflective glass.

The continuity of the monolithic form was achieved with a unitized system at equal height to the floor-to-floor dimension.

The vertical mullions were laid in an English bond pattern, which accentuated the three-point definition line. Curved walls, gradually increasing in height, define the unique form of the building.

Energy Complex

Location: Vibhavadi Rangsit Road, Bangkok, Thailand
Client: Energy Complex Group
Area: 177,000 square meters
Year: 2004–2009
Contract Winning Design
Associate Architect: Design Concept

This project was designed as the location of the offices of the Ministry of Energy, and of the petroleum authority of Thailand (PTT).

The parameters for the architectural design and the engineering were that it should be distinctive and that it should be a model of energy conservation for other large buildings to emulate.

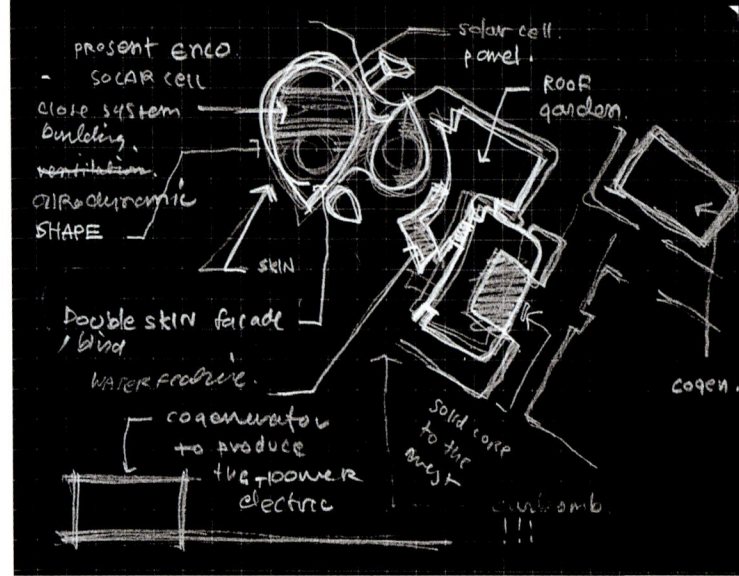

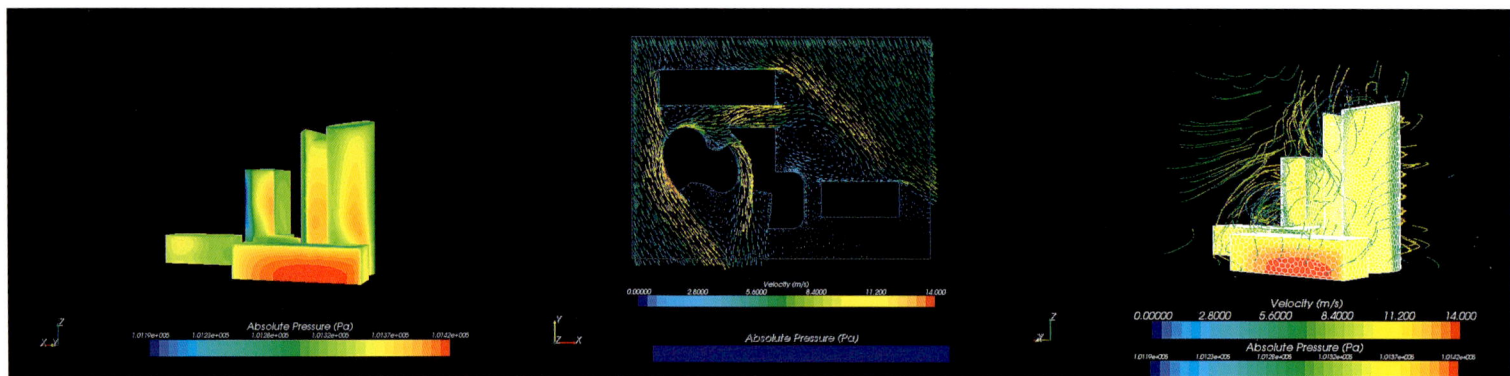

Wind and pressure study

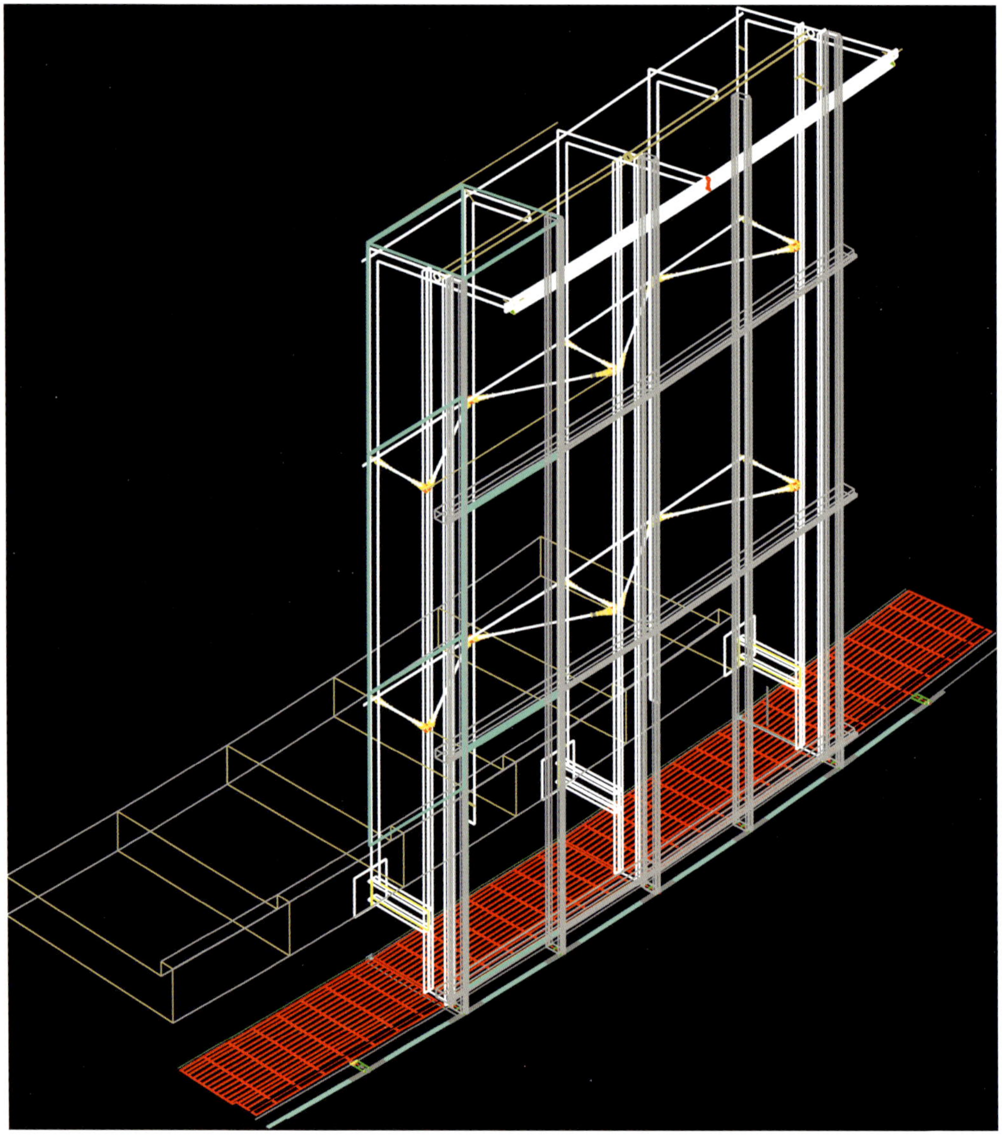

Façade study

  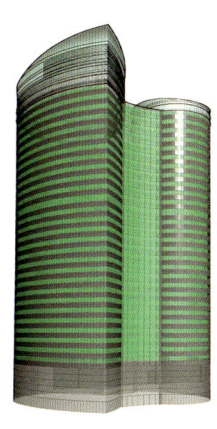

In consultation with engineers and energy conservation experts, several design options were considered, including one in the shape of a drop of oil. Ultimately, two concepts were submitted. The strict energy conservation parameters necessitated careful consideration of the exterior wall covering and the use of multi-layered windows.

The middle zone was also required to connect the PTT offices with the Ministry offices and to provide access to shared facilities, such as an auditorium, a library, and a recreational area.

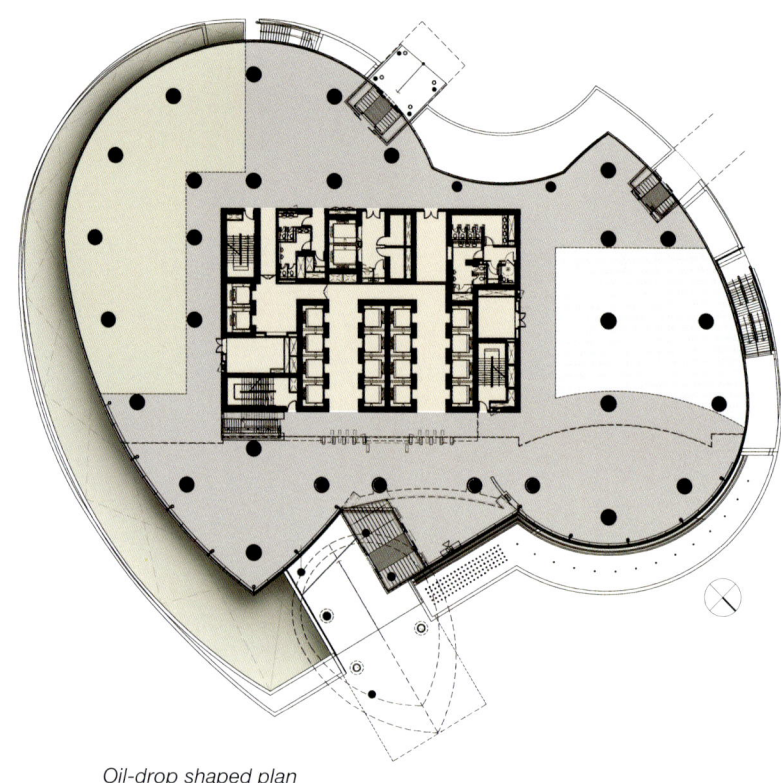

Oil-drop shaped plan

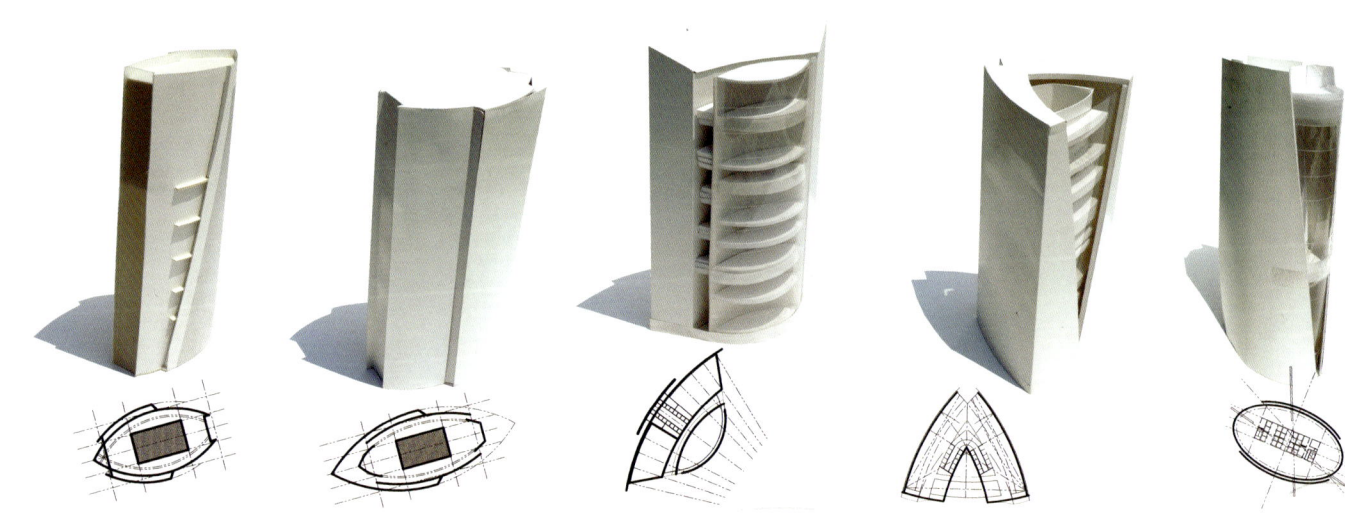

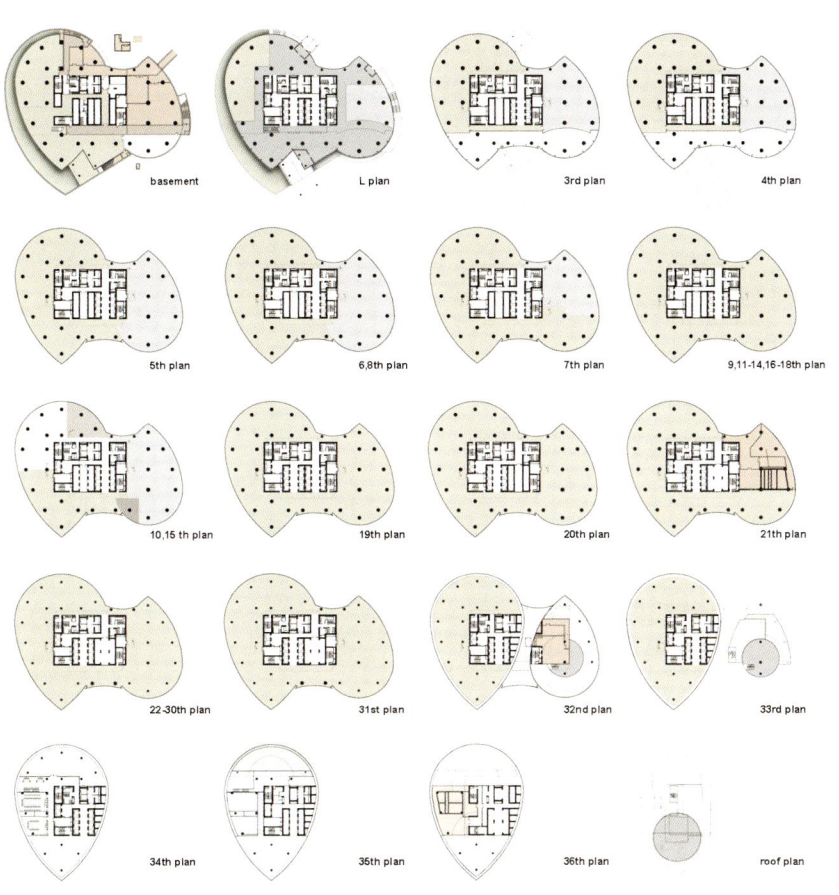
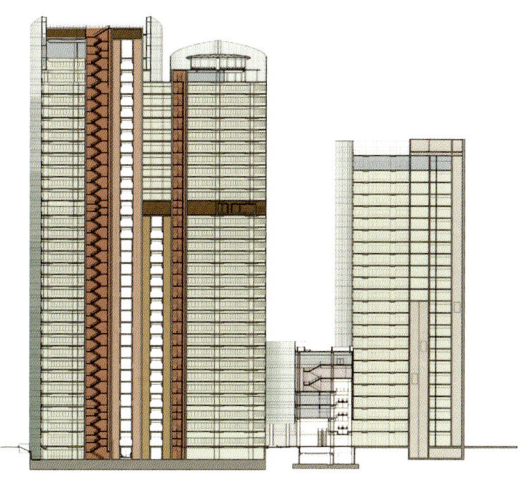

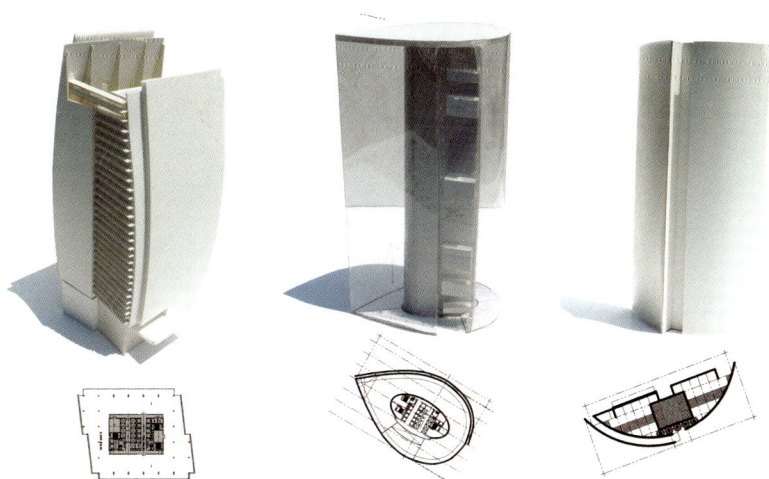

Preliminary stage: tower shape study

The Thai Red Cross Society Museum

Location: Rama IV Road, Bangkok, Thailand
Client: The Thai Red Cross Society
Area: 11,415 square meters
Year: 2005–2008

Located on Rama IV Road, the historic campus of the Thai Red Cross Society includes the 40-year-old French colonial building that formerly served as an anonymous clinic.

Development was initiated via collaboration with experts to determine the content of the museum, which later unfolded to become seven halls of exhibitions that present a lifetime of the Thai Red Cross Society in sequence. The seven halls comprise a route: clockwise circulation leads visitors up and down to the exhibition space distributed throughout the three levels of the building including the temporary exhibition area. The existing building will be used as a multifunction hall and will also house the souvenir shop. An elevator and staircase are provided in each wing and all are connected to the underground parking space for 60 cars.

The design proposes multiple access points by surrounding the existing building with four L-shaped buildings. The cruciform space provides a hub for activities and is covered by an overhanging structure that is suspended without columns. No truss intersects the cross.

Tapered edges reduce the massing of the building and give an extra dimension by way of red terracotta cladding, also in cruciform. The proposal undoubtedly offers a challenging innovation in museum typology.

Thailand Cultural Center

Location: Huai Khwang, Bangkok, Thailand
Client: Ministry of Culture
Area: 173,831 square meters
Year: 2006–2009
Contract Winning Design

This project was an award winner in the design competition organized by the Ministry of Culture, to erect an international center intended to become the gateway for Southeast Asian culture. The 4.8-hectare site is adjacent to the existing main national cultural center complex in the Huai Khwang district of Bangkok.

The first phase of the construction began with two major buildings, the museum and the ministry office; the grand theater and the zenith assembly will be assembled later to complete the complex. The guiding principle from the competition was that the center was to embrace the identity of Thai culture. One of the proposed manifestations is the gable roof of the museum, which resonates over the entire complex.

While preserving the north–south axis of the existing structure, some intersecting lines are applied onto the museum to create an exciting trajectory that points to and embraces the rooftop pinnacle. In contrast, the ministry building is rather unpretentious and tranquil, in line with the elegance of the entry colonnade. Its rectangular organization maximizes the efficiency of its operations.

Cementhai Building Products Gallery

Location: Bang Sue, Bangkok, Thailand
Client: Cementhai Building Products
Area: 48,250 square meters
Year: 2005
Contract Winning Design

The Siam Cement Group was founded under the Royal Decree of His Majesty King Rama VI in 1913 as Thailand's first producer of cement, a construction material critical to national development. The Cementhai Building Products Gallery includes exhibition halls, product showroom, training center, Cementhai Home Mart, and an educational area. Inspired by the logo given by His Majesty King Rama VI—a red hexagon containing a white elephant within—the exhibition building incorporates a red floating exhibition space symbolizing a hidden gem. Advanced construction methods using concrete reflect Cementhai's achievements as an expert manufacturer of the product.

The Cementhai Building Products Gallery comprises five sections: a showroom to educate and provide the public with information about construction materials, an exhibition hall to exhibit new products and set up conferences with the capacity of 5,000 persons, a training center to offer both common and specialized training, the Cementhai Home Mart for selling merchandise, and basement parking.

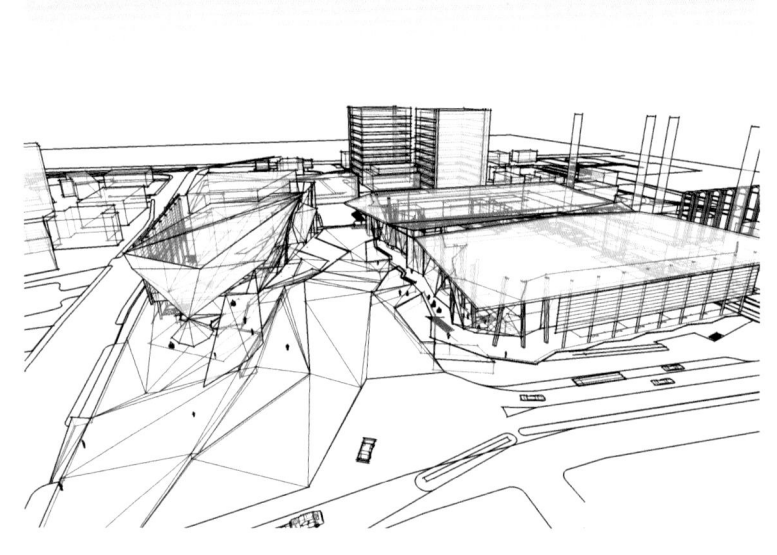

The design concept is the modern image of Cementhai in the new global market, showing its future development as a hub of new creations for Thai society and Cementhai employees. The design not only celebrates the company's historical elements but also presents an example of how to save natural resources in construction.

99

In addition to displaying Siam Cement Group products, the center also serves as a museum and as a venue for exhibitions of innovations in construction materials that demonstrate the capabilities of the group. Since the project is located in the grounds of a former cement plant with a long history, there are some original architectural features still in place, including about 60 tall chimneys. In the proposal phase, Architects 49 recommended that the chimneys be preserved as a symbol of the project.

 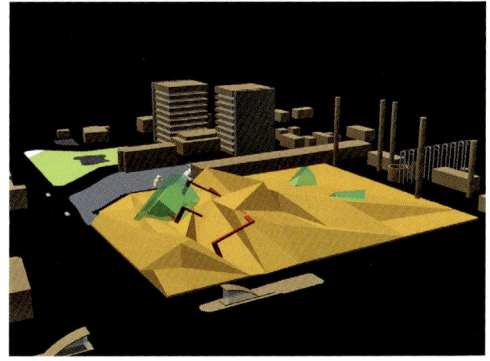 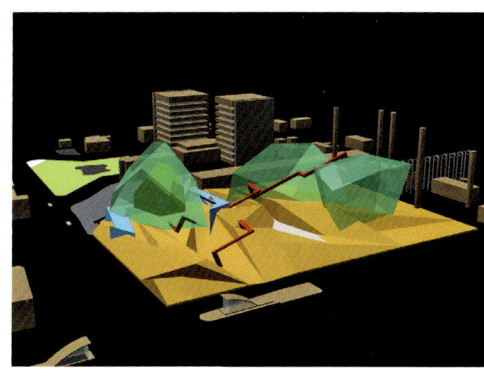
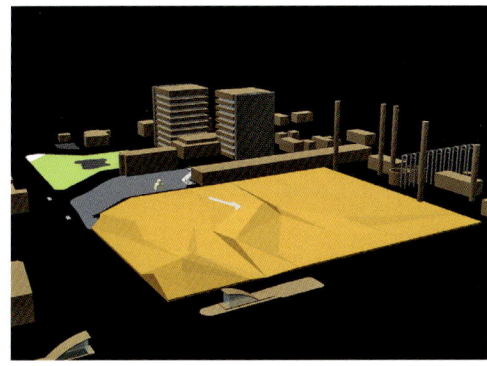 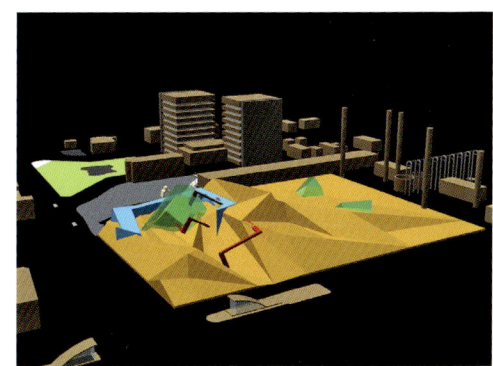 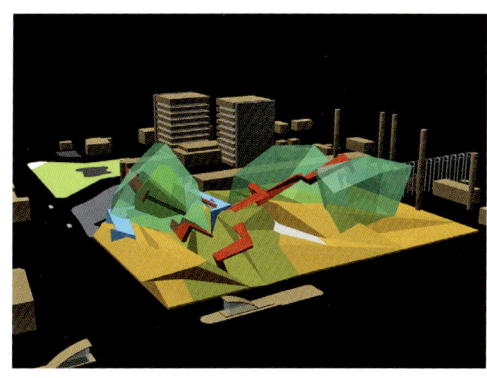
 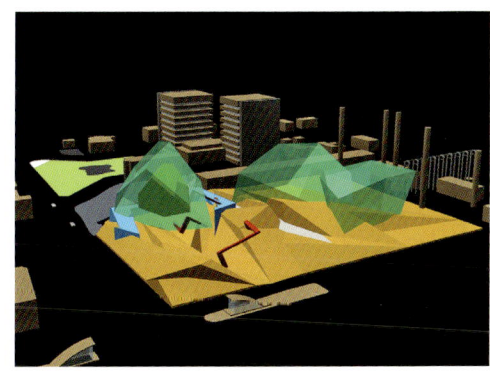 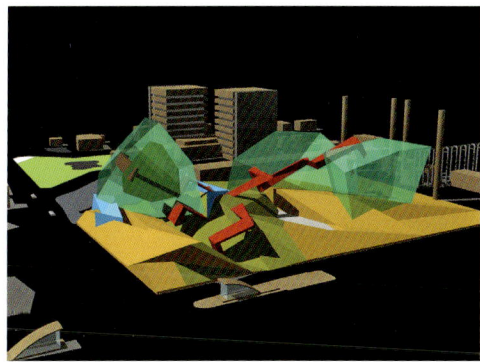

The ultimate design proposed a layout for the 100th Anniversary Siam Cement Museum in the shape of the corporate logo with the group's corporate color of red used for the main edifice, clearly visible from the multipurpose areas at the front of the project. An architectural consideration in the design phase was to demonstrate a structural feat that exemplifies both the company's achievements in product development and its wide variety of products.

SCG Experience

Location: At Narong Road, Bangkok, Thailand
Client: Cementhai Building Products
Area: 6,200 square meters
Year: 2007–2009

This project originated as a winning scheme in the design competition for the Cementhai Building Products Gallery, which was later adopted and relocated to the construction site for Project CDC, or Crystal Design Center, located at Praditmanudham Road. The center will display products used for all aspects of building construction design. Located at the front access point of the 11.2-hectare campus, the building's 20-meter-high glass façade welcomes visitors at first glance. Cementhai is a public company with a long reputation as the nation's first cement producer and has expanded continuously to become the largest and most advanced industrial conglomerate in Thailand. The design takes inspiration from the history of the company.

An enormous concrete slab gradually leans away from the floor slab to become the wall, then expands and "pierces the sky" to become the roof above its point of origin. This symbolism, in a way, reflects the advanced innovation of the company. Together, as a composition of the concrete plane, they form the three-story building containing the exhibition space, the reading area, and expert product consulting service on the first floor. The second floor comprises a library, designers' club, materials library, and display area for Cementhai's own products. The third floor will function as the administrative office and a display area for some more oversized products.

Although the shape of the building is largely defined by the perimeter of the property, the concrete of the building is liberated, elemental, and freeform. The edge of the slab also defines the shape of the floor plan and provides open space in the building by connecting all of the elements together.

All components of the building will be assembled exclusively from products made by Cementhai company and its affiliate groups.

Mae Fah Luang University

Location: Doi Ngam, Chiang Rai, Thailand
Client: University Affairs
Area: 180,000 square meters
Year: 1997–2002
Contract Winning Design
Co-architects: SJA+3D; Architects 110

Located in a mountainous area 15 kilometers from the urban center, the university was founded not only for students in the northern part of Thailand, but also for those from the economic rectangle including Myanmar, Laos, and the south of China, in accordance with the wishes of Her Royal Highness Somdej Phra Sri Nakarindra Baromraj Chonni, or Her Royal Highness the Princess Mother.

The plan followed campus-town concepts, developing the university and surrounding community at the same time.

Faculty office building and lecture hall

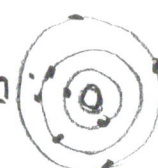

Conceptual sketches by Dr. Sumet Jumsai

The master plan concept lies on an east–west axis called "Chalermprakiate Axis," literally meaning the King's prestige enhancement axis. To the west the Doi Ngam mountain provides a beautiful background. The building compound lies along the axis in the following sequence: the main auditorium at the front, the offices of university affairs on both sides, and a multipurpose plaza in the middle, drawing the eye toward the office of the president.

The classroom buildings are formed as curved shapes in response to the plaza where *Hor Kamrai Mae Fa Luang* is located; the architecture is inspired by the heritage of Lanna. The metaphor of HRH the Princess Mother as the center of the universe with the surrounding buildings radiating in her aura is unavoidable. From this point, the Chalermprakiate Axis expands to encompass a secondary southward line of buildings including an academic services building, a research building, a canteen, and an area for student activities.

To foster energy conservation, natural light is diffused through a skylight in the middle of the building. Architectural shading devices were used along the west elevation to reduce heat together with layers of sloped roof. The plan offers thorough ventilation and flexibility. Every element was designed to comply with a simple architectural form and a prefabricated system substantially reduced the construction time.

Office of the president

Academic services

The Bhumirak Dhamachart,
The Royal Nature Conservation Center

Location: Nakhon Nayok, Thailand
Client: Old Vajiravudh Student Association and the Chaipattana Foundation
Area: 2,900 square meters
Year: 2002–2004

This project was initiated by Her Royal Highness Princess Maha Chakri Sirindhorn, who gave her approval to the Chaipattana Foundation and the Old Vajiravudh Student Association to create a center to exhibit His Majesty the King Bhumibol Adulyadej's idea and theory of development on the land site behind the Klongtadan dam. The project was named the Bhumirak Natural Preserve Museum.

A group of buildings with a total area of 2,900 square meters sits on the front portion of the 2.2-hectare site, leaving the majority of land for outdoor exhibition and future expansion. The rectangular buildings are connected to form an L-shape for the main indoor exhibition and open-air auditorium, while the staff's residences are located further to the west.

The project is an example of sufficiency architecture, where anything unnecessary is eliminated in accordance with the economic philosophy of His Majesty the King Bhumibol Adulyadej.

Simplicity and modesty form the core of the design idea, which unfolds as a modern Thai tropical aspect protected from harsh sunlight and rainwater.

Surat Osathanugrah Library

Location: Rangsit, Pathum Thani, Thailand
Client: Bangkok University
Area: 19,410 square meters
Year: 2000–2003
Citation, ASA Architectural Design Awards, 2004

This five-story library containing almost 800,000 books is located in the center of Bangkok University and accommodates 1,200 students each day. Recreational facilities such as a student lounge, a cyber center, and a contemporary art and design gallery are included in addition to the adjacent museum, which holds a privately owned collection of Southeast Asian ceramics.

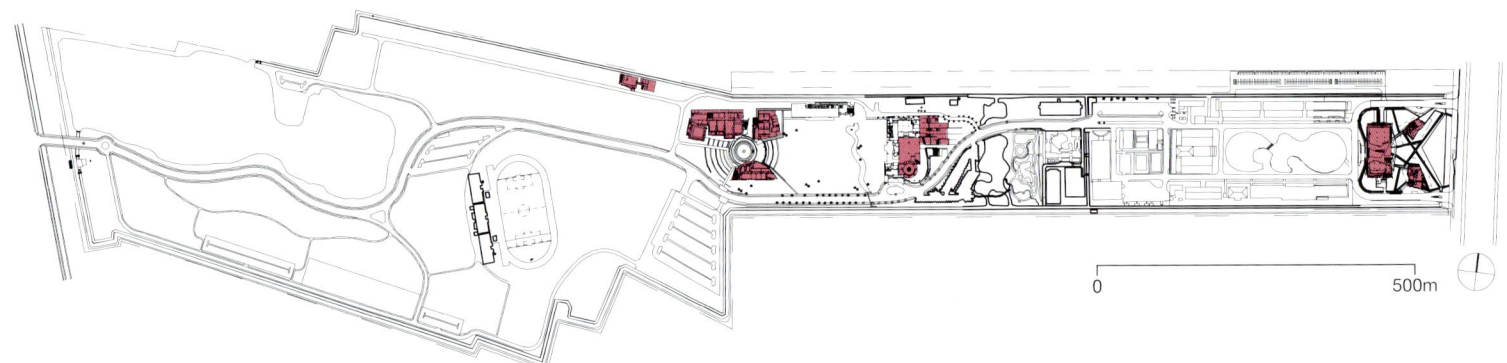

The box-shaped building is raised above the ground to liberate an elegant space for activities. Integrated within the box, the multistory atrium contains a circular ramp that, with the roof structure, collects and distributes natural sunlight into each floor of the building. Active areas such as the student lounge and gallery are located on the lower floor, and activities that require a quiet environment are on the third, fourth, and fifth floors.

The university's brief called for a design that reflects its image and the lively atmosphere experienced within the campus.

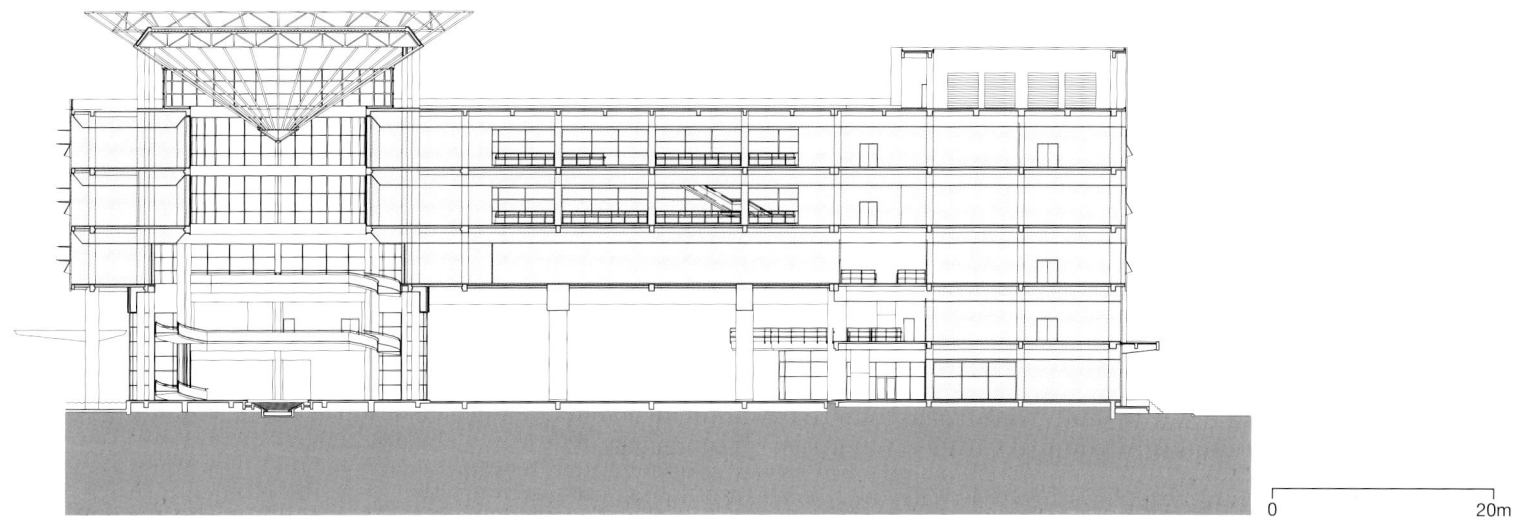

The emblem of the university, composed of a book, a cassia fistula bouquet, and a diamond, has been metaphorically transformed. The book as the spirit of knowledge is expressed by the function of the building. The bouquet as the essence of legacy is epitomized by the nature that is introduced into the building. And the sculptural roof form of the atrium represents the diamond, as the quintessence of preciousness and strength.

Southeast Asian Ceramics Museum

Location: Rangsit, Pathum Thani, Thailand
Client: Bangkok University
Area: 1,740 square meters
Year: 2000–2002
Gold Medal, ASA Architectural Design Awards, 2008

This project was conceived as a result of concern about the exploitation of ancient Sukhothai ceramic ware, which dates back 800 years and has highly specific characteristics. The orientation of the building had to accommodate the university's future master plan and embrace the elegance of Surath library, while still retaining some individuality.

The museum offers a modern appearance while also reflecting the essence of Sukhothai art and architecture; in particular the "Tao Turian Kiln," a special kiln used to produce Sukhothai ceramics in a baking process that involves digging down into the earth.

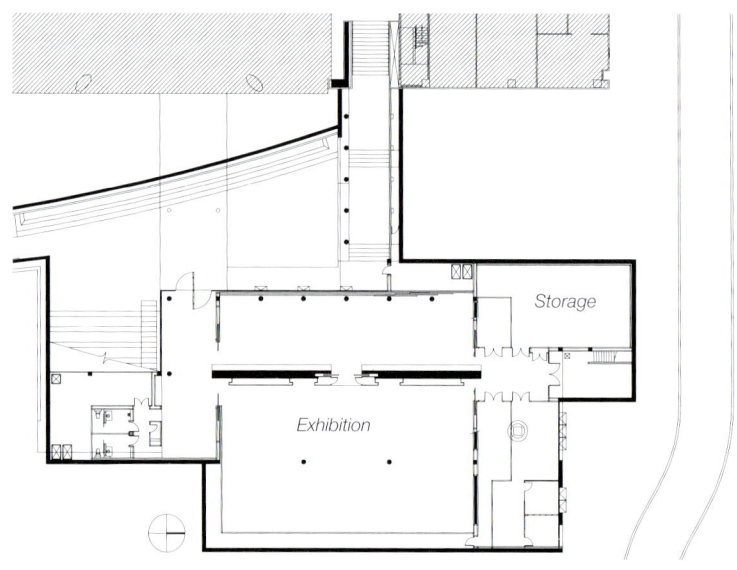

Basement plan

BUILDING ROOF PLATE
INTERIOR SPACE
BUILDING FLOOR PLATE
SERVICE CIRCULATION
TO SERVICE
TO MAIN ENTRANCE
TO MAIN LIBRARY
TO SUB ENTRANCE
TEMPORARY EXHIBITION
PERMANENT EXHIBITION
SUPPORT
OUTDOOR EXHIBITION
AMPHITHEATER

SECTION G
SECTION E
SECTION D
SECTION C
SECTION B
SECTION A
PROJECT CONCEPTUAL CONTOUR II

GROUND LEVEL
GROUND LEVEL
Half by digging
TAO TURIANG
Half by building up
GROUND LEVEL
Half by digging
TAO TURIANG CONCEPTUAL LINES
ELEVATION CONCEPT

NATURAL INDIRECTED LIGHT
SECTION

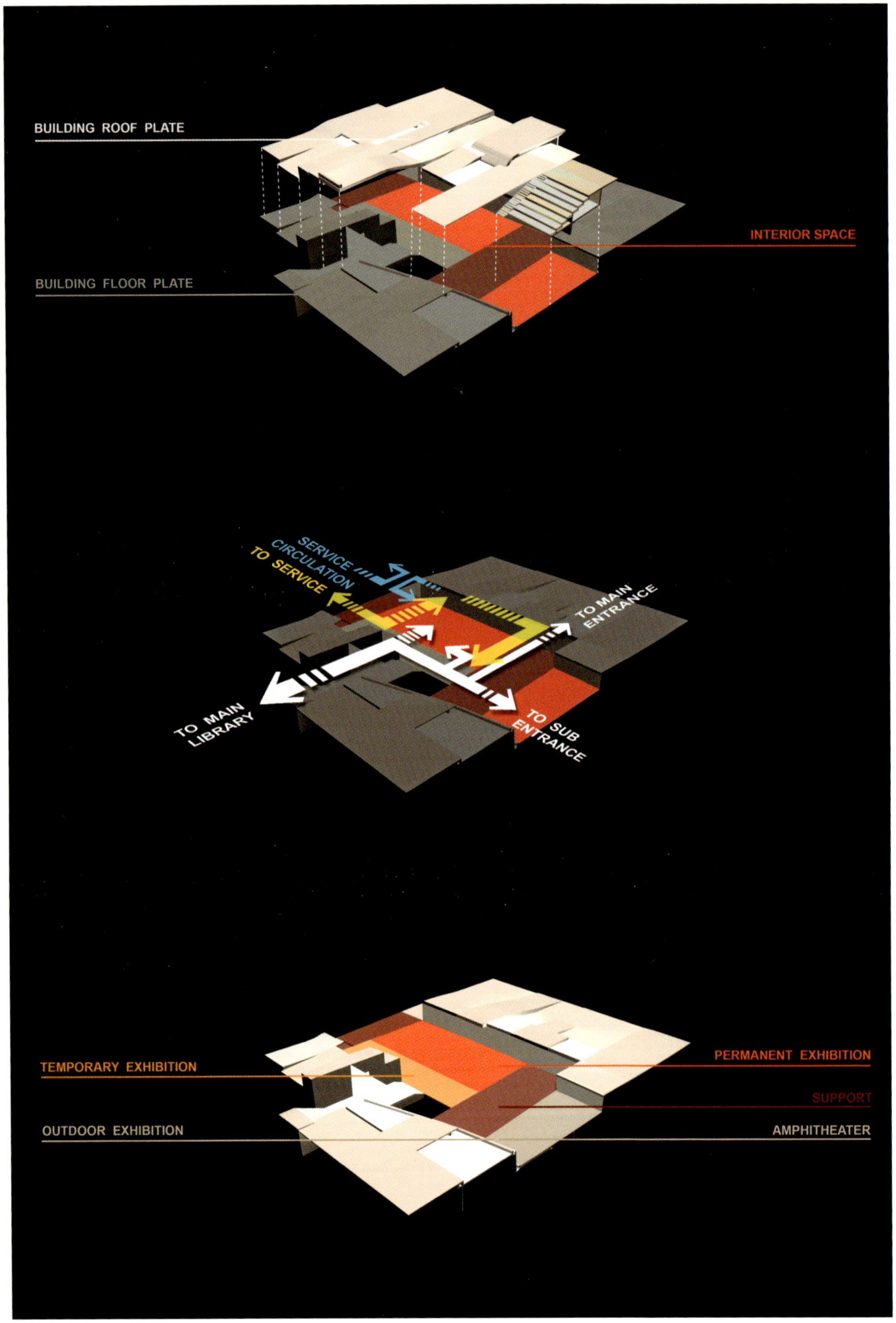

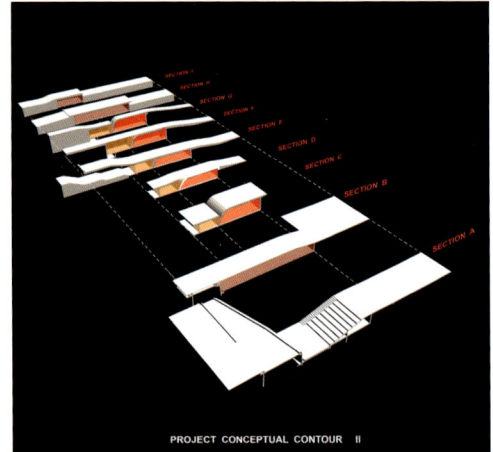

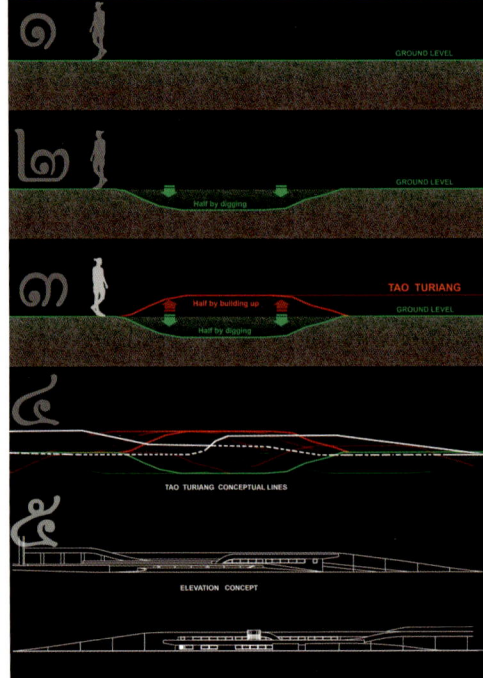

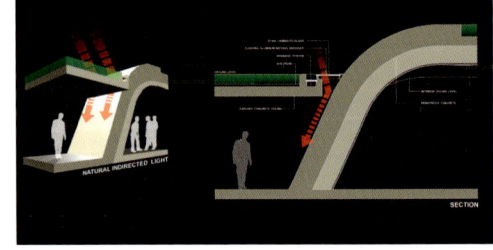

This one-story museum is sunk 2.8 meters below the ground level. The design prevents entry of moisture via double-layer walls and an air-conditioning system with efficient humidity control. The portion of the building below grade also offers energy efficiency with less exposure to harsh sunlight.

The museum consists of temporary and permanent exhibition spaces, study space, an administration office, and other support facilities. All are covered by a sculptural lawn roof, which appears to emerge from the landscape. The design also includes a 200-seat outdoor amphitheater and outdoor exhibition space.

Pongthip Osathanugrah Communication Arts Complex

Location: Rangsit, Pathum Thani, Thailand
Client: Bangkok University
Area: 18,000 square meters
Year: 2001–2004

The Communication Arts Complex represents Bangkok University as one of the finest facilities in the country. A group of buildings was planned around the central area of the campus, where the main library is also located. The central area, or inner pedestrian court, will be surrounded by future buildings. It starts its trajectory from the space underneath the central library, passes through a soon-to-be-erected building and finishes at the Communication Arts Complex space where it serves as a node to the expanding section of the campus.

In contrast with the tranquil space underneath the central library, the Communication Arts Complex space will be filled with an array of dazzling and lively activities including an amphitheater for the performing arts—one of the most important events in the complex's academic program.

Around this space, the complex splits into three buildings for three different purposes and with three different engineering limitations. The first building, housing a classroom and the faculty office, is approached from the main access thoroughfare and has a rather simple but sleek structure with curved forms that catch the eye and lead to the central circular space. The second building contains the studio, conference room, and black box in a wide structure with compartmentalized service areas. The facilities inside are erected with the appropriate dimensions for perfect acoustics and for broadcasting performances. The third building, a multipurpose classroom and laboratory, is a nine-story high-rise building (to reduce the footprint). The first three stories interconnect with the other buildings in the complex. The fourth to eighth floors contain classrooms and are served by vertical circulation, including elevators.

Inspired by media walls and billboards, the articulation of the buildings is treated as a floating solid mass on top of a glazed wall, or freestanding column. The warehouse appearance of the black box is achieved with corrugated-steel cladding, which is also applied to other parts of the building. The performing studios were also planned on the second floor so that they could be seen from the central court or as far away as the central library.

Rajini School

Location: Phra Nakhon, Bangkok, Thailand
Client: Rajini Foundation
Area: 10,000 square meters
Year: 2006–2009

This new four-story secondary school building for 1,500 students on a 1.7-hectare campus was created after the existing building was demolished.

It is located on the corner of Maharaj Road. To the southeast are Ku Muang Canal and the flower market—one of the busiest districts of Bangkok—and to the southwest is the Chaophraya River, which provides both vista and ventilation. These elements were important factors in the master-planning phase and in the manipulation of open space.

The concept derived from retaining the axis of the statue of Queen Prasripatcharindara, consort of King Rama V, and was designed as linked and connected open space to open the vista toward the Chaophraya River.

The architecture is characteristically modern yet tropically oriented and includes cross ventilation with good protection from the harsh sunlight via artificial wood screening, which also provides space for leisure and recreation activities.

Three schematic designs

Much thought was given to the building's sequence, which included placing the administration zone close to Mahanak Road for public access. The classrooms are laid along the central courtyard, and the boarding students are housed at the deepest point, close to the river.

Bangkok University Landmark Complex

Location: Rangsit, Pathum Thani, Thailand
Client: Bangkok University
Area: 25,000 square meters
Year: 2006–2009

This landmark complex originated from the university's policy to improve access to the front area of the campus and to offer students one of the finest facilities in the region.

The complex is composed of four buildings. The first two buildings are organized as single rectangular boxes yet offer a variety of different planes with glazing at uneven angles. Together they enclose the functional spaces including a seminar room and a 1,500-seat auditorium on the fifth floor. An unairconditioned atrium links the two buildings, where interwoven vertical-circulation elements such as the escalator and the elevator become magnificent forms. The more solid elements such as the service core are placed on two side edges of the slab, opening up the vista toward the rear of the building to the entire west area of the campus.

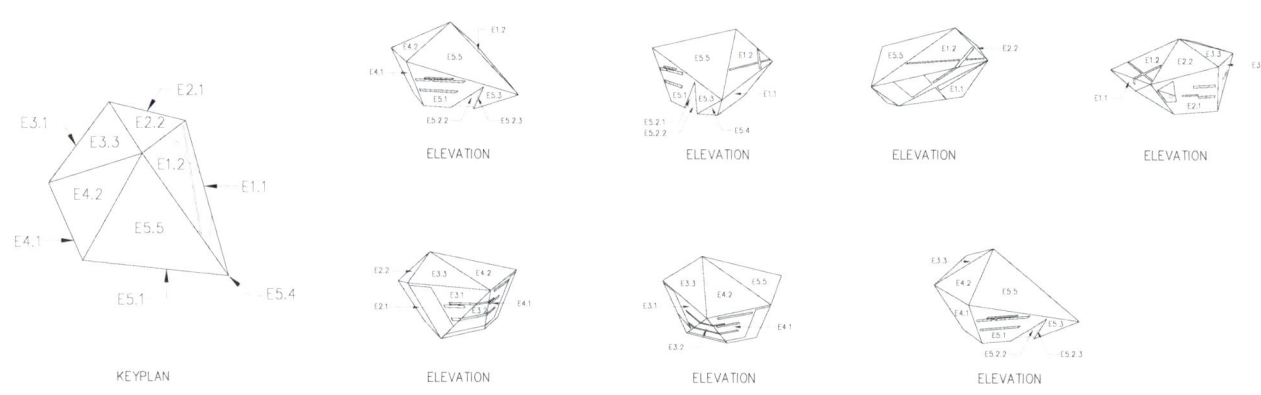

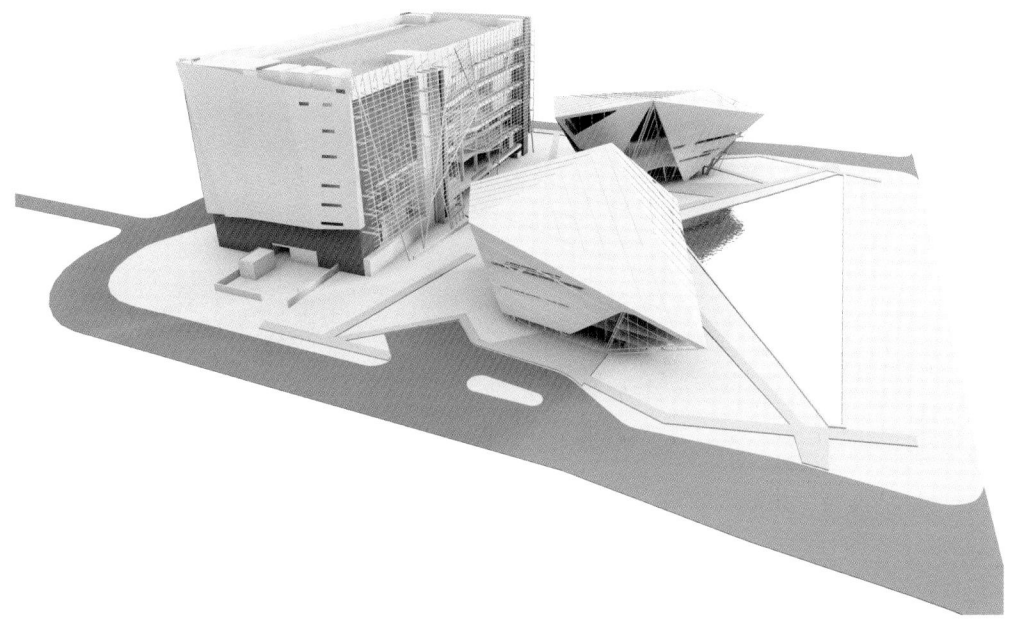

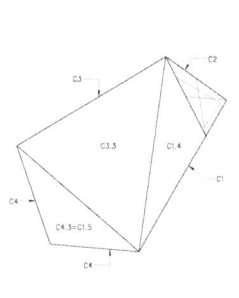

KEYPLAN

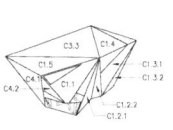

ELEVATION

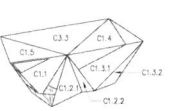

ELEVATION

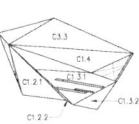

ELEVATION

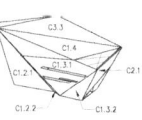

ELEVATION

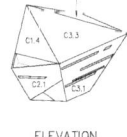

ELEVATION

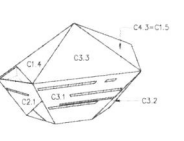

ELEVATION

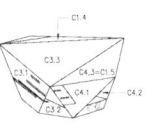

ELEVATION

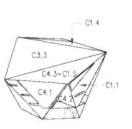

ELEVATION

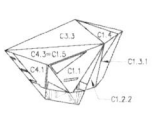

ELEVATION

In contrast to their reflective backdrop, the two front buildings embrace the visionary image of the university through the art of architecture.

They are formed as a group of cut diamonds, metaphorically implying the crystalline body of knowledge created by the many students who have been shaped by their education at this university.

While all buildings stand separately on the ground, they are connected by the underground parking lot that accommodates up to 300 cars.

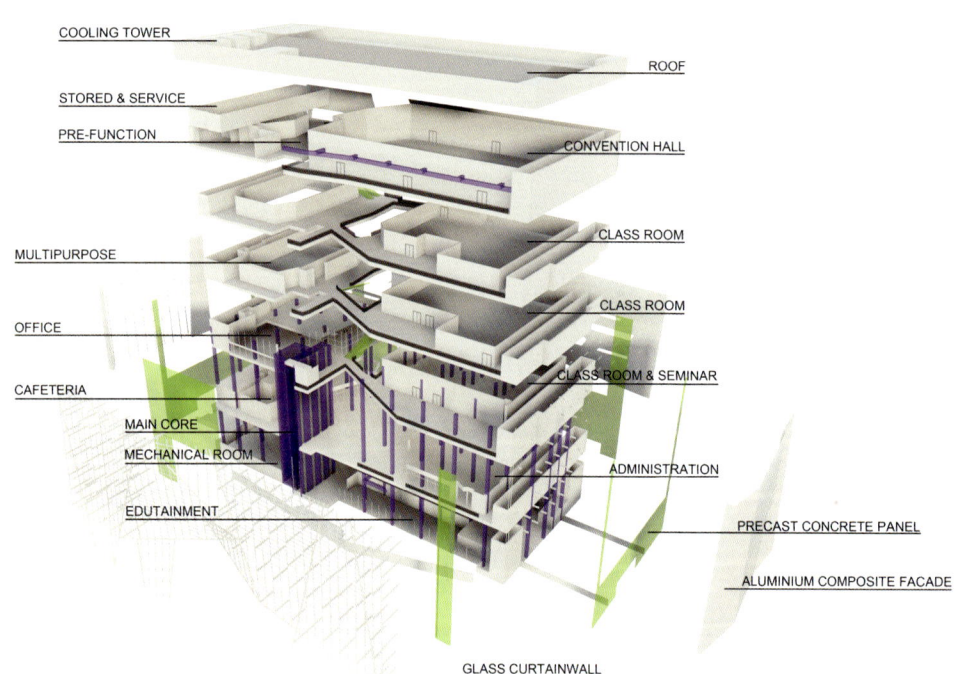

Mahidol University Technology Innovation Center & Main Auditorium

Location: Phutthamonthon, Nakhon Pathom, Thailand
Client: Mahidol University
Area: 15,000 square meters
Year: 2006
Contract Winning Design

The brief called for a 2,000-seat auditorium for art performances, academic gatherings, and ceremonial events, as well as a multipurpose hall to serve as a convention center for exhibitions and other events.

Mahidol University wanted the auditorium to be more than just a functional building. The aim was a symbolic structure, to help define its character as one of Thailand's best-known medical institutions.

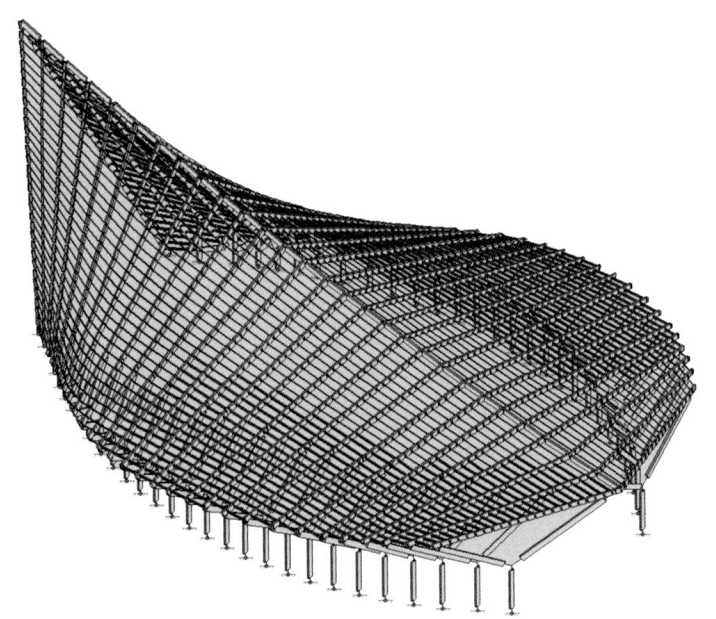

Moreover, the fact that *Mahidol* is actually the name of the late prince father of His Majesty the King inspired the quest for a modern contemporary Thai architecture that would elegantly reflect his status. In order to promote the university's prestigious medical background, organic shapes inspired by nature, such as leaf veins, were chosen to create the dramatic form of the auditorium roof. The main hall, with an elliptical plan, is made from steel; the convention center, on the other hand, is more modest, and serves to enhance the main axis and the main hall. The skin of the main foyer of the convention center is clad with the Kanpai Mahidol vine, the emblem plant of the university. The green color of the vine changes into shades of purple during flowering season, adding an interesting dimension to the façade. In addition, light and shadows cast into the foyer mimic the pattern of the screen motif in traditional Thai architecture.

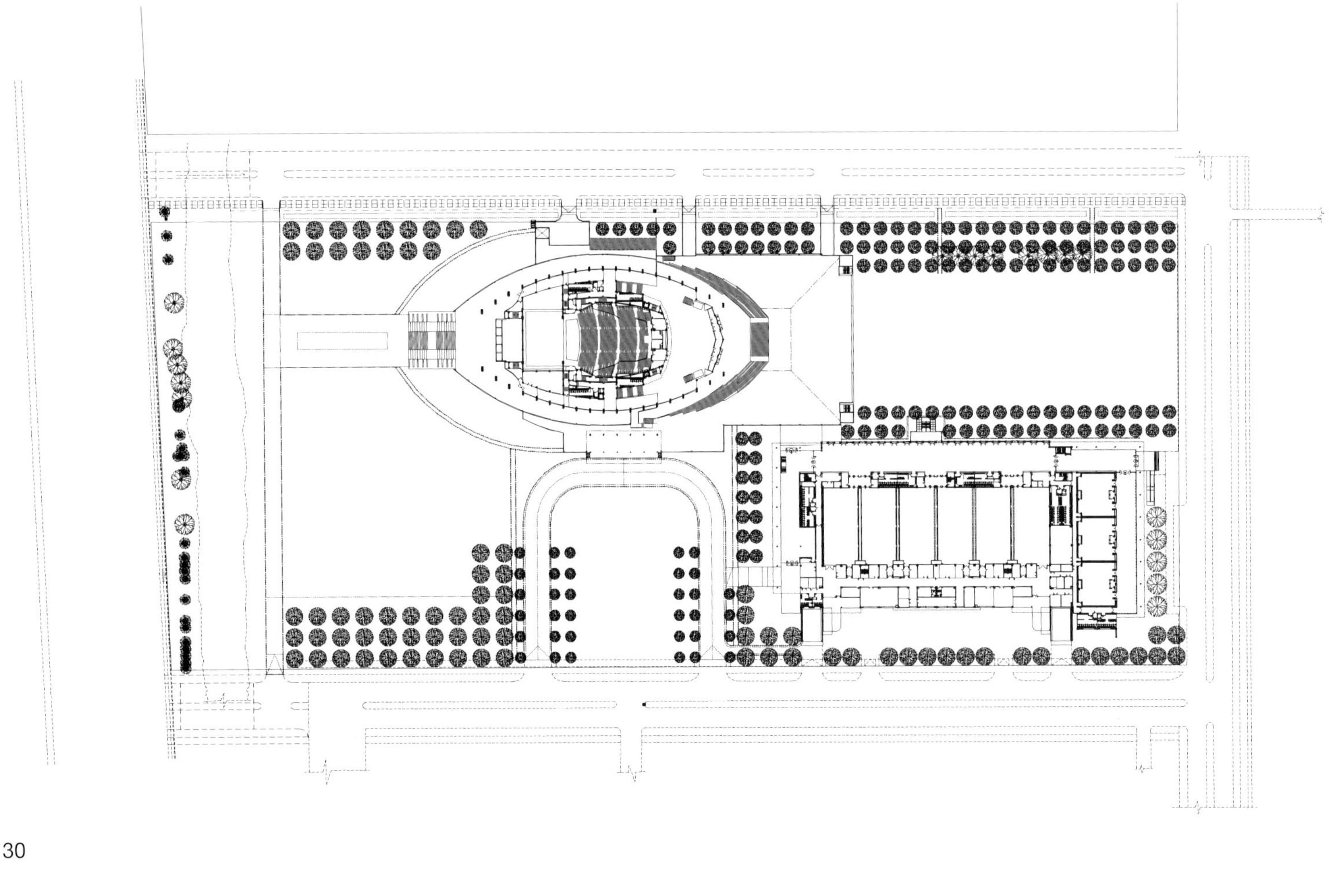

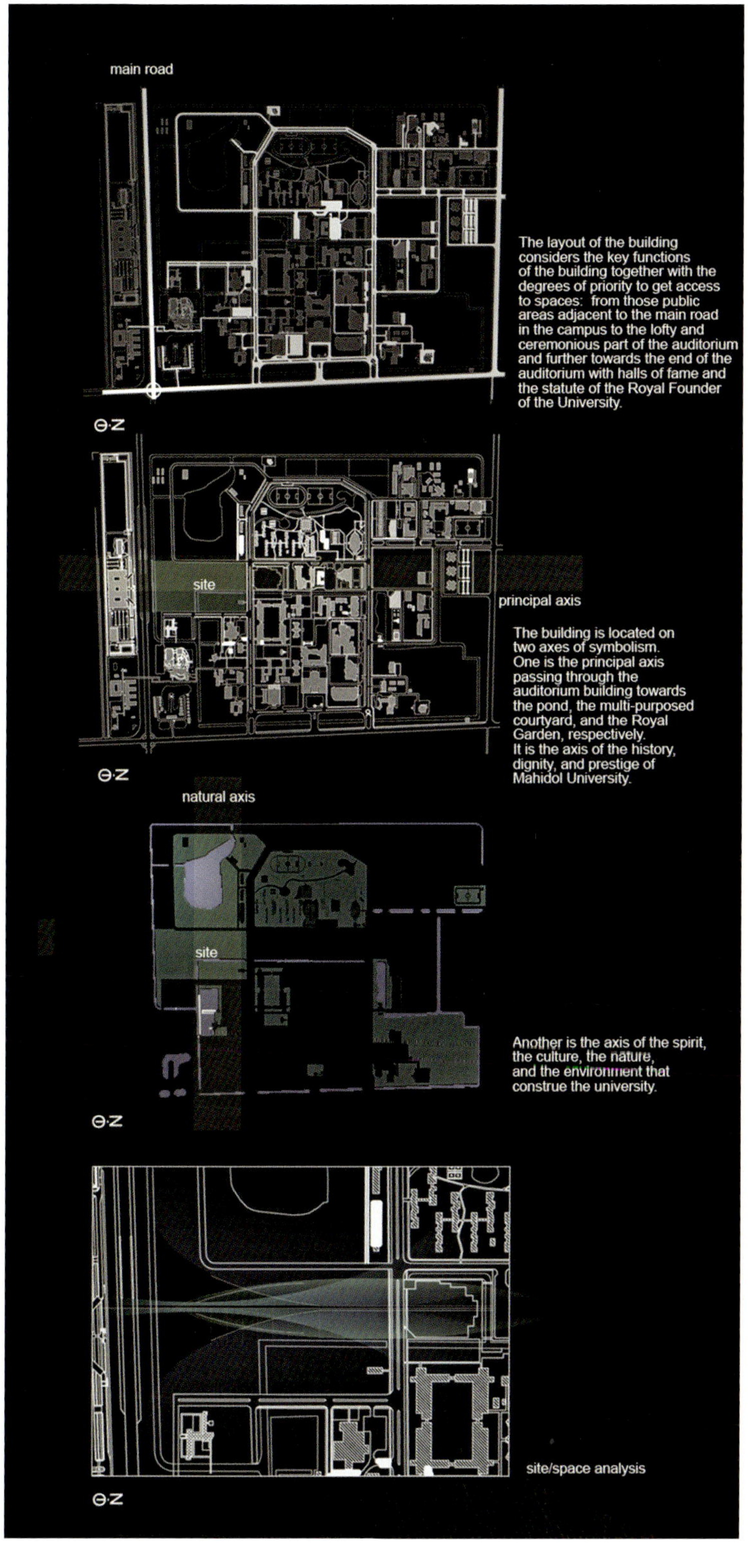

main road

The layout of the building considers the key functions of the building together with the degrees of priority to get access to spaces: from those public areas adjacent to the main road in the campus to the lofty and ceremonious part of the auditorium and further towards the end of the auditorium with halls of fame and the statue of the Royal Founder of the University.

principal axis

The building is located on two axes of symbolism. One is the principal axis passing through the auditorium building towards the pond, the multi-purposed courtyard, and the Royal Garden, respectively. It is the axis of the history, dignity, and prestige of Mahidol University.

natural axis

Another is the axis of the spirit, the culture, the nature, and the environment that construe the university.

site/space analysis

In terms of site planning, the existing open space and waterways were taken into consideration, as well as the axes of the campus master plan. The location of the auditorium enables the scale of the skeleton roof form to appear more imposing on the highway side and more "humanized" on the campus side. The strong axis of the form consequently dictates the positioning of the main plaza, water feature, and the convention center's compound, in turn reinforcing the presence of the main hall. The open-air lobby and naturally ventilated spaces in the buildings not only consume less energy but are also low maintenance. The use of vines on the façade helps lower ambient temperature and promotes the use of green concepts on the campus.

PLAZA · ENTRANCE PLAZA · LOBBY · PROJECTOR ROOM · FOLLOW SPOT · EXTERNAL ROOF

PARKING · CONTROL ROOM · M&E ROOM

Faculty of Arts, Mahidol University

Location: Phutthamonthon, Nakhon Pathom, Thailand
Client: Mahidol University
Area: 15,200 square meters
Year: 2007
Contract Winning Design 2007

To overcome several operational problems and to avoid having to limit the addition of new courses, Mahidol University's Faculty of Arts made the decision to construct a new building for classes and related activities. The facility is to include a national and international information and research center, and is designed to accommodate the current and future curricula for Thai, English, French, Chinese, and Japanese language studies, including a program for translation and interpreting. The design had to accommodate many forms of instruction, including regular classrooms, language labs, a library, multimedia studios, and rooms for academic services and support.

The building design provides an innovative identity for the study of languages and art with a wide range of electronic and telecommunications capabilities to facilitate global interactions, both people-to-people and people-to-computers.

A new, flexible architectural design approach was needed to support new language learning methods, such as a central communications hub to store information for all languages.

In addition, the design had to give prominence to Mahidol's emblem and be sensitive to the surroundings while accommodating the university's overall development master plan. The façade resembles the appearance of books in a stack and the lamp circulation represents the Samud Koy—the long book made of pulp from trees of the family Urticaceae, which Thai people used in the past.

Pine Valley Golf Resort & Country Club

Location: Beijing, China
Client: Pine Valley
Area: 9,000 square meters
Year: 1999–2003

Located in the suburbs of Beijing, the Pine Valley Golf Resort and Country Club consists of a golf course, a resort hotel, and a residential development. The project is fully equipped with superior standard facilities within the finest atmosphere.

The master planning incorporates all existing terrain features, including mountain ranges, pools, waterfalls, and cliffs. The resort hotel is composed of a single-load three-story slab and clusters of two-story detached residential hotel villages. Other functions integrate aspects of the local lifestyle, such as the Poker Room in the clubhouse, which is considerably larger than comparable Western clubhouses.

The design emphasizes flexibility and efficiency by splitting the plan into several buildings to distribute room occupancy, while reducing the footprint of the building appropriate to the site's geography.

A lengthy cantilevered roof in tropical-architecture style creates shade and shadow, giving a sense of the serenity of the East.

While the roof forms are harmonious with the clubhouse, the repeated rhythm of the architectural elements enhances the clusters of buildings as unique yet similar. The design is also appropriate to the climate, which is affected by the Gobi desert toward the northwest. The solid stonewall was inspired by the club's greater surroundings including the Great Wall of China, which is visible on a clear day.

The Royal Bangkok Sports Club

Location: Henri Dunant Road, Bangkok, Thailand
Client: The Royal Bangkok Sports Club
Area: 14,344 square meters
Year: 1998–2002
Contract Winning Design

The Royal Bangkok Sport Club (RBSC) has more than a century of history. His Majesty King Rama V donated the site and gave permission to found the club in 1901. Since then, Bangkok's city planning administration has also set aside the site for exclusive use by the club.

The brief was to reinstate the existing public stand for the horse racetrack and offer space for almost all indoor sporting activities, including the multipurpose hall that can be reconfigured to cater for basketball, volleyball, and takraw (a ball game incorporating aspects of volleyball and soccer, originating in Asia) and for use as a 500-seat banquet hall in addition to courts for badminton, squash, table tennis, billiards, snooker, bridge, chess, a changing room, library, spa, and the club's administrative office.

The site for this building is rectangular. The slab is elongated parallel to the perimeter of the golf course and racetrack. The land form and the dimension of the sport field initiated the design concept with their simple, matchbox-like forms. Structurally the building can be divided into two wings. The first wing has a long-span structure that houses the multipurpose space topped with the badminton court. The other wing is a shorter-span structure, which also contains more floor slabs. The core containing the elevator and staircase connects the two wings.

The façade is composed with a degree of solidity to ensure appropriate international standards of environmental control for specific sports. Areas of transparency in various parts of the building are designed to be meeting places with natural ventilation and are reminiscent of the former clubhouse.

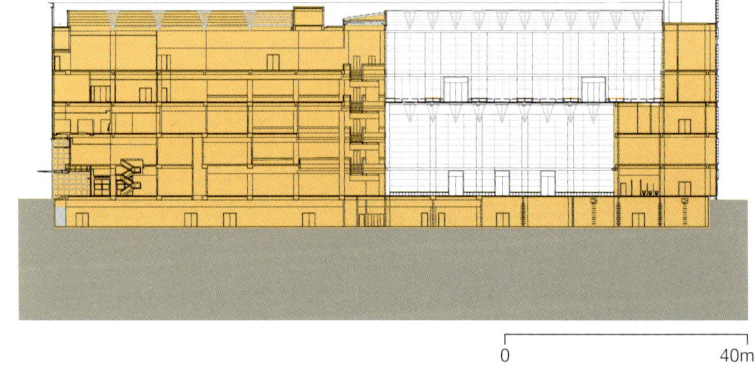

The primary material for the exterior cladding is beige limestone with dry process installation, which contrasts beautifully with the greenery of the golf course and gives the building a timeless appearance.

The Tubkaak Krabi Boutique Resort

Location: Krabi, Thailand
Client: Teicon
Area: 4,800 square meters
Year: 2000–2002
Citation, ASA Architectural Design Awards, 2004

The Tubkaak Resort is located on a site facing a spectacular beach with a chain of islands in the distance. The rear of the site is also adjacent to a national park. A natural creek flows from the nearby mountain through the site, which is lush with plants and trees. The beach also features a natural stream flowing through from the valley.

The master plan emphasizes as much preservation as possible of the existing environment. Buildings were clustered with their views directed toward both internal and external spaces. Internal spaces were designed in relation to the existing topography and environment while maintaining guest privacy. Landscape walls were integrated into the design in order to further enhance privacy. Behind the walls is an internal garden where guests can enjoy bathing outdoors without being disturbed by others. While each building was individually designed to fit and to blend into a specific location, they all feature a first floor elevated a meter above the ground.

The curved-edge gables and ridgepoles create a unique character to the roof of the Tabkaak resort.

The roof form was inspired by the unique forms of traditional *Ko Lae* and *Naga* boats. Detail elements, designed in a tropical vernacular style, appear on items such as bed screens, door locks, and so on, while also maintaining four-star resort hotel standards. Water is retained in the onsite reservoir, with the overflow directed across the site as part of the landscape design.

Mission Hills Phuket Golf Resort & Spa

Location: Phuket, Thailand
Client: Rung Sin Construction
Area: 7,500 square meters
Year: 2001–2003

The Mission Hills Phuket Golf Resort & Spa was built on a former Para rubber tree plantation, 20 minutes from Phuket airport. Located on the shoreline of Andaman Sea, the 18-hole golf course, designed by Jack Nicklaus, is the only one of Phuket's four golf courses to have views of the Andaman Sea from its fairway.

The layout of the golf course starts from the first hole next to the clubhouse and approaches the sea. A highlight is the green of the 9th hole, which is right in the middle of a sand dune, offering a view of Pangnga far beyond in the background. The layout guides the golfer around the course to the 18th hole in front of the clubhouse via the fairway parallel to the national mangrove reserve. The project also includes a driving range, clubhouse, and a 70-room resort and spa. The design utilizes an exaggerated traditional Thai vocabulary, which becomes the backdrop and wayfinding device for golfers on the course.

Traditional Thai architectural decoration can be found throughout the building, including columns, roof edges, and pediments.

These elements were designed in collaboration with experts from Thailand's Department of Fine Arts to ensure precise hierarchy and appropriateness.

Sofitel Patong

Location: Patong, Phuket, Thailand
Client: Phuket Income
Area: 34,000 square meters
Year: 2005

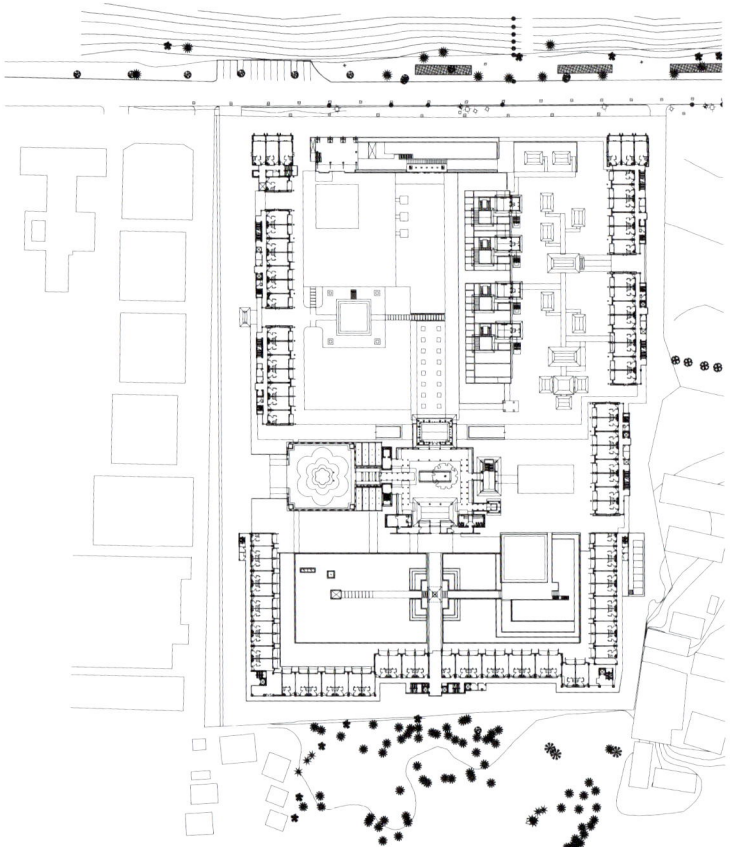

This five-star resort, on a 3.6-hectare site, anticipates the potential of nature and the continuing support of Thailand as an international tourism gateway to Southeast Asia. The preservation and support of cultural heritage were key considerations in the project's development.

The project consists of 320 guest rooms, spa, restaurant, swimming pool, and parking space for 80 cars. The average height of four stories was stipulated by a planning code affecting buildings built from the shore to 150 meters inland. Thus the ceiling height is also restricted to 2.6 meters. Surrounded by commercial buildings, the building's courtyard arrangement provides privacy for the guest rooms. The lobby creates a calm and elegant first impression for guests.

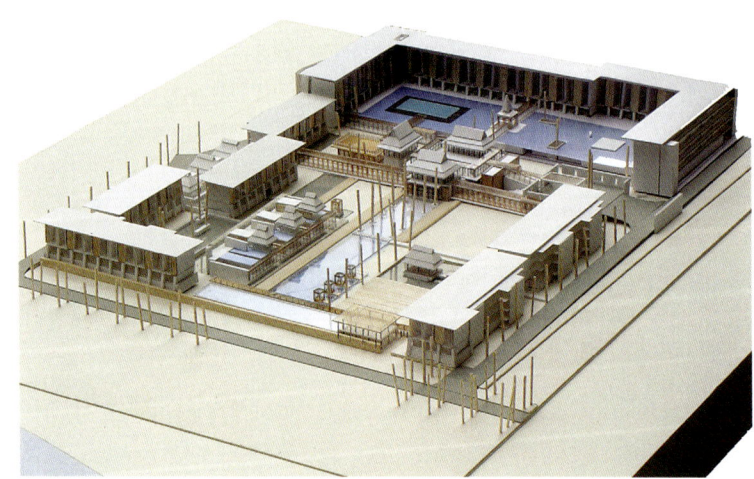

The design uses the architectural language of *Sukhothai* and *Ayutthaya* and the southern Thai vernacular to integrate and express the identity of the nation.

The infrastructure, including the parking area, is designed to have minimal impact on the environment—both in the resort and in the wider area. A major security concern was the evacuation plan in the event of another tsunami or natural disaster. To minimize potential damage and ensure safety for the guests, all guest rooms are elevated to a safe level, a feature which, in addition to the service area that is considered the heart of the design, has become a hallmark of the project. Views toward the sea are offered in all guest rooms, adding a further distinctive feature to the design.

Maldives Resort & Spa

The Maldives has long been known as the world's ultimate travel destination. From the spectacular lagoon to the long, white, sandy coral beaches and undisturbed natural flora and fauna it is the perfect location for three dream island resorts: Funama, Lunudhua, and Maavelavaru.

An acute environmental concern was that the latter two resorts are situated where sea turtle nesting sites are found around the island. The major idea behind the development concept was the notion of a great escape to an unseen natural seascape on a virgin island. Of equal importance in the development was to care for the area's natural resources by ensuring that any buildings blend in and seamlessly coexist with the natural environment.

The use of natural materials such as coconut thatch, terra cotta tiles, and plastered walls with good ventilation supports the idea of energy savings via reduction of heat gain while creating a natural ambience for the space. Other interesting and distinctive materials include coconut tree trunks and coconut shells, which are transformed to become part of the buildings' features, such as columns, as well as other gadgets and apparatus.

The Funama Resort & Spa

Location: Funamaudua Island, North Huvadhoo Atoll, Maldives
Client: Aminath Shafia – M. Park Lane
Area: 16,055 square meters
Year: 2004

The design focuses on creating a new experience of island dwelling, which allows visitors to enjoy the touch of pure Funamaudua spirit. The romantic round hut is the symbol of the simple lifestyle of a native islander. The interior ambience is relaxed and cozy luxury with a color scheme of light beige with accents of bright coral fish colors to warmly welcome guests.

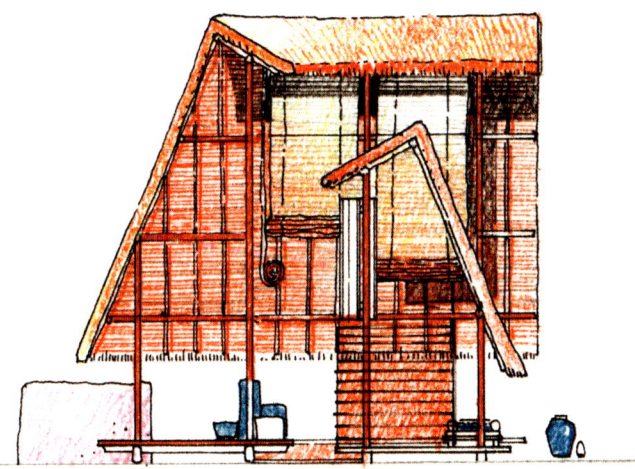

The Lonudhua Resort & Spa

Location: Lonudhuahuttaa Island, South Huvadhoo Atoll, Maldives
Client: Ahmed Hamza Ma. Kinbi
Area: 15,248 square meters
Year: 2004

The architectural expression blends sea life with local Maldivian character. The shape and form of the stingray echoes the sound and sense of the Maldivian sea like a welcoming whisper. The interior ambience offers a sense of modernity with a color scheme of white, bone, and gray tones, offsetting the surrounding natural colors—the turquoise ocean and lush green landscape.

The Maavela Resort & Spa

Location: Maavelavaru Island, South Miladhunmadulu Atoll, Maldives
Client: Ali Shiyam M. Fenfiyaazuaage
Area: 25,639 square meters
Year: 2004

The image of the sea turtle features in the guest villas to urge visitors to understand, appreciate and respect the value of nature and its inhabitants.

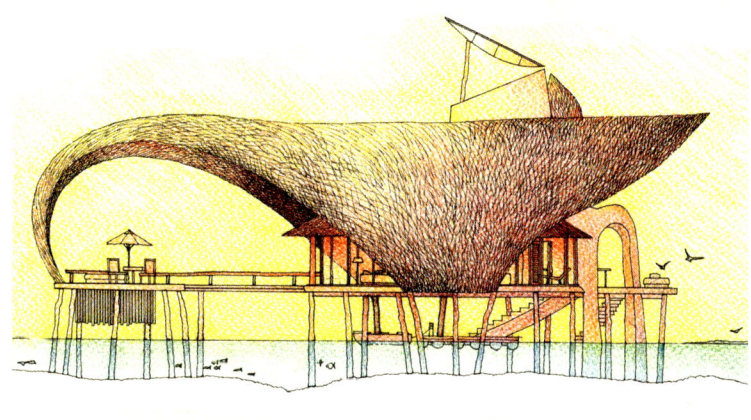

Inspired by the starfish, the exclusive stand-alone villas are reached only by boat and are the most luxurious type of accommodation. The ambience of the interior design offers serenity and understated modern luxury with a color scheme of warm and sensuous earth tones to welcome the sophisticated traveler. The interior decoration includes indigenous fabric crafts and artworks, which enhance the unique architectural setting and reflect the Maldivian cultural heritage.

Koh Kood Resort

Location: Koh Kood, Trat, Thailand
Client: Summit Auto Seats Industry
Area: 19,212 square meters
Year: 2006

This six-star resort, on Koh Kood Island in the Gulf of Thailand, is one of the premium destinations in the country. Located close to Bangkok, only one-and-a-half hours from the shore to the island, Koh Kood Resort offers the most perfect natural reserve in Thailand's Gulf.

From Tapoi Bay, there is no road access to Koh Kood Island—entry is exclusively by boat. A creek and waterfall are found on the east of the island, and a peninsula to the north. As the site runs parallel to the shore, the buildings were planned in a linear arrangement, with connections at both the beginning and the end of the site where the exclusive villas, special restaurant, and the wellness spa are located. The villas are grouped in unique clusters, and include the presidential suite villa, executive suite villas, superior beach villas, superior deluxe clustered villas, and deluxe stand-alone villas.

The design of the resort aims to preserve the island's environment, which includes a vast natural forest.

Natural elements such as rocks, leaves, waves, sand dunes, butterflies, and other insects were the inspirations in designing this project, Thailand's last remaining tropical paradise. The value of the architecture lies in the integrity of its natural form and characteristics, generating sensual and relaxing lines that perfectly fit the resort's luxurious ambience.

Phuket Renaissance

Location: Phuket, Thailand
Client: Seacon Hotel & Resort
Area: 22,000 square meters
Year: 2007–2009

Mai Kaw beach, site of the Phuket Renaissance Hotel, stretches for 10 kilometers along the northern coastline of Phuket. The hotel site includes sand dunes on the shore area, and a large lake and public road access at the rear of the property.

The Renaissance hotel consists of 220 guest rooms including 22 pool villas, with two restaurants, a large banquet room, spa, a kids' club, and business center. The circulation is divided into three distinctive and separate zones: the public, private, and service areas. The hotel is composed of various scales of building, starting from five stories at the rear, three stories in the middle section and one story for the villas close to the beach.

The hotel was designed to cater for visitors of all ages, offering unique experiences for family recreation and opportunities for more intimate interaction with the natural surroundings. Flexibility was the main criteria for the design of the master plan with a wide assortment of the room types on offer, and a variety of views toward the beach.

The layout also generates a sense of freedom and, together with the swimming pools and water gardens that are distributed over several areas, creates multiple recreation areas.

Restaurant

Lobby

Villa

Guest rooms

Spa

Jumeirah Phuket Private Island

Location: Phuket, Thailand
Client: Dilokpol Sundaravej
Area: 35,500 square meters
Year: 2007–2009

Located in the untouched tropical island of Koh Raet, just 500 meters offshore from Ao Po Bay, northeast of Phuket Island, this new development offers breathtaking views of Pangnga. The island is reached by a four-minute private motor yacht ride or island ferry from the access point on the mainland, just 15 minutes from Phuket International Airport. The undulating site features changes in level of up to 15 meters and has abundant existing trees.

The building code limits the height of the structures to 6 and 8 meters. From the pier to the reception—at the highest point of the island—the circulation branches to distribute visitors to the various rooms and facilities. Included in the resort are 65 lavishly appointed deluxe pool villas, each with private infinity pool and Jacuzzi, 12 three-bedroom luxury residential villas, four restaurants and bars as well as extensive leisure, spa, and fitness facilities including a large freeform swimming pool and a 400-meter stretch of private white sandy beach.

The project also offers a marina, a private yacht club, a tennis court, several boutiques, a business center and a library with dedicated reading room.

The design experiments with the contemporary Thai roof to counter the height limitations.

Pullman Bangkok King Power

Location: Rang Nam Road, Bangkok, Thailand
Client: King Power International Group
Area: 41,490 square meters
Year: 2004–2007

The 388-room Pullman King Power Hotel occupies a 21-story tower on the south wing and a six-floor L-shaped low-rise on the west and north sides, all gathered around a grand inner open courtyard. On the first level, guestrooms benefit from the intimate touch of a long and narrow lotus pond, which enhances the oriental sense of living by the water.

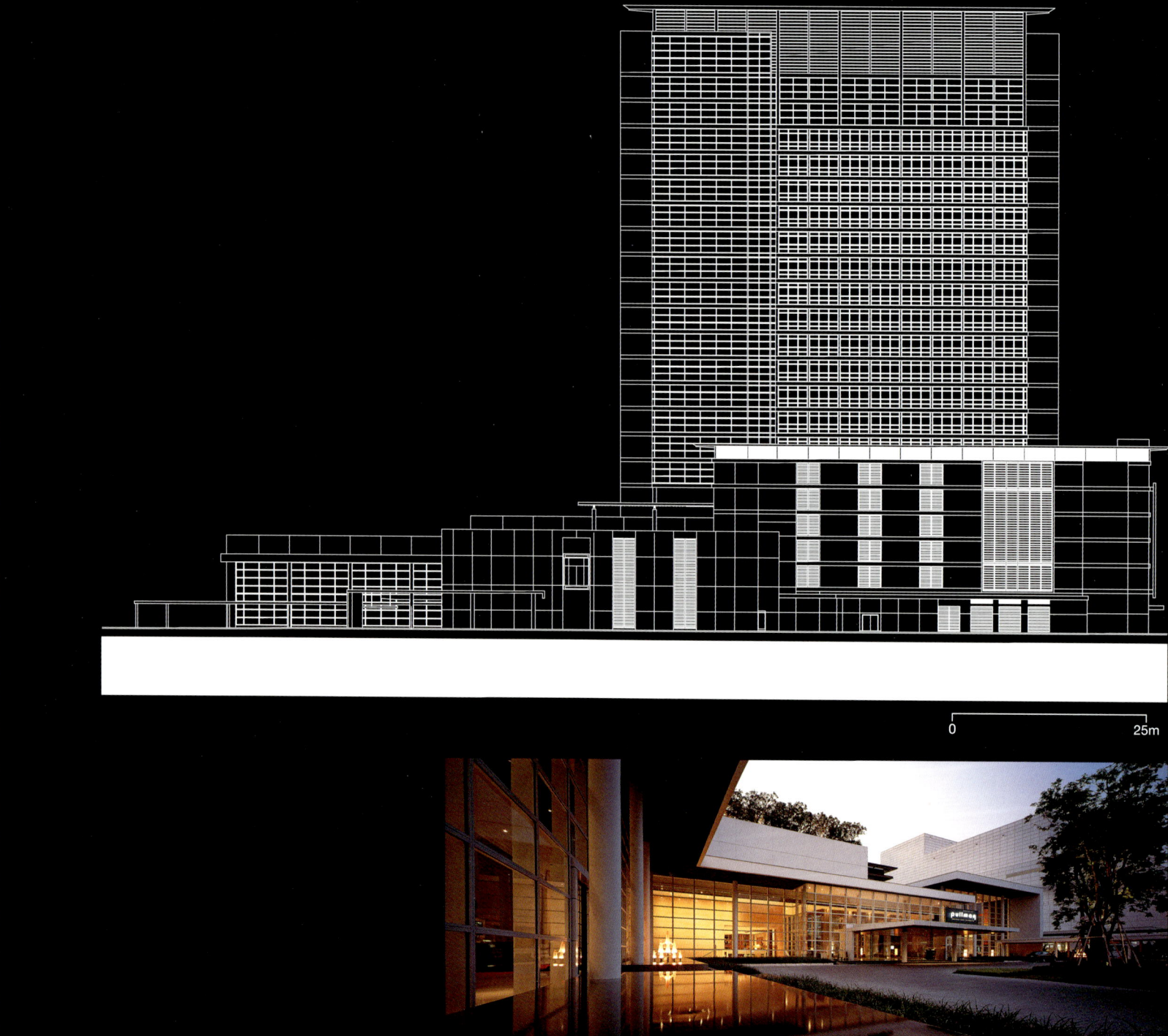

0   25m

From the inner boulevard, the Pullman King Power Hotel welcomes guests at the colonnaded arrival courtyard, which defines the border between city chaos and tranquility. Guests are dropped off under the shade of rain trees before being led to the grand lobby, which is connected to the banquet hall, from where they can glimpse a smaller inner courtyard that offers all-day dining and a lobby lounge. On the upper floor the glazed-edge swimming pool overhangs the grand courtyard. A spa, meeting facilities, and an Asian fusion restaurant are also located around the hotel.

The Pullman King Power is intentionally designed as a resort-like hotel in the heart of Bangkok. The design breaks through the stereotype of typical urban hospitality projects by providing large open areas such as the central courtyard and including waterscapes and ample plantings of local vegetation. Natural light diffuses through trellises and shading screens to amplify the tropical ambience in most of the public areas.

Holiday Inn Express

Location: Rama I Road, Bangkok, Thailand
Client: Holiday Inn
Area: 20,160 square meters
Year: 2008–2010

Located in the heart of Bangkok, the Holiday Inn Express is a recent, rapidly expanding innovation from the Holiday Inn chain. The three-star hotel offers reasonably priced yet stylish accommodation.

The front area is preserved as an open space with access from the side drop-off area. In the high-rise tower there are 20 guestrooms per floor, with a central service core and a structural span of 8 meters on a black granite base.

The design of the tower resembles shifting boxes and creates the illusion of animation.

The façade articulation brings together precast concrete and patterned glazing to offer gradual changes in the degree of transparency while reducing the construction costs of glass application.

Schematics of façade design

Red Mountain

Location: Phuket, Thailand
Client: MBK
Area: 22,000 square meters
Year: 2008–2010

This project is situated on a mountain overlooking the famous Bangtau Beach. The cliff faces reveal layers of the reddish rock that were the inspiration for the name of the development. The project also includes one of the best golf courses in Southeast Asia, while the combination of hotel and spa offers visitors the finest hospitality service with the atmosphere of a natural hideaway.

The guest rooms vary from the deluxe, on three-story stepped slabs, to the twin-unit type with an extra-wide balcony. The rooms are oriented around the manmade lake. Planning is interwoven with the natural context, by, for example, placing water closets in the midst of trees, where such activity can become part of nature. The three-bedroom villas with flat overhanging roofs are located on the rather steep slope. The clubhouse also comprises executive member lounges for golfers, a spa, and a restaurant beside the swimming pool.

The architectural language is a simple interplay between the vertical and horizontal planes.

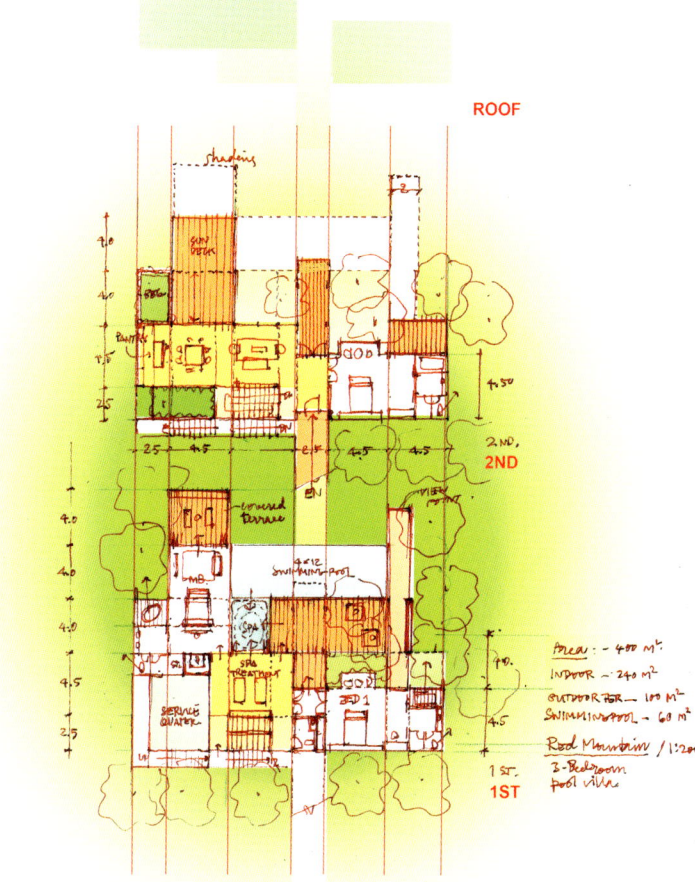

The roofs are designed to be as flat as possible to reduce the visual massing. The pattern of the trellises mimics the rhythms of a tree. A natural color scheme was chosen to relate to the surrounding lush vegetation.

Oasis at Mulberry

Location: Upper Aljunied Road, Singapore
Client: Tan Chong Land
Area: 23,028 square meters
Year: 1999–2004
Contract Winning Design 1999

Upper Aljunied Road is a new residential area of Singapore, composed mainly of rather traditional town houses. This development offers a new concept in response to the demands of Singapore's current generation of homebuyers by offering an alternative approach to the architecture. In addition, the developer determined that the construction of all units be completed before they were available for sale.

The project offers seven variations of typology in 76 town homes. All homes are two stories high with a sub-basement and attic floor underneath the roof.

The project was designed with the underlying idea of a garden accessible to all units; this was achieved by separating the access road from the central garden, which allows each unit to have two front façades.

The articulation of the architecture embraces crisp, ultra-modern lines, producing openness and clarity.

Overcoming the limitation of the shared walls that generally characterize townhouses, the design incorporates a skylight at the middle portion of the houses to let natural light into areas such as bedrooms, bathroom, kitchen, and pantry. An interesting feature of the Singapore building code required that the sub-basement floor incorporate thick concrete walls, strong enough to resist a bomb blast and that the attic floor underneath the roof be connected by a door to the adjacent unit for use as a fire escape route.

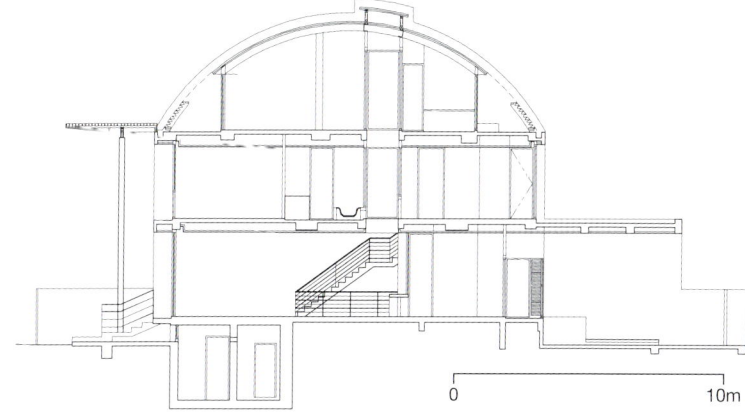

Bukit Gita Bayu

Location: Kuala Lumpur, Malaysia
Client: Yee Seng Heights
Area: 14,680 square meters
Year: 2002–2004

Bukit Gita Bayu is a 48-hectare exclusive residential development in Seri Kembangan, Serangor, 15 kilometers from Kuala Lumpur and accessible via the Kuala Lumpur–Seremban highway. Gita Bayu, which translates to "windsong", lives up to its name by evoking images of rustling leaves, running streams, and a picturesque lake. Situated on the former Kelton Estate, the second-oldest rubber plantation in the country, the development was first proposed in 1997 to cater to the demand for homes in a setting that was more than green in name only. This was the catalyst for developers and architects to practice minimal disturbance of the site's flora and fauna and to retain the existing trees wherever possible.

The hill villas area contains 34 two-story bungalows and four three- and four-story walk-down condominiums, perched on stilts on the hill.

Every effort was taken to build around the existing foliage as opposed to building over it.

In the master plan, building and pathways had to occasionally be aligned around the plants, while some trees were transplanted to other locations within the development.

With the master plan and landscape design blurring the line between residence and resort, the long overhanging roofs and the sensitive, tropical-style architecture allow the buildings to nestle within the green backdrop. The end result is homes scattered amid woodlands, characterized by a majestic collection of trees that provide the impression of living in a luxurious tropical retreat.

Samui Pavilion

Location: Samui Island, Surat Thani, Thailand
Client: Nawarat Patanakarn
Area: 450 square meters per unit
Year: 2006

Situated on Samui Island, Thailand, this 6.7-hectare hillside development provides panoramic views of the Gulf of Thailand from each of its 40 villas.

Existing vegetation was preserved as much as possible, as was the natural geography of the land and the natural surroundings. Minimizing the roadway gave each house maximum privacy without blocking views toward the sea. The houses offer tropical Western lifestyle with the comfort of three bedrooms plus guest houses, and infinity swimming pools that blend with the horizon.

Careful consideration was given to the low-maintenance properties of natural materials, and local rock available around the area was used for architectural detailing.

Local building codes in Samui required that the buildings have a pitch roof, to preserve the identity of the island. With the curved-edge signature roofs, the architectural language embraces both a sense of modernity and the local vernacular.

Cocoon Life Style

Location: Phuket Country Club, Phuket, Thailand
Client: Anupaspirom Resort
Area: 600–800 square meters per unit
Year: 2003–2006

Cocoon Life Style is an executive residential development in the middle of the golf course at the Phuket Country Club. The site is slightly elevated to offer extensive views of the surrounding area. This presented a challenge for the design since all parts of the houses, including the service areas, were subject to 360-degree visibility.

Designed for elderly residents, the housing typology is limited to single-story, one-and-a-half story, and two-story buildings, with ramps inside for convenience. The buildings' orientation creates an inner courtyard, with a tropical modern atmosphere to complement Phuket's climate, and accentuated by wooden terraces, marble, and sandstone walls.

Inspiration for the courtyards came from the Sino-Portuguese architecture of houses in downtown Phuket, creating a comfortable atmosphere while reflecting local culture and identity.

Cheras Residential Development

Location: Kuala Lumpur, Malaysia
Client: Hong Leong Properties
Area: 500 square meters per unit
Year: 2006–2010

The design of this development of detached houses was inspired by the lush, green, modern tropical lifestyle of Kuala Lumpur. Each individual design has its own characteristics, ranging from contemporary designs to the more modern.

One feature that all designs have in common is an open plan that orients internally toward a private courtyard.

Entry from the carport is dramatized through a series of steps and spaces. Each design will have its own individual entry experience. Relaxing in the main living space, one can enjoy the view out to the private pool and landscape beyond.

From the deck by the pool, families can enjoy the tranquility or unwind with friends, the kind of experiences that generated the design concept from the outset.

The Peak

Location: Kuala Lumpur, Malaysia
Client: E & O Properties
Area: 1,500 square meters per unit
Year: 2008–2010

The brief called for luxury private villas of 800 to 1200 square meters each. The approach to the design is to utilize as much as possible of the land plot while exploiting the view toward Kuala Lumpur city center.

Each component in the villas is composed in a modern arrangement with a courtyard and swimming pool as the focal point. All the units feature large fully glazed living and dining rooms. The deck area adjacent to the swimming pool is carefully laid out to provide extended outdoor living areas.

The folded roof with standing seam metal deck forms a key visual element to the architecture, which is unmistakably modern. The exterior color palette provides a warm ambience to the residential compound.

The Clover

Location: Thonglor 18, Bangkok, Thailand
Client: Top Line Living
Area: 42,000 square meters
Year: 2005–2007

Located in Thonglor 18 Lane, one of the finest residential locations in Bangkok, The Clover comprises five nine-story buildings on a 10-hectare site. It offers a metropolitan lifestyle for the young white-collar market.

The group of buildings orient their elongated façades toward the north and the south to reduce heat gain from the west while taking advantage of the wind direction. Surrounded by public streets and other high-rise buildings, the design arranges the group of buildings around a large courtyard inside the project where the garden, swimming pool, and other sport facilities are located. The 589 residential units are available in studio, one-bedroom, and two-bedroom configurations.

The addition of an articulated frame wrapped around two floors gives a distinctive accent to the façade and reduces the mass of each of the building blocks.

Vertical wooden louvers are installed to express the vertical circulation that ascends to the roof. These two features together produce an urban element that demonstrates modernity and simplicity.

Jumeirah Park Apartments

Location: Dubai, United Arab Emirates
Client: Nakheel
Area: 500,000 square meters
Year: 2007–2009

Located in Dubai, this high-end residential development offers a range of duplex residential units.

The buildings form a crescent more than a kilometer long around a man-made lake, mimicking the curve from the larger master plan. Each building is composed of three sections, organized like double-loaded corridors to maximize the perimeter of the building. The height of the buildings varies from 12 to 24 stories. Parking for 2,000 cars is provided at the underground level. The critical design issue is how to deal with the massive scale and repetition of the project.

A Southeast Asian sensibility is integrated into the design with large terraces, loggias, and plunge pools, while an Arabic flavor is provided by the application of the motif screens made of glass fiber reinforced concrete (GRC) and precast concrete.

Urbana Langsuan

Location: Langsuan Road, Bangkok, Thailand
Client: Urbana Estate
Area: 23,822 square meters
Year: 2003–2005

Like its predecessor, Urbana Sukhumvit 15, this 36-story condominium was built on the site of a former structure in Langsuan Lane, one of the finest residential locations in Bangkok.

The tower consists of 152 privately owned units that occupy the 9th to 29th and 32nd to 37th floors and serviced apartments that occupy the 2nd to the 8th and the 30th to 31st floors. These apartments are available in single- to three-bedroom and also the penthouse. Shared facilities include a restaurant, tennis court, basketball court, squash court, gymnasium, business center, and luxury swimming pool on the 31st floor.

Efficiently utilizing the space while providing panoramic views to the nearby Lumpinee Park were the major considerations.

The curved towers feature a façade articulation that expresses their verticality; the two towers are connected by the sky-high swimming pool and the distinctive roof that is a trademark of the Urbana condominium series.

The Fraser Suites Urbana Sathorn

Location: Sathorn Road, Bangkok, Thailand
Client: Urbana Estate
Area: 40,860 square meters
Year: 2003–2007
Citation, ASA Architectural Design Awards, 2008

This 36-story residential tower on Sathorn Road in the heart of Bangkok is accessible from the Bangkok Mass Transit System's sky train and elevated expressway. The tower consists of 208 residential units: 145 units from the 15th to the 36th floor are for sale, and 63 units from the 8th to the 14th floor are serviced apartments. Common areas include the reception hall, restaurant, tennis court, mini basketball court, squash, physical fitness, aerobic room, swimming pool with jet whirlpool, locker with sauna, playground, and the business center.

The common areas are visually exposed to the exterior by a 14-meter-high glazed curtain wall; the rest of the façade is clad with a composition of laminated glass, precast concrete, and aluminum louvers.

The tower can be divided into three parts. First is the lower seven floors, with a front façade in glazed curtain wall, and aluminum louvers wrapping the rear parking space. Second, the residential units span from the 8th floor to the 36th floor, where vertical columns interweave with the horizontal bands of louvers and balustrades. Third is the overhanging roof, supported with pairs of tilted columns to lighten the visual massing of the tower top. Together, they form a remarkable edifice that embraces the Bangkok skyline along with Urbana Sukhumvit 15 and Urbana Langsuan.

citi
EVERGREEN LAUREL HO

0
25m

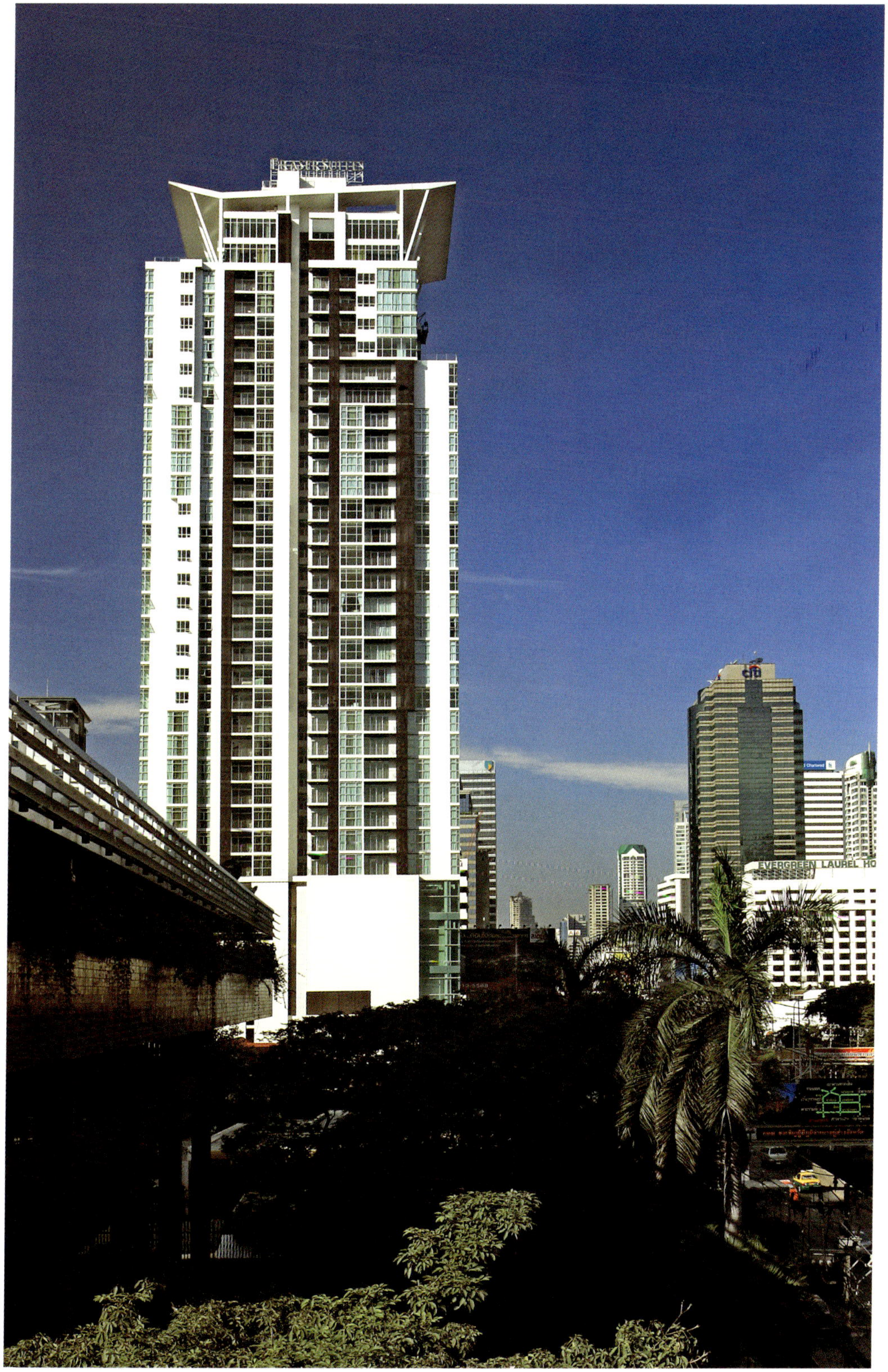

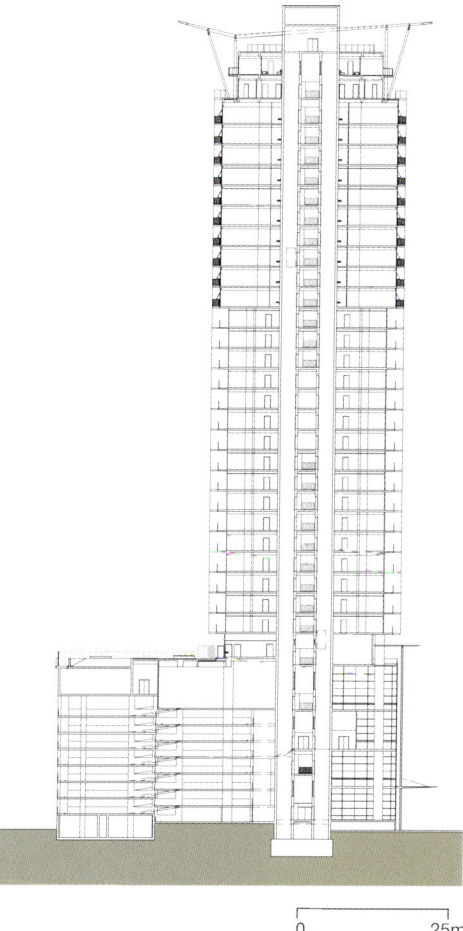

SK 41 Condominium

Location: Sukhumvit 41, Bangkok, Thailand
Area: 39,538 square meters
Year: 2003–2007

Rising 37 stories on Sukhumvit Road in the heart of Bangkok, the Madison comprises 151 residential units, four of which are penthouses, and community areas that include a 30-meter swimming pool, fitness facilities, spa, and banquet hall.

The tower offers a variety of unit types, catering to the multiplicity of urban life.

The building is expressed as a composition of smaller forms with different exterior finishes, creating a distinctive identity from the surrounding visual approach.

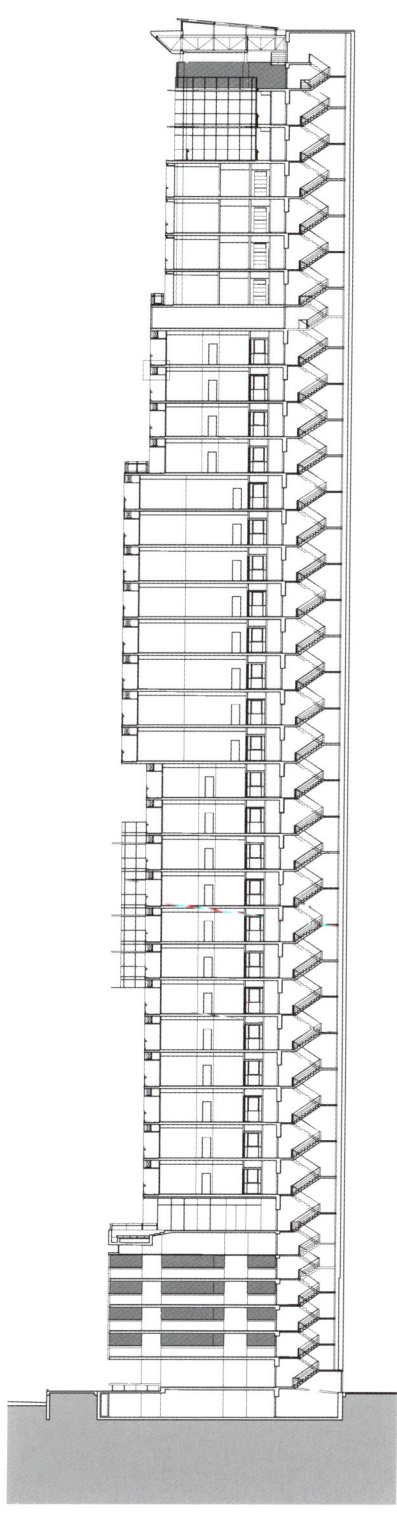

Although the overall articulation is simple, more delicate details are applied on an intimate scale, such as tactile textures, handrails, and ceilings. The building structure is generally reinforced concrete with a post-tension floor system and a steel roof structure.

Along with other high-rise residential building in the Sukhumvit area, the Madison offers a unique character that adds to the variety of the Bangkok skyline.

Athenee Place

Location: Wireless Road, Bangkok, Thailand
Client: TCC Capital Land
Area: 180,000 square meters
Year: 2004–2008

Athenee Place is located in Wireless Road, in the center of Bangkok. Its development continues from that of the late 1990s, catering to the demands of local and international business.

The project consists of three components: a 38-story office tower with three floors of retail, meeting rooms, and an 800-square-meter grand ballroom; a 41-story condominium with 219 residential units including seven penthouses; and the existing Athenee Plaza hotel. Together they form a complex of 180,000 square meters with shared parking for 1,650 cars. The plan incorporates a generous green center court that links the three main buildings to the recreation area on the seventh floor of the residential building; an open-space garden surrounds all three buildings.

The design embraces the language of Art Deco architecture, integrated with the lines of the existing hotel.

The tower's signature swooping roofline is inspired by the hand gestures of traditional Thai dance. The hand evokes a sense of protection for residents and the gentle curve offers a soft counterpoint to the tower's linear and vertical dynamism.

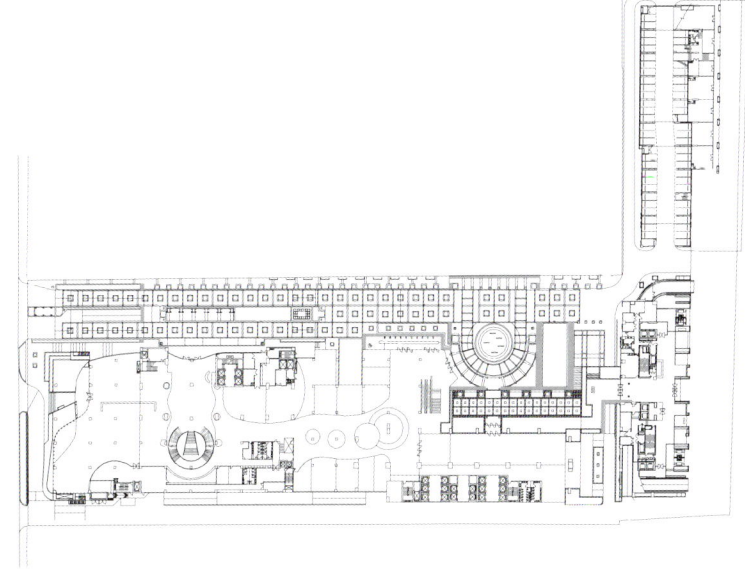

The Emporio

Location: Sukhumvit 24, Bangkok, Thailand
Client: TCC Capital Land
Area: 70,125 square meters
Year: 2005–2008

Emporio Place is a cluster of towers on Sukhumvit 24 in the center of Bangkok. Rising 42 and 35 stories, this project combines the finest elements to offer the highest standard of living.

The unique architectural aspects of Emporio Place include specially selected materials with tasteful finishes. Usable areas are efficiently designed for maximum functionally and total privacy. Most of the 329 units are enclosed by three exterior walls; huge bay windows in all living areas provide fantastic full views. A ceiling height of 2.8 meters provides additional space. Extra large living and dining spaces span over 7.5 meters in the larger units.

The façade design emphasizes the vertical architectural elements, enhancing the sense of elegance and luxury inspired by elements of Eastern culture and tradition.

The Emporio is where two disparate cultures meet in their finest forms. The modern Western design yields optimum functionality for easy living, which is further enhanced by the rich Oriental values discreetly expressed in the rhythms of the architecture.

1

1,2,3 *Schematic designs*

2

3

Wireless Road Project

Location: Wireless Road, Bangkok, Thailand
Client: Thai Contractor Assets
Area: 34,817 square meters
Year: 2007

This project, located in Bangkok's CBD, comprises prestige serviced apartments and office space for the Thai contractors' association. The surrounding greenery provided inspiration for the composition of the building. Hence, all the important public functions, such as main lobby, food and beverage outlets, lounges, and swimming pool, are composed to take advantage of the views. In addition, these composed spaces and architectural elements enhance the modern urban feeling of Wireless Road.

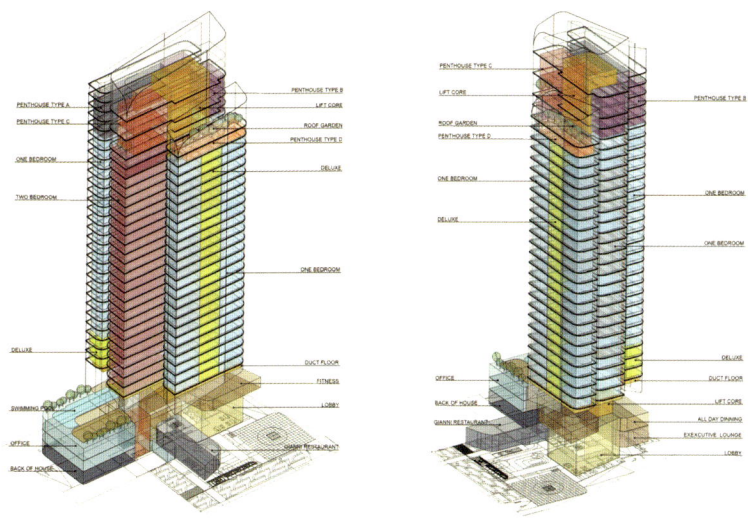

SIMULATION MODEL

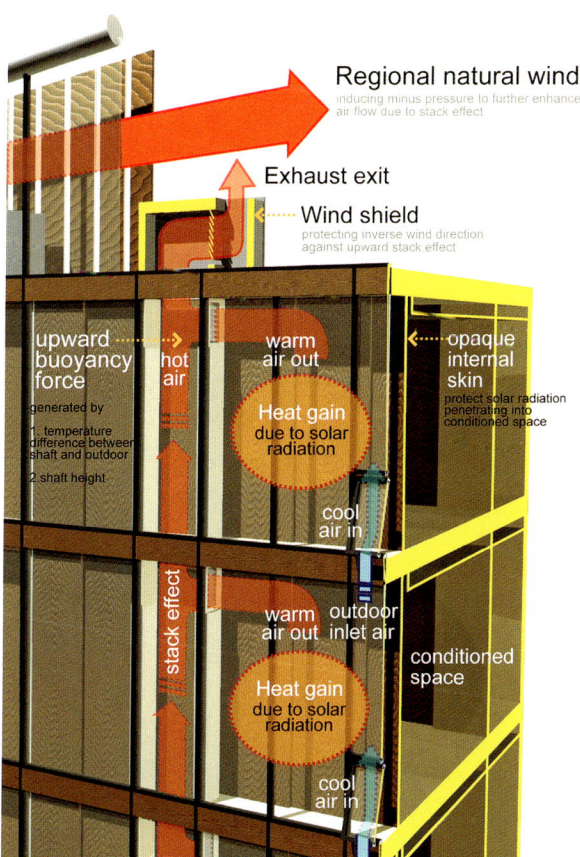

MECHANISM OF PROPOSED FACADE DESIGN

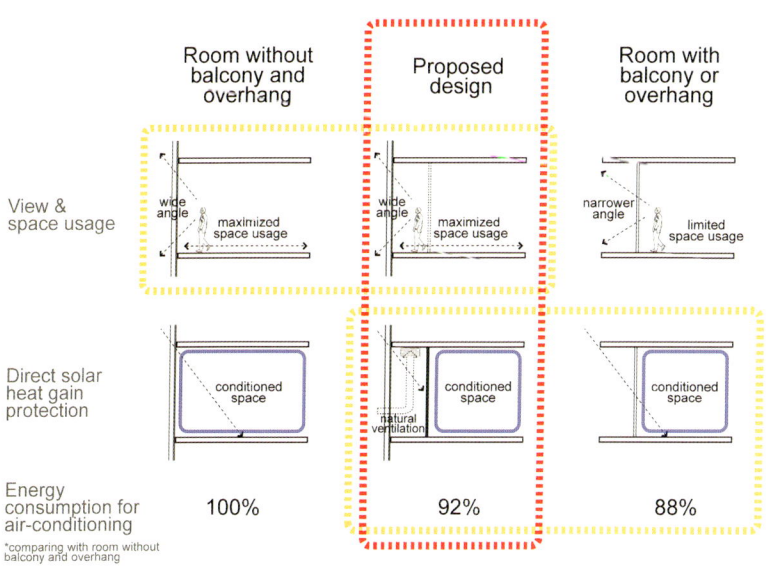

COMPARISON ON ENERGY CONSUMPTION

205

The building skin was initially inspired by the character of timber screens used in the past. These timber screens, combined with a modern aluminum and glass curtain wall and an energy-saving design, create a unique façade that is modern, warm, and lively at the same time.

The aluminum and glass façade imparts a modern feel, while the second layer of timber screens provides warmth. Residents add to the dynamism of the façade by opening the screens from the inside, creating a random pattern on the façade. The liveliness continues after dusk with the endless varying patterns of light and shadow of the timber screen.

The curved lines of Thai arts and crafts as well as the Thai alphabet provided inspiration for the building. The outcome is a building with unique characteristics and a memorable form.

King Power Complex

Location: Rang Nam Road, Bangkok, Thailand
Client: King Power International Group
Area: 145,000 square meters
Year: 2004–2007

Located on a 4.8-hectare site in the heart of the city, the King Power Complex comprises four components: a 12,000-square-meter duty free mall; a 570-seat theater and dining facility; the King Power headquarters; and a 388-room, four-star hotel.

The entire complex sits above the basement parking floor, which accommodates approximately 1,000 cars. The planning of the complex is divided into two components: first, the duty free mall, theater and office, and second, the hotel. The two components are connected by a tree-lined inner boulevard that features a texturized path and a calming pond. A drop-off canopy strip can accommodate four to five coaches at the same time while 40 coaches wait in line in the shade underneath the building at the rear of the complex.

1 Atrium
2 Restaurant
3 Foyer
4 Parking
5 Office lobby
6 Office
7 Executive office

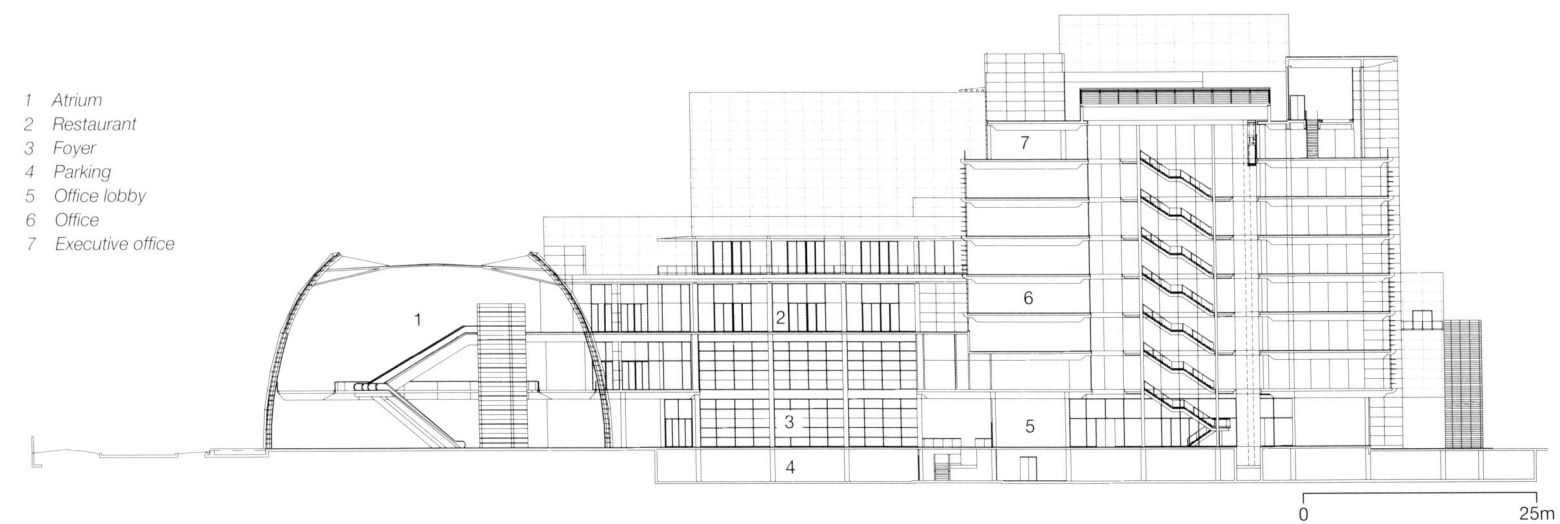

The complex

The King Power Complex is a well-programmed tourist destination where the architecture enhances a revolution in the shopping experience while celebrating the expression of Thailand's golden heritage.

Headquarters

The office center atrium spans eight floors and features a glazed elevator and exposed staircases. This tremendous void generates an exciting working atmosphere, which is humanized by the transmission of natural sunlight and ventilation. The elegant 4-meter floor-to-floor height of the work areas creates optimal working conditions. On the eighth floor, where the executive offices are located, the perimeter of the floor is recessed back to provide an outdoor deck area.

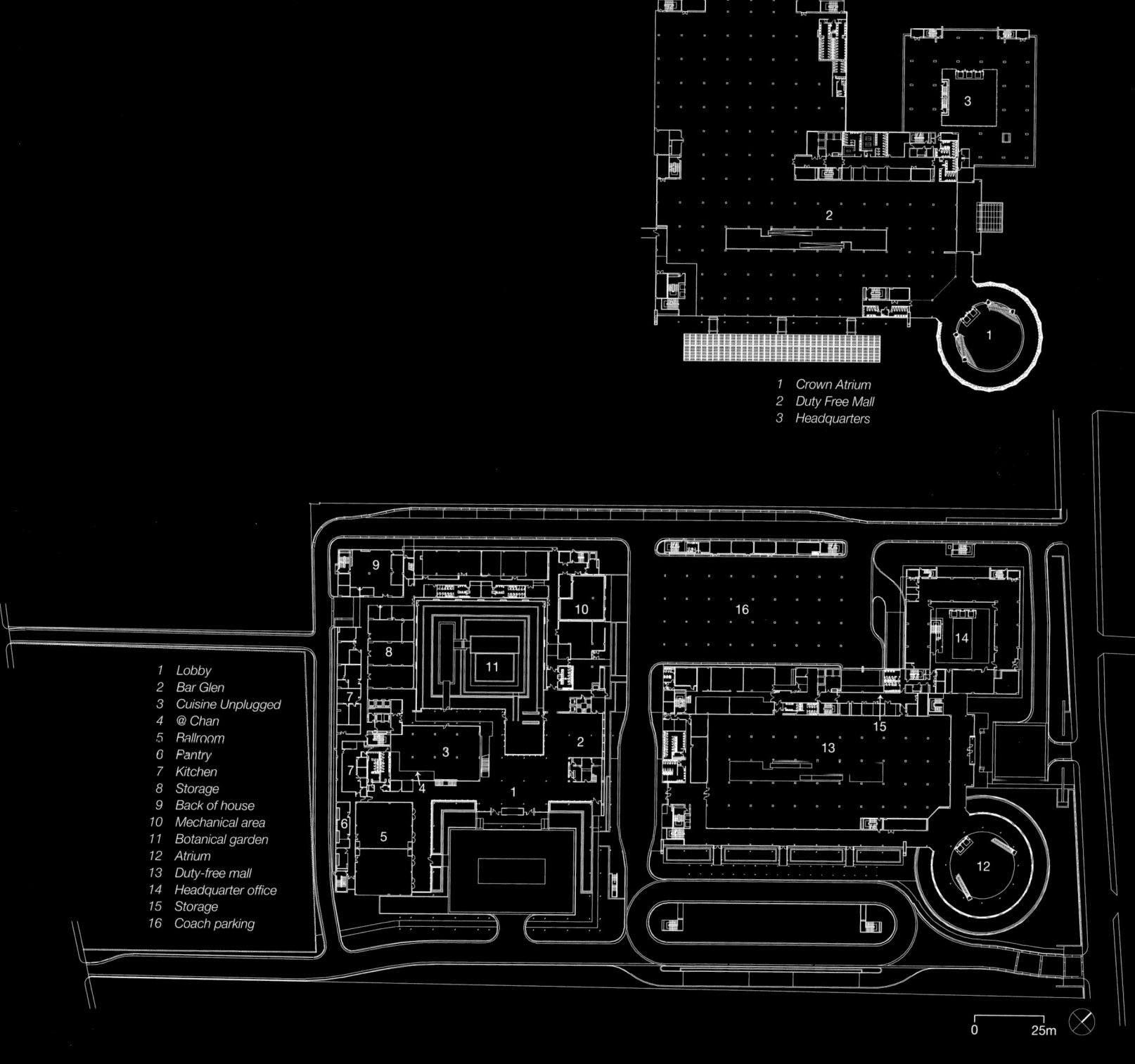

Crown atrium

The crown atrium is designed not only as the central circulation core, but as an expression both of Thailand's rich cultural heritage and its modernization.

Inspired by the craft, motifs, and patterns of ancient Thai goldware, the crown atrium's elements are high-tech engineered to achieve equilibrium between the construction methods, the energy used, the light and temperature conditions, and the construction cost.

With its scale and context condition, the crown atrium will eventually become a commanding presence in the area and serve as a symbol of Bangkok and its region.

- Compression Ring
- Steel Rafter
- Steel Transom
- Steel Column
- Aluminium Shading Device
- Laminated Glass
- Stainless Steel Tension Rod

Duty free mall/theater/dining facility

From the drop-off strip, visitors gather along the interior colonnade to proceed to the crown atrium. At the mezzanine level, visitors find their way into the duty free mall, which occupies almost the entire 8,000 square meters of floor area on the second floor. The mall is also connected to the 4,000-square-meter first floor, and the two floors are connected by the void and escalator. From the mezzanine level, four escalators and two glazed elevators serve the three floor levels, including the third-floor theater and dining facility.

Siam Square Commercial Development

Location: Pathum Wan, Bangkok, Thailand
Client: Chulalongkorn University
Area: 73,196 square meters
Year: 2007
Competition Design

The area around Siam Square and Rajprasong has long been one of the main commercial and business areas of Bangkok, featuring department stores, massive shopping centers, hotels, restaurants, shops, tutoring schools, public transportation waiting zones, and other areas.

The proposed development calls for a variety of activities to form nodes connected by a network of sidewalks and walkways that start at the Mah Boon Krong Shopping Complex side on Phyathai Road and go through the Henri Dunant Road, passing by the project area.

This major commercial opportunity is situated at the rear of Siam Square. It connects with the various nodes and is a landmark visible from the sky train junction station and anywhere in Siam Square. In effect, it is like an axis with all paths leading to it.

Realizing the project's full potential can include many possibilities, such as a major concentration of tutoring schools, parking, shops, and a hotel. The project's open spaces can also serve as a major passage point, as well as for a variety of buildings.

CIRCULATION DIAGRAM

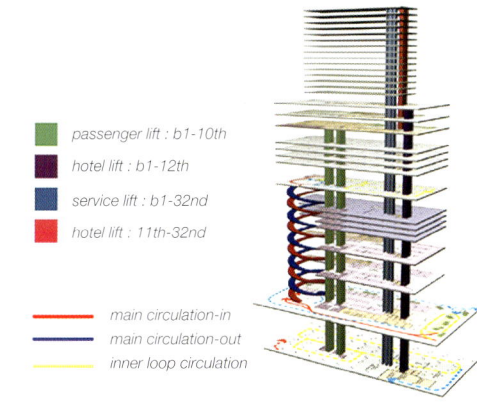

passenger lift : b1-10th
hotel lift : b1-12th
service lift : b1-32nd
hotel lift : 11th-32nd

main circulation-in
main circulation-out
inner loop circulation

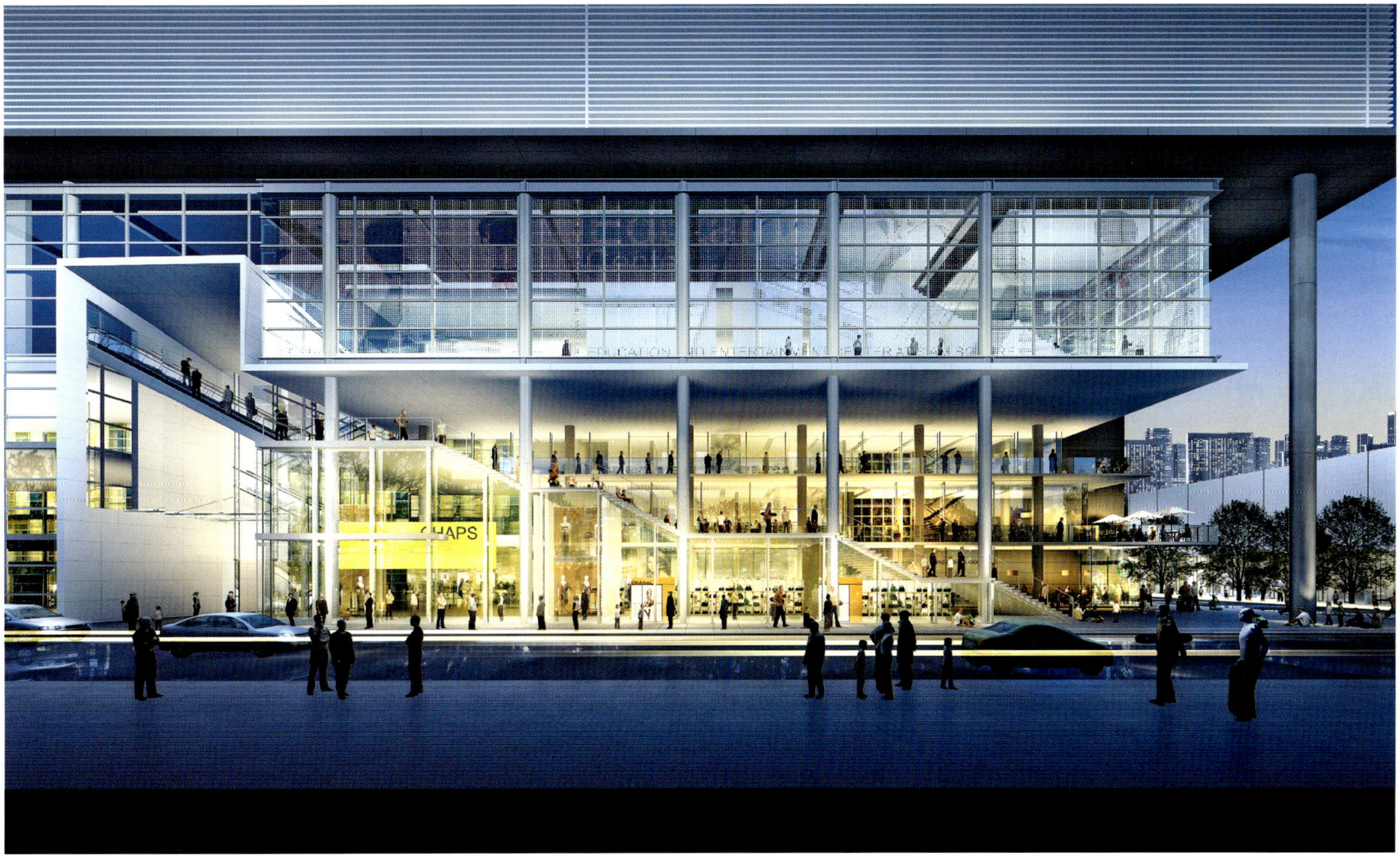

Waterfront Development at Khlong Toei

Location: Khlong Toei, Bangkok, Thailand
Area: 3,764,800 square meters
Year: 2004

This project is a study of development in the Khlong Toei Port area, the last large piece of land in the inner part of Bangkok. When a significant load of the port was diverted to Lamchabang Port, this area, with its long river frontage, was left vacant, offering Bangkok enormous potential for a first-class development.

The proposal consists of office buildings, hotel, retail, convention center, park, museum, and a port for tourism. The ratio of the building floor area to the land area is taken into consideration to control the density of the land usage and allow open space for the public. Each residential apartment offers an open courtyard for recreation with a green belt around the residential zone. The multipurpose plaza and the public park along the riverbank offer a fine perspective and respond to the city's public effort. The mid-size park in the center of the development provides some privacy for the residents and visitors.

The commercial buildings are arrayed as two street walls to blend with the low-rise shopping street. The convention center and the mid-size theater serve social, cultural, and business activities. The sports field in the area of the former port is to be improved to become a modern sports and recreation center; the city library close to the river will be the center for information. The plan also includes the Bangkok sky park, inspired by the sail and the river to celebrate the area with a new landmark.

Land & Houses Urban Development at Chiang Mai

Location: Chiang Mai, Thailand
Client: Land & Houses
Area: 115 hectares
Year: 2005–2010

This 115-hectare site is located on the southwest of Chiang Mai, just one kilometer from the airport. The development of the site will incorporate a low-rise resort, a boutique villa resort, serviced apartments, condominiums, a sport club, commercial area, an international school, a hillside housing project, and a canal type housing project.

The initial master planning concept proposed the creation of the largest man-made lake in Chiang Mai to provide a unique atmosphere that would differentiate the project from other developments. Landfill removed to create the lake will be reused in landscaping other parts of the project.

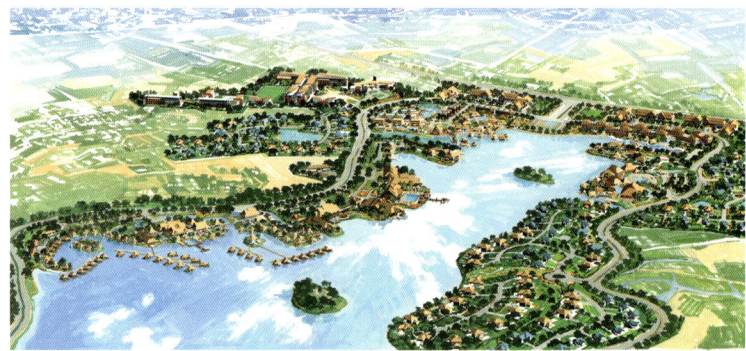

The hotel project is located to the east, providing views to the west, with Mount Suthep in the background. The hotel compound includes a 5- to 6-star boutique villa resort with 71 units on an 8-hectare site. Villas are one or two stories, designed as water bungalows on the lake in a traditional Lanna Thai style. The low-rise resort has 330 rooms, no more than four stories high. This development, on a 6.4-hectare site, has a contemporary Thai appearance and is also close to the lake. The serviced apartments and condominiums are part of a medium-density development on a 1.6-hectare site.

The residential sector comprises the Hillside Residences and the Canal Residences. In the Hillside projects, landfill from the lake is used to create berms that provide a hillside atmosphere. Hillside houses have views either toward Doi Suthep, or across the lake to the resort hotel on the east. The Canal Residences are located away from the lake.

The Commercial complex is situated at the southern portion of the site, along the Sompoj Chiang Mai 700 Years Road, close to the site entrance.

Given Chiang Mai's 700-year history and the richness of its cultural heritage, the project is inevitably endowed with Lanna Thai philosophy and architecture. This indigenous style can be perfectly applied to each part of the project to embrace the new urban atmosphere.

Boutique villa resort

Resort hotel

Retail

Condominium

Boutique villa resort

The Danet Gateway

Location: Danet, Abu Dhabi, United Arab Emirates
Client: Al Tamouh
Area: 1.15 million square feet
Year: 2006–2010

Developed as part of the Danet Abu Dhabi development, The Danet Gateway is a mixed-use project with offices, serviced apartments, and shopping with underground parking. Complementing the unique characteristics of the site at the entrance to the Danet development, the symmetrical gateway concept was planned from the outset. This final scheme features 10 towers on both parcels of land.

Rather than being arranged into a large residential block with hundreds of units, the 24-story-high residential towers are laid out to form the gateway concept with a spectacular glazed roof above the main road. The proposed architecture will eventually become not only the gateway to the Danet Abu Dhabi development, but will also become an important landmark between downtown and the airport.

The Danet Gateway complex features four residential towers, one office tower, two levels of retail, and three underground parking levels on each parcel. The grouped arrangement of the towers animates this high-density project with natural light, ventilation, and shaded areas throughout. The office towers, located on both sides to form the gateway effect to the Danet urban area, accentuate the 21st-century living and working environment concept of the development.

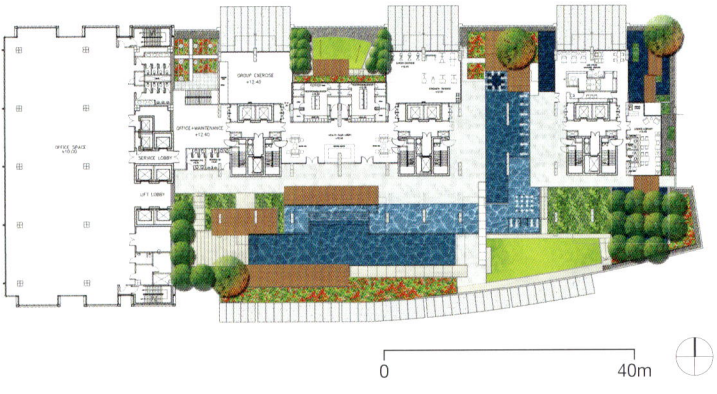

The landscape composition and theme for The Danet Gateway embodies a spirit of commercial exuberance and residential vitality along with a combined respect for nature and sense of place. Landscape patterns and forms emphasize this unique urban setting and combine to create a signature address and sense of direction. Linking together and unifying the gateway, the landscape elements, including paving, water features, and planting, are interwoven to differentiate The Danet Gateway as a modern, accessible, and convenient world-class landmark in Abu Dhabi. The Danet Gateway is certain to emerge as one of the most important and recognizable destinations in the region.

Thu Thiem New Urban Area

Location: Ho Chi Minh City, Vietnam
Client: Al Tamouh
Year: 2008–2010

The Thu Thiem New Urban Area is the only preserved green area in Ho Chi Minh City. The 50-hectare district consists of an iconic tower, a commercial residential development, a stadium arena, and some green areas along the waterway.

The elevated boulevard is an important public space and will be a major attraction for the city, like the iconic tower on the river side. The mixed-use iconic tower, comprising offices, a hotel, and observation decks, is the main component of the project.

Inspired and synthesized from the shape of the star on the national flag of Vietnam, the tower spirals up toward the sky, symbolizing the progression of the nation into the 21st century.

The aim of the project is to create a distinctive identity to the neighborhood as well as creating a contemporary lifestyle that is uniquely Vietnamese. It is hoped that this dynamic and vibrant project will also benefit the broader community of Ho Chi Min City.

Wat Pa Sunantawanaram

Location: Kanchanaburi, Thailand
Client: Wat Pa Sunantawanaram & Mayakotame Foundation
Area: 1,100 square meters
Year: 2001–2002
Citation, ASA Architectural Design Awards, 2004

Kanchanaburi is Thailand's third-largest province, about 130 kilometers west of Bangkok. Wat Pa Sunantawanaram is a Buddhist temple intended especially for the study and practice of meditation.

The temple's central multipurpose hall is a single-story structure inspired by the province's local religious architecture. It features a main hall for meditation and two wings with semi-open rooms for prayer. These structures enclose an open courtyard used primarily for meditation. Its appearance is unostentatious compared with traditional Thai temples, which are huge complexes decorated with glittering ornaments and symbols of Hindu Buddhist cosmology. This temple's plain appearance underscores the Buddhist philosophy of simplicity as a way of life. It contains only essential structures and eschews ornamentation. The wooden roof structure branches into different directions as a metaphor for the form of a tree. Natural light passes through selected areas of the translucent roof tiles to illuminate the image of Buddha.

Construction materials were mostly sourced from the local area and have been left in a raw or lightly processed form that reveals their natural textures and finishes. Materials include bamboo awnings, reclaimed timber flooring, and polished cement floors.

This is a place where people come to seek truth and enlightenment. The architecture reflects the principles of Buddhism, in particular the teachings of Luang Pu Chan, the late respected Buddhist monk.

Maharattanaviharnkot Wat Pra Dhammakaya

Location: Klong Luang, Pathum Thani, Thailand
Client: Dhammakaya Foundation
Area: 1,000,000 square meters
Year: 2005–2007

Each side of this grand two-story square building for religious events is one kilometer in length. The building surrounds the grand courtyard of the central Dhammakaya Cetiya.

The thin shell structure covers an area of 200,000 square meters, while other areas are made of reinforced concrete and precast concrete. The depth of the stand, wrapped around the central courtyard, is 99 meters. It includes 32 staircases. Each wing houses a support area comprising restrooms and mechanical and control rooms. Meditation rooms, seminar rooms, and storage areas occupy the space in the corners. The center can accommodate an event involving up to one million people.

Because the project is built to last for more than 1,000 years, low-maintenance construction materials, such as stainless steel and exposed concrete, are used.

The design offers openness while remaining strong and elegant as it embraces the central Dhammakaya Cetiya, the symbol of world peace.

World Peace Valley

Location: Khao Yai, Nakhon Ratchasima, Thailand
Client: Dhammakaya Foundation
Area: 10,000 square meters
Year: 2007–2008

Established by the Dhammakaya Foundation on an 80-hectare site in Khao Yai, Nakhon Ratchasima, Thailand, the World Peace Valley offers more than 10,000 square meters of space for meditation and can accommodate up to 1,500 visitors at any one time.

The complex consists of an administrative office, meditation house, assembly hall, seminar space, canteen and kitchen, and a residence with separate areas for females, males, monks, and instructors. An outdoor recreation space features several reservoirs that provide a serene and calm atmosphere for meditation.

The architecture was inspired by the shape of mountains, trees, leaves, and insects; together with the earthy color scheme of the materials, it conveys the sense of being in a forest.

Guan Yin Shrine

Location: Saphan Hin, Phuket, Thailand
Client: Phuket Municipality
Year: 2008–2009

The Guan Yin Shrine is located in Sapan Hin on the eastern shore of Phuket, and is the location of the events held on the last day of the *Kin Jay* Festival. The site was selected using precise considerations of *Feng Shui*. The island is 108 meters offshore—its positioning in the Bay provides a metaphor for the two arms of the *Bodhisattva*.

Inspiration was taken from the eight-petalled lotus that is often seen alongside the *Bodhisattva Guan Yin*. The number eight was used as the design principle for every detail of the project, which consists of a reception hall, a plaza for paying homage to the *Bodhisattva Guan Yin*, and an exhibition hall beneath the plaza.

As with much sacred architecture, a great deal of attention was paid to the selection of materials and colors that conform to the principles of *Feng Shui*. White terrazzo, white stone wash, and white concrete offer a sense of pristine beauty in contrast with the black-framed windows. The lotus petals are made from white glass reinforced concrete, exposing a rougher texture in contrast with the sensual curved form.

Pra Bhothiyanathera Pagoda

Location: Ubon Ratchathani, Thailand
Client: Wat Nong Pah Pong
Area: 300 square meters
Year: 1992–1996

Wat Nong Pah Pong is a Buddhist forest monastery located in the province of Ubon Ratchathani, in northeast Thailand. The pagoda is a memorial to Ajahn Chah Subhaddo (a venerable monk) and provides an architectural example to help future generations understand and appreciate the history of the Buddhist Sanctuary and vernacular architecture in general.

The function of this pagoda is slightly different from the traditional use, since the program requires the space to hold spiritual ceremonies involving up to 300 people. The form and simple decoration of the pagoda reflect this function; the tranquility and serenity reflect the philosophy of Ajahn Chah himself.

The black granite floor contrasts with glittering gold columns, adding resonance to the interior lighting. New methods of construction, such as prefabricated elements, allow efficient and safe construction, while most of the elements are composed of simple materials that facilitate handling and maintenance by the Buddhist monks.

Wat Pa Sunantawanaram Pagoda

Location: Kanchanaburi, Thailand
Client: Wat Pah Sunantawanaram
Area: 149 square meters
Year: 2007–2009

The pagoda is part of the campus of the Wat Pa Sunantawanaram monastery in Kanchanaburi, one of Thailand's lush provinces. Its primary purpose is to be the sentinel of the sacred Sareerikathat, or Buddha bone relic, a venerated artifact found in Buddhist temples.

Initially, the shape of the pagoda appears to have been influenced by nearby Burmese architecture. However, as an additional feature to conventional pagodas, the round-shaped plan is transected by four axial porches, which create entrances to the functional space inside.

Further enhancing the expressive form, red mosaics are applied as a finish to increase the degree of contrast with the green surroundings while offering an enigmatic sense of calm and tranquility. While the use of bright color may seem inappropriate, this effect is surprisingly found in many examples of ancient Thai architecture.

Wat Pah Nikhotharam Pagoda

Location: Udon Thani, Thailand
Client: Wat Pah Nikhotharam
Area: 80 square meters
Year: 2008–2009

This new pagoda in Udon Thani in northeast Thailand will be erected to pair with an existing pagoda on the site. The new building accommodates new functions and includes practical space to pay homage to the relics of Buddha.

Octagonal in plan, the body of the pagoda is split into three sections with a stainless steel pinnacle. The exterior material is brick, which is cemented and plastered and finished in white. Efficient air ventilation and moisture protection to the interior is ensured.

Rising 20 meters, the new pagoda stands elegantly yet pays respect to the existing building by not exceeding its height.

Mahaviharn Pramongkol Thepmunee Memorial

Location: Song Phi Nong, Suphan Buri, Thailand
Client: Dhammakaya Foundation
Area: 4600 square meters
Year: 2006–2009

The Dhammakaya Foundation initiated this project in homage to Pramongkol Thepmunee, the founder of Dhammakaya meditation. It is intended that the memorial should stand for another 1,000 years.

The island compound on which the memorial stands consists of a crystal globe on the water, which contains a reception office and a memorial shrine. The shrine is in the hexagonal pyramid shape of the Golden Mountain, designed to protect the 1.5-scale image of Pramongkol Thepmunee. It also includes a fully equipped mechanical system, service area, and a water-based heat reduction system.

The base is clad with Burmese marble, which has heat-resistant qualities. The rest of the structure is made from concrete. Mosaic cladding on the sacred golden stone glitters with the lighting on the pinnacle.

Pra Bhothiyanathera Pagoda

Wat Pa Sunantawanaram Pagoda

Wat Pah Nikhotharam Pagoda

Mahaviharn Pramongkol Thepmunee Memorial

Baan Sukhumvit 38

Location: Sukhumvit 38, Bangkok, Thailand
Area: 2000 square meters
Year: 2000–2002

This residence combines the simple forms of modern architecture with functional spaces arranged according to the principles of *Feng Shui*.

To fit almost 2,000 square meters of functional space into a confined site, while maintaining a conceptual synergy of the modern and the traditional, results in an extremely large mass. Therefore, much consideration was given to ways in which the brashness of the house's four-story mass could be softened. To achieve this, two large rectangular forms were introduced to the façade to simultaneously establish focal points and lend the house its unique character, while also making it appear as a two-story building. The exterior frames and walls are also designed to make the private living areas feel light, airy, and comfortable. In contrast, they are more solid and elegant in the more public zone around the reception area.

247

Baan Lat Phrao

Location: Lat Phrao, Bangkok, Thailand
Area: 800 square meters
Year: 2000–2001

This garden-living-style house in the midst of the city was designed so that interior and exterior spaces are linked, bringing the shady exterior into the interior spaces.

A geometrical volume, unfolding from the two-dimensional plane, is juxtaposed vertically and horizontally according to the program and hierarchy of functions. The form was conceived so that the arrangement of wall openings and materials responds to, and takes advantage of, the climatic conditions. Walls that are exposed to direct sunlight are solid, while others are made of glass to provide transparency, interconnection of indoor and outdoor spaces, and regulation of natural ventilation.

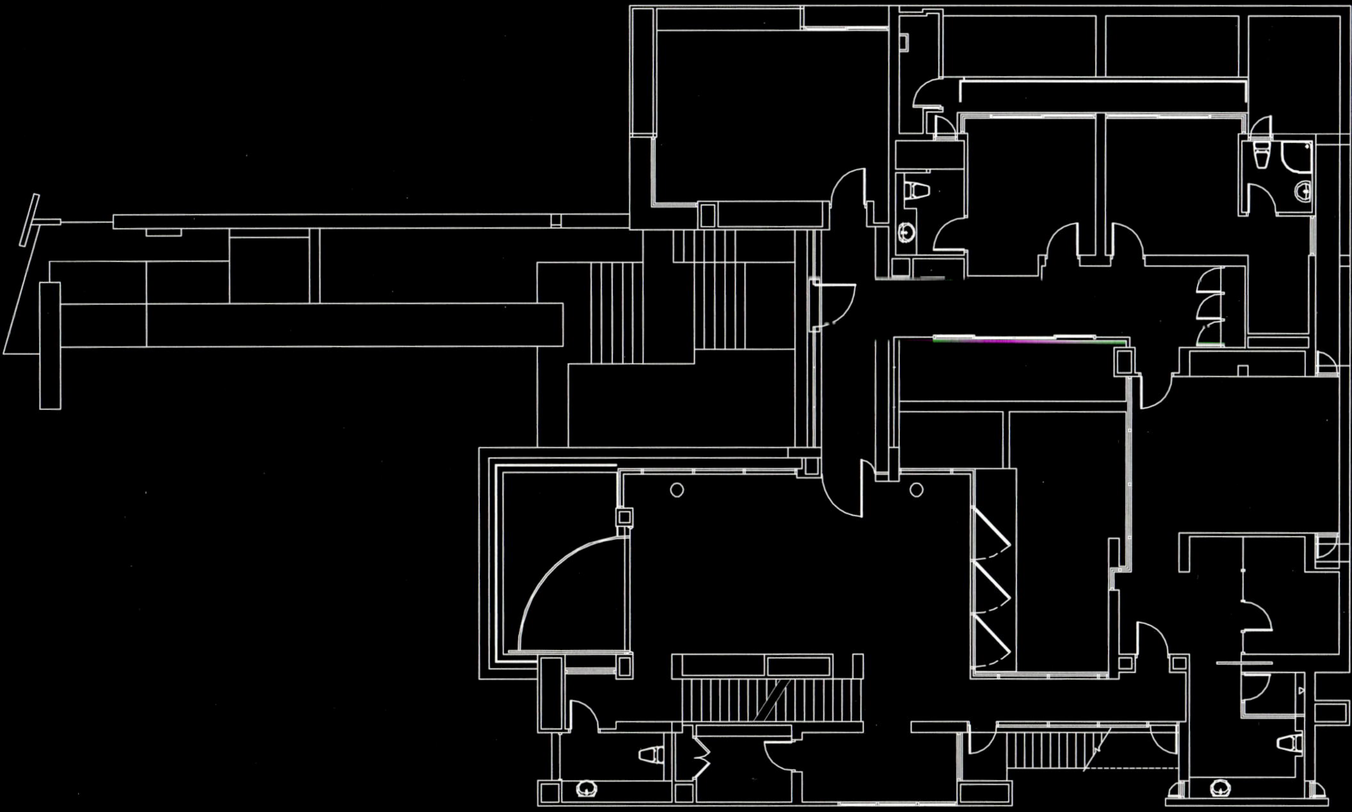

Baan Muang Thong 3

Location: Muang Thong 3 Village, Nonthaburi, Thailand
Area: 1,350 square meters
Year: 2000–2002

This two-story house is composed of two buildings—the main house and the service quarters. The site is approximately 1,600 square meters, with a moat to the west and an expansive lake to the southwest. The layout is designed to preserve the project's green spaces, which have been arranged into two open areas: the main entrance, and the south side of the residence, which has the best view of the lake. The main building has been placed slightly off the site's north–south axis. As a result, its façade looks squarely over the lake on the southwestern side, where a large aluminum louvered overhang helps protect the interior from the strong sun.

The designer has transformed the otherwise large and heavy mass of the house by incorporating a variety of architectonic forms. At the same time, the multiplicity of forms lends a mysterious feel to the spatial dimensions as one moves around inside the house.

255

Baan Windmill

Location: Windmill Project, Bangna-Trad Road, Samut Prakan, Thailand
Area: 1,270 square meters
Year: 2001–2004

The house is configured with four stories, including a basement floor. The house was designed to maximize gross floor area and to ensure that every space enjoys views to the lake, the focal point of the site. A veranda provides a relaxing atmosphere in the open courtyard in the middle of the house. A particular design aim was to visually link the surface of the swimming pool with the surface of the lake at the rear of the site.

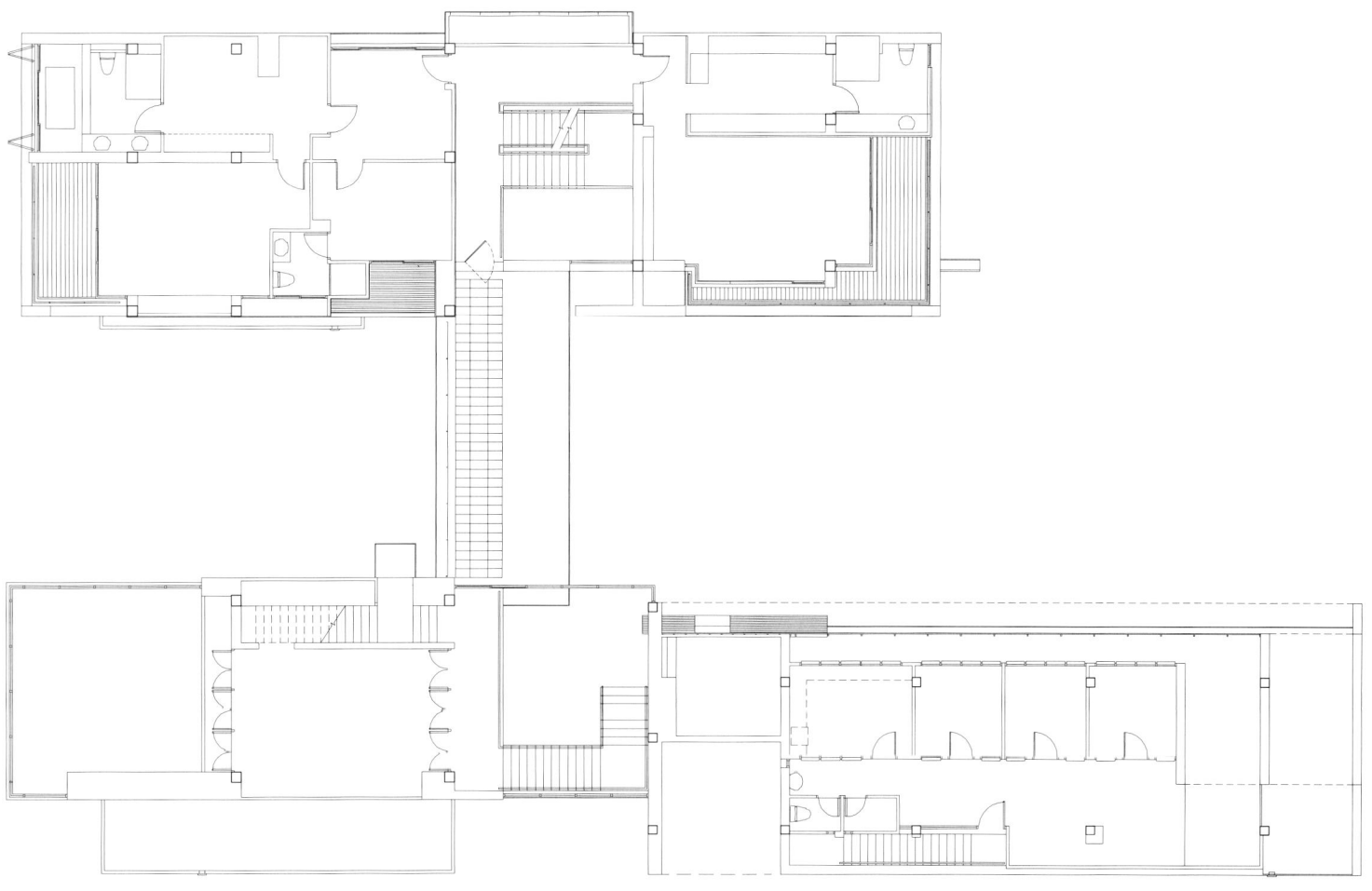

The geometrical architectural composition is achieved by connecting the horizontal and vertical planes, which alternate between open and opaque.

Harmony is provided with materials of complementary colors and textures. For example, wood is blended with other materials such as glass and concrete to create a modern house with a welcoming atmosphere.

Baan Hua Hin

Location: Hua Hin, Prachuap Khiri Khan, Thailand
Area: 1,800 square meters
Year: 1999–2005

Hua Hin, a district in Prachaub Kirikan, is a two-hour drive south of Bangkok. It has been a favorite weekend sanctuary for Thai familes since King Rama VII built Wang Klai Kangwon in the early 1900s. It greets visitors with miles of golden sandy beaches. This project is a weekend and vacation retreat for a Thai businessman and his family to escape their busy lives in Bangkok.

The client's initial brief was for a design that reflects the history of Hua Hin while creating its own environment, and for a house that is easy to maintain, with a variety of interior spaces. Views are scarce, blocked by the rows of bungalows and houses that face the beach. The narrow site—100 meters at its widest point—is flanked by neighbors on either side, leaving only a linear path to the beach.

Three pavilions—the service pavilion, sleeping pavilion, and communal pavilion—are stretched over the site, facing toward the sea.

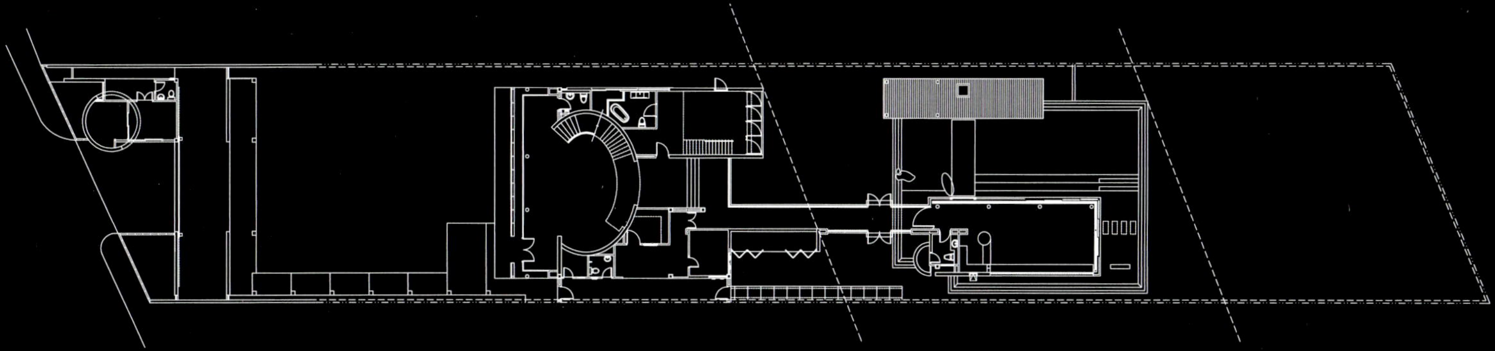

Courtyards between the pavilions provide alternative views and leisure spaces and feature plantings to soften the geometric lines of the house.

The outer skin of each pavilion responds sensitively to each wall's orientation to ensure comfort for the occupants. The living and dining rooms, which are located closest to the beach, are mostly transparent, bringing nature into the rooms. The bedrooms are located in the middle pavilion and introduce an untreated wooden slatted skin to provide shade and harmony with the surroundings.

IA49

Interior Architects 49

Central World

Location: Rajprasong Road, Bangkok, Thailand
Client: Central Pattana
Area: 71,500 square meters
Year: 2004–2006

The Central World Plaza project is a combination of the existing zones A, B, and C (Atrium, Beacon, and Central Court) and the new zones, D, E, and F (Dazzle, Eden, and Forum).

Central World Plaza is a "lifestyle" shopping mall that features a variety of shops and different brands. In order to counter the main issue of customer orientation in a floor plan of more than 50,000 square meters, the interior architects worked closely with the marketing team to divide the zoning by type of shop and brand image.

The design concept paid attention to clear planning, easy circulation, and emphasis on zone identity.

This was accomplished by the use of color and graphic patterns. Working together with Graphic 49, the interior architects created floor and column patterns, railings, and counter details that reflect the graphic signage concept of each zone.

Lighting and natural light were problematic in zones A, B, and C of the existing building. This problem was resolved by creating skylights and increasing lighting levels to make the interior atmosphere more pleasant. The overall interior architecture design was based on continuity with the architecture, to emphasize the space and make it more interesting.

3

4

In Zone A, there were two open wells, one larger and one smaller, which cut through level 1 to level 7. A new feature was designed to float through the two open wells, creating an attraction for this zone that can be seen from every level.

Zone C is the center of the mall and features two glass elevators that travel from level 1 to level 7. The escalators were positioned around the open well, improving circulation within the mall. This also had added benefits of improved customer orientation and views of the event hall on level 1.

The jewelry zone is located on the first floor and has an Indian-inspired design. Checked marble floors, vaulted ceilings, and crystal chandeliers create a luxurious ambience.

The new Zone E has three levels with a central open well. The interior architects created a ceiling pattern in a curved, S-shaped design that is lower at the shop fronts of the open area enabling a more dramatic look and minimizing floor depth.

Opposite:
  Zone C – view of Central Court, from level 1 to the skylight above
3 *Zone C – Central Court, an open well with escalators as the main circulation for the plaza*
4 *Zone E – Eden, the new zone, viewed from level 3*

Ramayana Restaurant

Location: Rangnam Road, Bangkok, Thailand
Client: King Power International Group
Area: 1,630 square meters
Year: 2005–2007

This 550-seat buffet-style restaurant was designed for visitors attending the puppet shows or shopping at the King Power Duty Free Mall. The design concept is based upon the Ramayana, one of the most important literary works of ancient India that has had a profound impact on art and culture in Thailand.

Three different environments within the restaurant are created by means of content, shading, and furniture. These variations create more interest and help customers find their own seats more easily.

The three themes are "ogres," "men and monkeys," and a tropical forest in the center, which links all areas. A huge mural, more than 60 meters long, occupies the back wall of the restaurant. It portrays the war between the ogres and the humans, in whose army the monkeys served as soldiers. Each force comes from its own side of the restaurant and meets for battle in the middle, simulating one of the best-known scenes of the Ramayana. The interior decor utilizes the distinguishing features of the ogres and the monkeys. Each side has its own colors, which are reproduced on the walls, the chairs, and other items in the restaurant, thus generating enough customer interest to overcome the spatial inertia of the restaurant's size and creating zones of fun.

1 Himapan room

1

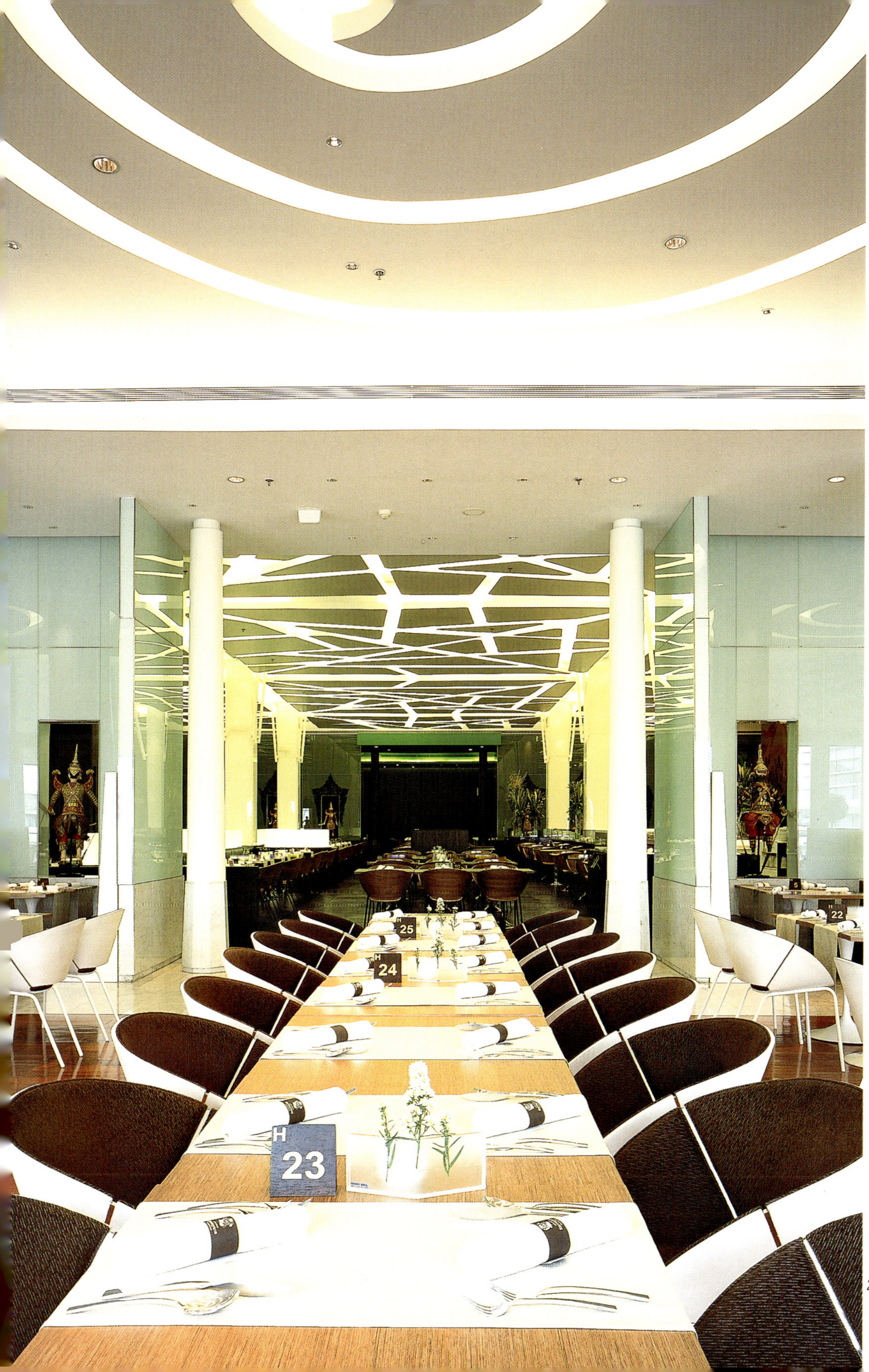

2

3

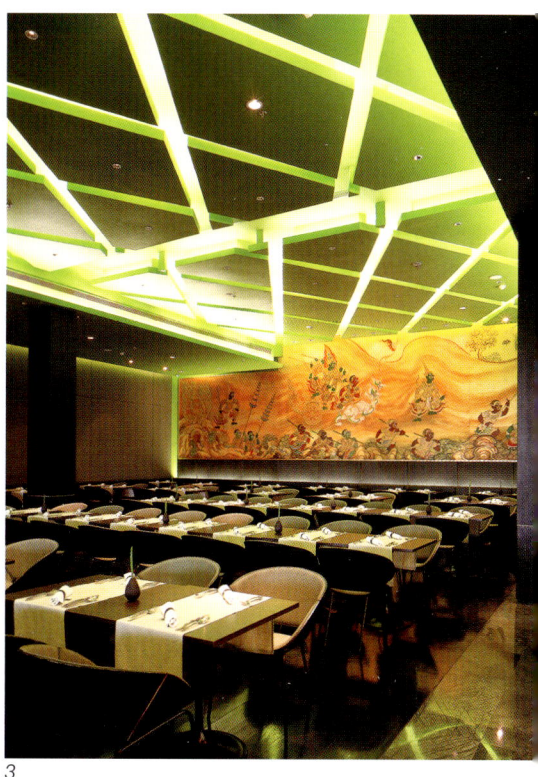

2 View from Hanuman room to Himapan room
3 Tosakan room

King Power Headquarters

Location: Rangnam Road, Bangkok, Thailand
Client: King Power International Group
Area: 17,549 square meters
Year: 2005–2007

This large, 9-story modern office building provides more than 12,000 square meters of usable space. The entire outer surface is glass, thus making maximum use of natural light to provide a bright work environment inside. A large atrium, 18 by 18 meters, occupies the entire center of the building, extending to the top. Traffic flows around this atrium on every floor, with each floor's walkway designed to provide optimum efficiency of movement and spatial use. The operational activities within the building are clearly visible between floors. The top of the atrium features fins designed to protect the interior from excess sunlight while the building's inhabitants enjoy the benefits of open, uncrowded space. On the ground floor, in the middle of the atrium, a large reflecting pool can be converted into a spacious event area when required. Movement within the building is facilitated by both stairs and glass elevators. Each floor has its own conference room, pantry, and copying room for added convenience.

1

2

1 Main entrance hall is nine stories high with transparent glass walls
2 Executive office
3 Executive boardroom
4 Manager's office

Bangkok University Landmark Complex

Location: Rangsit, Pathum Thani, Thailand
Client: Bangkok University
Area: 13,090 square meters
Year: 2007–2009

1 Administrative building hall
2 Pre-function hall
3 The School of Business Administration hall
4 Stock Exchange classroom

This project for Bangkok University comprises a group of three buildings ranging from three to seven stories with an area of 25,000 gross square meters and an interior area of 13,000 square meters. The functions are entertainment, seminar rooms, a 1,400-seat multifunction room, the business administration office, and the dean's office. The architectural design is inspired by the shape of the diamond, which is a symbol of the university. It is designed to intentionally stand out from the urban landscape.

1

2

3

4

The interior language complements the architecture to ensure a flow from outside to inside. Advanced technology is used throughout the interior, aligning the project with growing public demands and expectations.

In order to create such an efficient use of internal space, communication with the client was key in the planning stages. Constant consultations with the sound engineers were also needed to ensure sound absorption was calculated correctly.

Materials chosen are low-maintenance and durable, in line with a limited budget. Environmentally friendly materials such as recycled plywood are used in conjunction with energy-efficient lighting. Color schemes are very light in tone to create airy spaces and optimum use of natural lighting. Photocopy machines are grouped together to free up more internal space and reduce widespread noise pollution. The design theory is oriented around three main principles: the architectural blend, an emphasis on the character of the university, and environmental efficiency.

Dholhiyadhoo Resort & Spa

Location: Dholhiyadhoo, Maldives
Client: Hotel & Resort, International
Area: 16,500 square meters
Year: 2006–2008

The Maldives is an island nation in the Indian Ocean, southwest of India and Sri Lanka. It consists of 1,190 coral islands grouped into 26 atolls, with a total of just 300 square kilometers of land. The Maldives is a famous tourist destination, with 74 of its islands now housing luxury hotels.

The five-star Zitahli Resort and Spa is constructed on Dholhiyadho Island, in the Shaviyani atoll, north of the Maldives' capital city, Male. The crescent-shaped island is 2.2 kilometers long and 500 meters wide. The resort itself includes 100 villas, a main restaurant, Asian fusion restaurant and bar, cigar lounge and library, champagne and wine bar, spa, reception building, and recreation building.

The Zitahli Resort and Spa's romantic atmosphere is created through the combination of the island's natural features and the five senses of sight, sound, smell, taste, and touch.

1

2

3

4

5

Sight: the design utilizes appropriate lighting control, taking into consideration natural forms, materials, and colors, in designing the interior spaces. Furniture is free-flowing and lightweight.

Smell: the smell of a scented candle, incense, wine, and interior materials from wood to woven mats, evoke the scents of the Indian Ocean. It is important to plan out the spaces that require adequate ventilation.

Sound: the sound of waves against the sandy beach, or of wind chimes, all the way to the sound of modern technologies such as the iPod, all contribute to the design process.

Touch: interesting textures and those with natural references, such as the softness of hand-woven cotton, the natural roughness of a woven mat, the textural feel of a woven rattan, are carefully chosen to add to the ambience.

The five senses of romance are also used in the design of the guest rooms, which are separated into two groups: "beach" and "aqua." The emphasis of the design is on comfort and nature. Beach-type rooms lean toward a green color scheme to represent refreshment obtained from surrounding trees, while the aqua-type rooms have a blue tone that reflects the Indian Ocean. Woven window treatments admit soft daylight while creating natural shadows that enhance the rooms' atmosphere.

The resort's facilities highlight reactions to nature in many ways. For example the different phases of the moon are used in the main restaurant and the lunar eclipse inspired the design of the Asian fusion restaurant and bar. The moon symbolizes nature and romance, while the crescent shape represents the island. The relaxing atmosphere of the sunken cigar lounge and library has the mellow feel of a cigar club but stands out due to its natural interior finishes. The color scheme of the champagne and wine bar reflects the colors of a sunset. The design process included planning everything from interior materials, color selection, and furniture selection in order to create a very relaxed environment.

1 Main restaurant
2 Champagne bar
3 Deluxe beach villa
4 Super deluxe aqua villa
5 Reception building

Pullman Bangkok King Power Hotel

Location: Rangnam Road, Bangkok, Thailand
Client: King Power Hotel Management
Area: 27,095 square meters
Year: 2005–2008

Pullman King Power Bangkok is a five-star hotel managed by Accor and is part of the Pullman business hotel brand. The building is separated into two zones—the garden wing spanning seven floors and the tower wing, which boasts 21 floors with 386 rooms including three restaurants, two bars, a spa, seminar rooms, ballroom, executive lounge, business center, and fitness room.

The interior design concentrates on a connection with the architecture and has an enduring, contemporary Thai style. Each area has a connection with Thai art.

3

4

5

The lobby is influenced by the King's throne. It features a high ceiling, linear column features, and modern materials such as steel mesh to provide a slick, contemporary feel.

The main feature lies behind the front desk: an over-scaled Thai sculptural pattern crafted from timber by award-winning local artist, professor Noniwan Jantana Parin. Wall wash lighting highlights the feature during the day and has a more moon-like ambience at night. Corridors are decorated with fine art murals painted by professor Son Srirntrang. Other parts of the hotel feature art pieces designed by a variety of award-winning local artists, which solidifies the contemporary Thai concept. The lobby lounge hosts the Glen Bar, which was designed under the concept of local river life and incorporates fireflies, reflections in the water, and moonlighting created from an opening in the ceiling and flashes on the walls to create an abstract Thai ambience. The design communicates to guests the feeling of a Thai hotel with a strong design concept.

1 Lobby, waiting hall
2 Déjà Vu restaurant
3 Wine Pub
4 Lobby lounge, Glen Bar
5 Cuisine Unplugged, all-day dining

So Bangkok

Location: Sathorn Road, Bangkok, Thailand
Client: Oak Tree
Area: 4,560 square meters
Year: 2007–2009

This five-star luxury business hotel managed by Accor is the first of the "So" brand in Thailand. Five Thai designers were selected to work on different areas of the project.

IA49 was given a set of guest rooms and hallway areas.

Using a contemporary Thai concept, all rooms were designed differently and all interior walls were designed with angles that would allow shadows to be cast on the plain walls.

Thai artworks were placed in each room to enhance the Thai atmosphere. Bathroom walls use the traditional Thai concept of *Phalai* (sliding panels) to open up the internal space when not in use. Headboards were made from sketches by company president and awarded national artist Nithi Sthapitanonda, and were etched into frosted glass. Hallways and stairwells were designed as traditional Thai terrace space. Timber and glass were used throughout. The ground-floor furniture also includes bronze details and sculptures designed by Nithi Sthapitanonda. The attention to detail throughout the design gives guests the definite sense that they are in Thailand.

1

2

3

4

1 Atrium and guest room corridor
2 Junior suite bedroom
3 Junior suite bathroom
4 Suite bedroom

Seri Tanjung Penang Condominium

Location: Penang, Malaysia
Client: E&O Property Development Berhad
Area: 149,200 square meters
Year: 2007–2008

This project is located on Penang Island, one of the most magnificent coastal areas in Malaysia. The building has 39 floors with two main typical units. All units provide panoramic beachfront views. The project is aimed at a high-end Asian and European expatriate target group with the idea that the units would be used as either permanent residences or short-stay second homes.

2

3

The designs of the two show units were slightly varied to serve potentially different ethnic groups. Layouts were arranged to be as open-plan as possible.

4

Much attention was given to furniture positioning to optimize views across the bay and less storage space was provided for both designs.

Unit A was designed as a luxurious contemporary getaway unit in a classical style. Three bedrooms, four bathrooms, and open-plan living, dining, and kitchen areas were spread over 198 square meters. Use of materials such as timber flooring and patterned wallpaper gave a natural aesthetic to each space. Classic furniture was used throughout. Architrave and fixture detailing provided the unit with unique characteristics.

Unit B, a two-bedroom unit, maintained a classic contemporary aesthetic. Bedrooms were treated with a classic Chinese concept. The combination of traditional oriental furniture and detailed architrave features establishes an impression of elegance within the space.

1 Living area and pantry, Unit A
2 Living area and pantry, Unit B
3 Master bathroom, Unit B
4 Guest bedroom, Unit A

Aksra Theater

Location: Rangnam, Bangkok, Thailand
Client: King Power International Group
Area: 4,017 square meters
Year: 2005–2007

This 574-seat theater was built for puppet performances in the Thai style. Traditional Thai decor is used for ornamentation along the passageway. Figures of ogres stand as sentinels in the entrance hall.

The inner hall has been designed for splendour, like that of a throne hall, with a ceiling height of 14 meters. The ceiling is decorated with a "sentinel" motif, along with a chandelier designed especially to display Thai ornamental themes. The Thai themes continue with typical Thai patterns drawn on various surfaces, the winding walkways on each side, reminiscent of Thai temples, and the main puppet figure occupying a covered throne in the middle of the hall.

1 Hall of Fame
2 Angels in high relief on side panels
3 View of theater from box seat

Gold, as has always been the case in Thai traditional architecture, is the predominant color in the decoration (with blue as a contrast color), and serves as a linking motif to the theater inside. For the theater itself, the Baroque style has been applied to the Intrapisek painting, modeled on that of the Temple of the Emerald Buddha, and the congress of the gods, painted on the theater ceiling.

House Design

1

2

3

1–2 Baan Hua Hin
 3 Baan Lakewood
4–6 Baan Ekamai 10

1

5

6

7   Halland Residence
8–10   Baan Krungthep Kreeta
11–12   Baan Sukhumvit 38

10

11

12

L49

Landscape Architects 49

Central World

Location: Rachaprasong Shopping District, Bangkok, Thailand
Client: Central Pattana
Area: 96,000 square meters
Year: 2003–2006
Associate firm: The SWA group

Located in the busiest central district in Bangkok, this project is one of the largest mixed-use developments in downtown Bangkok. Central World comprises a high-rise office tower and luxury hotel, a grand convention center, a shopping and entertainment center of almost 700,000 square meters, and the city's largest urban public plaza above massive underground parking.

Rows of royal palm were chosen for their majestic height, which can reach 25 meters. The palms have large crowns that provide shade to the space below while allowing visual penetration at ground level. They are also used to define the perimeter of the project along two major roads and the main plaza. Vast open space on the main plaza is anchored by shrines of Hindu gods and an outdoor semicircular seated theater, which appears to spin out of the center water fountain that mimics the image of the project's logo.

After the initial concept had been proposed to the client, many more studies and alternatives were presented in order to determine how to best treat the design for such an important downtown civic space. The main concern was whether this plaza should incorporate more hardscape or more softscape areas. The district has been promoted as a center where the New Year countdown events can be celebrated and the plaza could be used for many other large events.

The final decision was made to design the plaza with maximum flexibility so that it can be transformed for multipurpose uses. A series of automatic height adjusted and dancing fountains, and water features including a mist fountain, provide animation and cool off the surrounding atmosphere when the water evaporates. The system can be turned off, either in sections or across the entire plaza, when there is a temporary setup for special events.

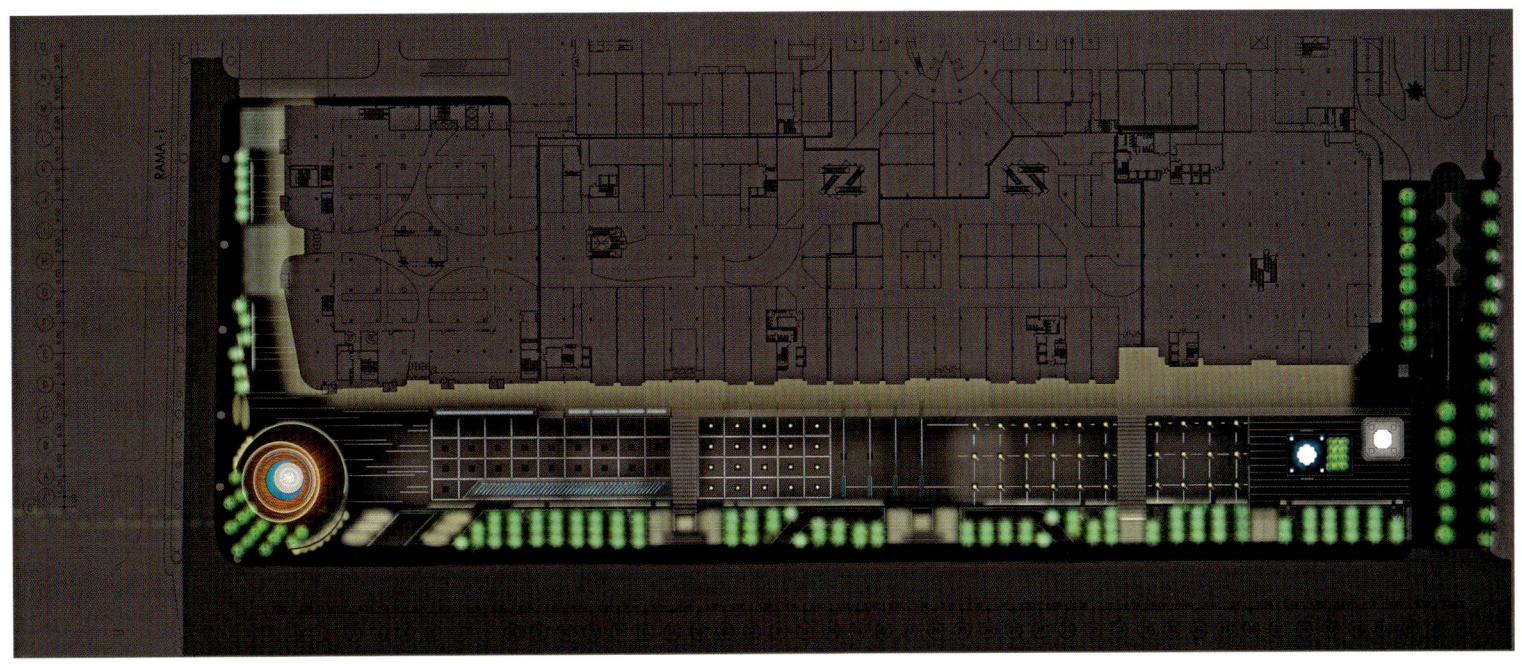

The project was designed with a very modern approach to allow all kinds of events and activities yet with the strength to express its own identity when no special events occur in the space. Black was chosen as the dominant theme for the materials in the landscape; touches of white or lighter gray are used as highlights and as wayfinding devices. A continual changing pattern of color and movement is added to the landscape by the presence of people in the space along with advertisements on building façades, a giant LED screen, and other events that occur in the space.

King Power Complex

Location: Rangnam Road, Bangkok, Thailand
Client: King Power International Group
Area: 48,000 square meters
Year: 2004–2007

This mixed-use complex comprises a duty free shopping center, offices, and a luxury hotel in a modern urban setting. To create a suitable landscape, a sequence of courtyards was used to move people from one space to the other. This sequence, in conjunction with the architectural design, takes visitors from the main courtyard of the shopping center to the hotel and office vehicular drop-off areas and into the courtyards, both indoor and outdoor. Each space is formed by the arrangement of architectural corridors or buildings.

Water features play a role in the landscape as connecting elements from one space to another and appear in several forms, including a serene reflecting pool, an energizing series of fountains, cascading water, lily ponds, and fishponds in various spaces. The design of hardscape elements employed the articulation of the strong and simple geometry of the architecture to provide harmony and a coherent design.

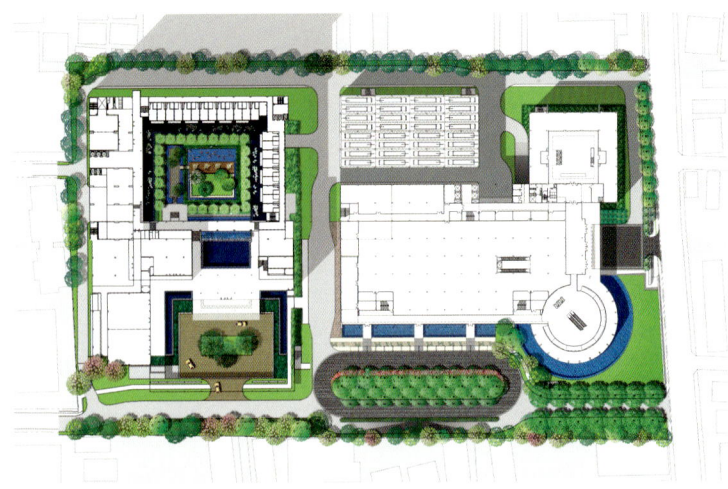

In contrast to the hardscape elements, the planting design was fashioned from lush mixed tropical foliage, which brings a more relaxed feeling to the space. An exception is the row of Toddy palms in the hotel's center court that were planted to give the aligned column effect found in classical Thai spaces.

MCOT Complex

Location: Rama IX Road, Bangkok, Thailand
Client: MCOT (Public)
Area: 48,814 square meters
Year: 2003–2007

Mass Communication of Thailand (MCOT) is a media organization that operates television and radio stations. Over its more than 50-year history, buildings and functions had been added without a master plan. When the organization was repositioning and re-branding its overall image, the 49 Group was engaged to determine how to reorganize the property for optimum utilization, as well as to renovate existing buildings and propose new functions. L49 was responsible for the overall study of land use, reorganizing open space areas, and traffic arrangement as well as designing the landscape architecture to achieve a more elegant, energetic atmosphere for the re-imaged organization.

Through the study and design process, many chaotic functions had been removed or relocated and a vehicular path was clearly defined. With the addition of a new parking building, much of the on-ground parking was turned into more pleasurable green open space.

Under the re-branded "Modern Nine" slogan, a modern design vocabulary was employed to create an overall atmosphere for the organization. A pedestrian pattern of intersecting lines, derived from the lines that used to appear on the television screen, was extended out across the open space. When the open space is viewed from the building, the lines become a network that recalls the signals sent out across the country. A series of fountains and water features were added to create a connection between the activities and sounds in the space.

The space is enclosed by rows of large-canopied trees and aligned arrangements of palm trees to replicate a scene of Thai paddy fields through which the signal is broadcast.

TALA 2007

The Thai Association of Landscape Architects (TALA) held its 2007 annual events at Central World with the theme of "landscape innovation." The main objective was to promote understanding of the profession and to provide inspiration to the public.

The exhibition contained show gardens, an area for student competition works, displays of student works from various universities and professional design offices, and professional design awards projects.

Within the theme of landscape innovation, *ma-ya* (illusion) and "maze" were the focal themes used to create a variety of rooms in the landscape. These included a maze room, water garden room, and indoor plant room. High hedge walls or green walls were used to create visual order. Large mirror panels were introduced to create illusionary effects in many forms including surprise trap doors and an infinity illusion. All the elements were interplayed and juxtaposed with the existing features in the plaza to create this event landscape as a borrowed scene.

The Tubkaak Krabi Boutique Resort

Location: Krabi, Thailand
Year: 2002

This site is located in one of Krabi's most superb natural settings. It faces Phang Nga Bay, with the large cluster of limestone islands in the middle of the bay as its main focal point. The site contained many existing large trees; one of L49's major goals in site planning was to locate all guest rooms and hotel buildings on the site with minimal interference to the existing trees, which were very valuable to the project's overall atmosphere.

The arrival area is on the high side of the site. Guests then walk across the boardwalk, high above ground, to the lobby reception area, which is located at the same level as the treetops. The main visual and pedestrian axes were aimed toward the cluster of islands in the bay, impressing guests with the magnificent view. The main open area in the site was designated for the resort's main swimming pool area, forming an open space and views for those guest rooms without a sea view.

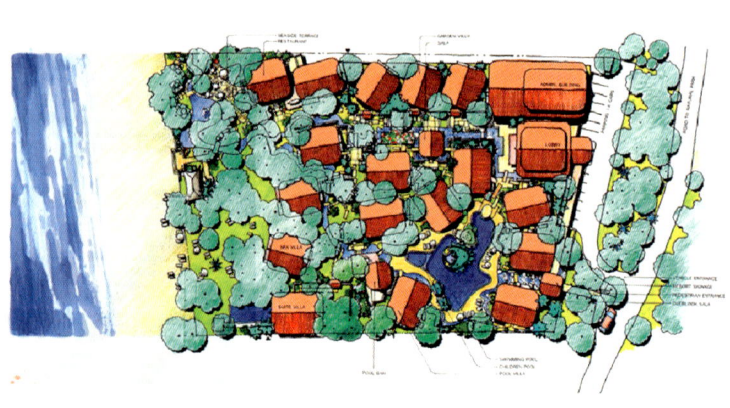

Domus

Location: Sukhumvit 16, Bangkok, Thailand
Client: Gaysorn Property Co., Ltd.
Area: 6,400 square meters
Year: 2004–2006

"Life in Balance" is the slogan for this project, from which all the design concepts were generated. The site is situated in a prime location in downtown Bangkok where most other projects are high-density, high-rise buildings, both commercial and residential. The owner of the Domus project had a vision to create one of the most luxurious living standards in the heart of Bangkok, and to develop this mid-rise low-density development as an urban sanctuary where the buildings cover about 40 percent and more than 50 percent of the area is designated for open space and recreational facilities.

In conjunction with the architectural concept, a minimalist tropical modern language has been reinterpreted in the landscape architecture design. With clean and simple lines of space and pattern in the hardscape elements, the planting designs, which form each space, are borrowed from the character of the mixed vegetation in the English garden style to give the project a domestic, warm atmosphere rather than one of stark minimalism.

Prime Nature Villa Hua Hin

Location: Pechkasame Road, Petchaburi, Thailand
Client: Prime Nature Villa
Area: 163,200 square meters
Year: 2004–2008

This seaside property is typical of the Hua Hin region. The site—500 meters long and almost 80 meters wide—has a narrow shape that stretches from a highway to the sea. The project aimed to create a seaside resort of second homes. The main concept, which was employed to generate the layout planning and the landscape, came from the ecological phenomena of the seaside landscape.

A series of dunes—existing, remnant, and re-created—were used to form the scene, which incorporated the erosion created by drainage that ran from the mountainside toward the sea. The pattern of the overflow channel remained as a main central corridor of the project's open space. Houses are located on the rolling landforms of the high plain, which then connects to the seashore via a footpath along the white-sand corridor. This broad sand corridor will give the residents a feeling of being deeper inland while still part of a seaside resort.

Boardwalks were added to cross the plain, also serving as the drainage corridor for rainfall to be collected at the lower level of the existing ponds. A further ecological concern of the design was that all the drainage in the project was designed to be collected by a natural open swale that allows water to penetrate underground while excess water runs off and is collected in the pond.

Prime Nature Villa On Nuch

Location: On Nuch Road, Samutprakarn, Thailand
Client: Prime Nature Villa
Area: 480,000 square meters
Year: 2001–2005

This site contains an enormous lake, almost one third of the site's area, in the middle of the property. The lake is approximately 500 meters long, 300 meters across, and has a circumference of almost 1.5 kilometers. It is surrounded by a moderately steep slope, creating a bowl in which the water level is at 16–20 meters below the surrounding land. This is quite an unusual sight for the general landscape in the outskirts of Bangkok, which is part of the large flat plain of the Chaopraya River delta. The soil excavated when the lake was created more than 20 years ago was used for landfill nearby. The low water level has since been maintained, and the slope stabilized with plantings of acacia trees.

From the beginning of the project, land planning was studied in terms of the landscape design of gardens and swimming pools in the show house units.

Many planning and parcelization layouts were presented to the client following an initial market study program, which aimed for smaller, single-family housing for a moderate-income market, since the higher-income market did not exist, nor was forecast, for the area. However, it was felt that this proposal would not suit the essence of the site's landscape. In order to maintain its unique landscape character, an alternative that could preserve the site's beauty was proposed: to maintain a much larger parcel on the slope side of the land and create a low-density development community rather than very high-density single-family housing, which already existed nearby. This was a very rare occasion where a landscape architect had intervened with a client's marketing program.

Residential Compound at Sukumvit 16

Location: Sukhumvit 16, Bangkok, Thailand
Site: 6,500 square meters

This site, surrounded by towering neighboring buildings, has been designated as a family residential compound. Instead of dividing the land into separate residences, the family decided to develop the site like a small village where they could share common facilities, including open space, gardens, swimming pool, main storage areas, and parking for excess cars and guests. Individual plots would be just big enough to build separate houses with minimum private garden space.

The main swimming pool courtyard is surrounded by 4-meter-high ficus hedges, forming the central space for the compound. In the symmetrical design arrangement, architectural features are located in the center of the east–west axis that progresses from the clubhouse to the covered pavilion and shading trellis at the end of the vista. The hedges provide the courtyard area privacy from occasional vehicles passing to enter each individual house, while the road also serves as a jogging and roller-blading circuit for the residents. A simple design character was chosen for the common area, to provide coherence with the different architectural styles of the individual houses within the compound, which range from contemporary to tropical contemporary and a minimal modern style.

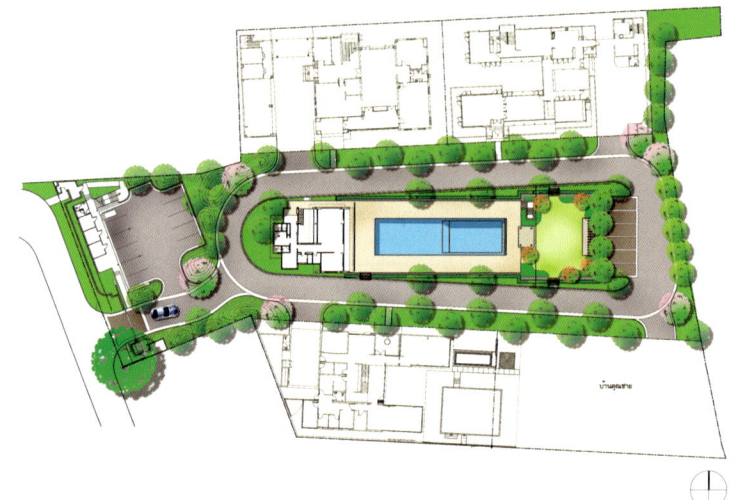

Garden Design for Private Residences

In addition to the larger land planning, urban and commercial landscape projects that it is involved with, private garden design has been a vital part of L49's landscape design profile since the firm was established. Working in private gardens has enabled L49 to explore many aspects of design that are tailored to the specific needs of each individual client while many aspects, such as materials (both hard and soft), can be applied to more public-scaled projects.

Though many projects may appear to be just very small back yards of town houses, some private gardens designed by L49 have in fact been larger in size than some of its public and commercial projects.

Master Planning

Throughout its professional work in landscape architecture, L49's main emphasis has been to design master plans that achieve the ultimate goal of creating a balance between the economic aspects of the project and the environmental concerns. The objective is to maintain and/or preserve the existing site's valuable natural resources and its ecology, such as water corridors and existing vegetation, so that they exist harmoniously with the development. A further aim is that these preserved natural resources will enhance the value of and pleasure derived from the development. Through careful observation and investigation of the site's basic features, a series of site analyses are explored to reveal its potential and constraints, enabling L49 to select the most suitable approach to the project.

Representative projects include Zhongsan, China; Sanya Luhuitou Residential, Hainan, China; Al Yasmeen Islands, Abu Dhabi, UAE; Maldives projects; Tubkaak Resort, Krabi, Thailand; Mae Fah Luang University, Chiang Rai, Thailand; and Prime Nature Villas.

L49 is often faced with sites, both urban and non-urban, that have suffered degradation or complete loss of their natural ecology. In these cases, much effort is made to restore the natural ecology of the area by using the past ecological environment as a core concept to create a better living environment for the development.

Representative projects include Prime Nature Villa Hua Hin; the former pre-cadet school site mixed-use development, Thailand; Parkland Srinakarin, Thailand; Land & Houses, Chiang Mai, Thailand; Jumeirah Park, Abu Dhabi, UAE; Seacon Renaissance, Phuket, Thailand; and Bangsar, Malaysia.

2

1

3

4

1 Jumeirah Park, Abu Dhabi, UAE
2 Residential, Bangkok, Thailand
3 Mae Fah Luang University, Chiang Rai, Thailand
4 Thailand Cultural Center, Bangkok, Thailand

5

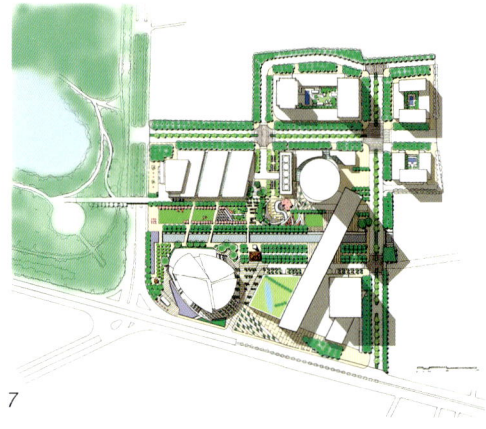

7

8

6

5 Mavelavaru 1 Island, Maldives
6 Koh Kood, Trat, Thailand
7 Former pre-cadet school site, Thailand
8 Land & Houses, Chiang Mai, Thailand
9 Seacon Renaissance, Phuket, Thailand
10 Bangsar, Malaysia
11 Danet Gateway, Abu Dhabi, UAE
12 Zhongshan, China

9

10

11

12

331

G49

Graphic 49

Logo Design

Year: 1989–2008

  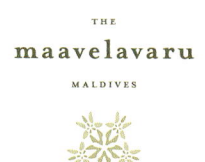 

Devarana Spa

Location: Dusit Thani Hotel, Bangkok, Thailand
Client: Dusit Thani
Year: 2004

Inspired by the name Devarana, which means "garden in heaven" in Thai-Sanskrit, the design of the Devarana Spa is based on the concept of the garden situated at heaven's gate. The god lays under the "Pho" tree in front of river before his enlightenment, as described in the *Traibhumikatha*, the ancient Thai literature written in 1345 AD (1888 BE). The Devarana Spa emblem is crafted in a traditional style similar to a historical printmaking technique, and the logotype is customized to match, to communicate and accentuate the sense and ambience of heaven and enlightenment. Elaborate and delicate graphics are an extra touch to emphasize the exclusive services and carefully detailed surroundings designed to stimulate all the senses at the spa.

G49 worked in close collaboration with brand consultant and renowned writer Ploy Chariyaves, and with interior designers, to create the spa's unique décor—imagined as "heavenly contemporary" Thai decoration. Collateral designs are very detailed and implemented along the same theme; for example, the spa menu is in Buddhist bible style. The spa's products are also promoted with the additional theme of "flowers in heaven," reflected in their scents, product variety, naming, patterns and label graphics.

Suvarnabhumi Museum Shop

Location: Suvarnabhumi Airport & King Power Duty Free Mall at King Power Complex, Bangkok, Thailand
Client: King Power Tax Free
Year: 2006

The Suvarnabhumi museum shop is a concept store selling Thai and Southeast Asian art reproductions, souvenirs, and publications. *Suvarnabhumi* is the name of the golden trading era in the Southeast Asian region, the "Golden Land" rich with cultural heritage and natural attractions noted in many sources.

The idea of logo came from mythical *naga* (snake, especially the cobra). The *naga* was believed to be the god of the river or water, the main trade pathway during the *Suvarnabhumi* period. The logo is simplified to resemble the letter "S." The form of the symbol and a custom logotype were crafted in the local art and artifact style. The logo is applied to all shop collaterals, printing, signage, packaging, and souvenirs and has been made into jewelry pieces.

Savoury Gastrocafe

Location: Siam Paragon Shopping Complex, Bangkok, Thailand
Client: Thippara
Year: 2006

Savoury Gastocafe is a new chain restaurant that changed from a local Thai food chain to a French–Thai influenced fusion restaurant. The chef character holding an oversized ladle and welcoming guests is a recognized original restaurant logo, sketched by the owner, a famous illustrator. Added elements are its shadows in active poses carrying a wider variety of food dishes that are additional to the offerings of the original chain.

Typography was selected to add simple, sophisticated value. Fresh, overlaying savory colors are continued in the signage, illuminating the layering of vividly colored Plexiglas in the interior design. The menu has been made with 3D prints that give the illusion that the chef is actually moving.

Alila

Location: Cha-am, Petchaburi, Thailand
Client: KS Resort & Spa
Year: 2008

At Alila Cha-am, the design of the graphics and signage was influenced by the prominent style of architecture, coupled with the strong corporate identity of the chain hotel. The architecture of private labyrinths, the opening and enclosing of walls, and associated rhythms, shading, and shadows led to the idea of edges and corners acting as wayfinding elements.

The design is simple, systematic, and unique to the place. The concept of natural and rustic materials is reflected in the use of natural aged brass materials for the signage. Corporate typography is customized with stenciling and specific proportions and spacing in conjunction with a new arrow, symbol, and pictograms to make a unique identity. Standard backlighting techniques complement the signage.

Outlet identity has also been created by the architect to emphasize and add a signature theme to each space: "cloud loft" restaurant, "the red bar," and "motion" all day-dining. The signage and collateral design for the outlet is minimal but elegant to create a memorable space and place.

R E D **BAR**
C L O U D **LOFT**
M O T I O N
W I N E **LIST**

Bank of Ayudhya

Location: Thailand
Client: Bank of Ayudhya
Year: 2005
Contract Winning Design 2001

The re-branding of the Bank of Ayudhya aimed to refresh its outdated traditional Thai corporate identity and re-establish it as a unique, up-to-date commercial banking organization. The bank's logo was refreshed to more resonant proportions and a new logotype designed to provide consistency with the emblem. The prominent fresh yellow color as a new brand signature was picked out from the bank's original gold and brown color scheme. It has added an aspect of youthfulness to the brand and has become a powerful part of the bank's identity. A new prototype for the visual identity of the branches has led to increased competition with other local financial retailers.

G49's role included design of all collateral material and the applications of brands, from stationery to promotional and advertising graphics. Further sub-identity, service marks, and auxiliary graphics were planned, created, and applied systematically to the bank's retail visual identity, including environmental graphic signage systems, branch bank façade design and lighting, typical ATMs, auto-lobby banking, and drive-through branches.

ธนาคารกรุงศรีอยุธยา
BANK OF AYUDHYA

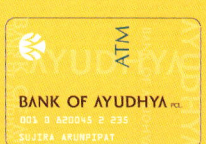

TMB Bank

Location: Thailand
Client: TMB Bank Public
Year: 2007
Contract Winning Design 2005

When the Thai Military Bank merged with two other major financial institutions, the Thai Dhanu Bank and the IFCT, in 2004, a major re-branding was necessary. The challenge was to reposition the existing brand, which had a long history and an established brand identity. The bank was also renamed (TMB Bank) and a new logo was created.

Before the merge, the bank's corporate identity incorporated the red, white, and blue of the Thai flag. The new logotype incorporates a refined graphic proportion and new refreshed colors: 70 percent blue, 20 percent red, with a white line between that come together as the bank's signature.

Given these three colors to work with, each color was given a distinct identity and used to create the bank's information system. A family of sub/service marks and pictograms established a more friendly commercial service. A hand symbol was formed to promote the concept of the bank being hand-in-hand with its customers.

The aim was to create a very bold and easy understandable graphic and signage system by representing the action of banking activities without excessive text. It was also hoped that the brand could be represented without the bank's main logo.

A challenge to the designers was the short period allowed to implement all exterior signage systems in each of the 250 branch banks spread over the country. The four-month deadline was accomplished by the use of a flexible, simple graphic identity system and signage production that was applicable to all the extremely different conditions. The work continues on interior graphics and signage for prototype retail branches, mini booth/ branches, printing and promotion publication design, and other publications.

Government Housing Bank

Location: Thailand
Client: Government Housing Bank
Year: 2008
Contract Winning Design 2006

The Government Housing Bank wished to promote a new image following a shift in focus from the original government bank funding the majority of housing and construction loans for government officers to a full-service government-funded commercial bank. The bank's emphasis remains on housing and construction loans. The majority of its business is with domestic clients, and it has outlets all over the country. Its vision is to remain friendly and accessible to the same group of clients and to attract a new generation of clients with the right image.

While the existing logo is well established, a totally new image was required to incorporate GHbank, the new abbreviated name. Custom logotypes in both Thai and English languages are proposed. Other proposals include a vivid palette of tropical colors, new typographic usage, sub-service logos so that all products are consistent in branding, and adding to the existing auxiliary graphic to represent abstract notions of dynamic space, construction, and a growing business.

A full set of new graphic standards for stationery, printing, and promotional items has been launched, as well as the signage system. A simple renewed branch bank façade, which can be used in all variations and environments as a shading device, is both energy efficient and functions as a plain background for new vividly colored signage and information. This is cost-effective while having a significant impact. A manual for both corporate identity and the signage/environmental graphics system has been produced for the client.

MCOT Complex

Location: Rama IX Road, Bangkok, Thailand
Client: MCOT
Year: 2007
Contract Winning Design 1994

MCOT is the major government television channel in Thailand and is known locally as Channel 9. A recent reorganization as an independent body led to the promotion of a new image: "Modern 9."

G49 was involved with the re-branding aspects of the complex and all related graphic signage elements. The first new item implemented was a new logo, which features the numeral nine with an eye, representing the channel's new image.

Applications of the graphic standard to items such as stationery and all signage in the complex then followed. The ideas for wayfinding and signage at the MCOT complex derived simply from an array of RGB television colors that are commonly recognized and which are used to represent an array of buildings within the complex. While the design of the signage system is very simple, it is easily understood and adds meaning and liveliness that complements the simple modern architecture of the corporate complex.

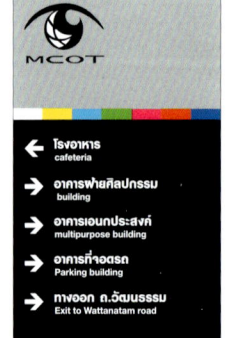

CP Lotus Superstore, Super Brand Mall, Shanghai

Location: Super Brand Mall, Shanghai, China
Client: CP's Chia Tai Group, China
Year: Design completed 2007; construction not completed

CP, the group owner of several superstores previously managed by the Lotus brand in major cities in China, has reorganized and wished to recreate its new co-owned brand as CP-Lotus. The first store to be upgraded is located at the Super Brand mall in Shanghai. In conjunction with the architects and interior designers, the aim is to renew this store as a prototype for other CP-Lotus locations.

A new corporate identity image and retail graphic system were created. The main concept is an upgrade to a modern new supermarket to suit the contemporary Chinese lifestyle, and to gather scattered information and promotional images into one system that could communicate the value and promotional aspects of products.

The logo and logotype have been adjusted to be used in conjunction with the new red, yellow, gold, and gray color scheme for a modern Chinese look. Promotional information is given a consistent hierarchy and format that associates the meaning of selected colors to speed the shoppers' decisions. The selection of new typography, both English and Chinese, is very important, as it is a large component of the graphic and signage information; chosen fonts are visually clean, interesting, and bold. Auxiliary patterns of systematic vertical lines will be used as the signature of the store's "everyday low prices and freshness." This additional graphic signage decoration is also an image separator solution in a flexible system for numerous product images that are required to be incorporated into walls, advertising, promotional, and signage systems.

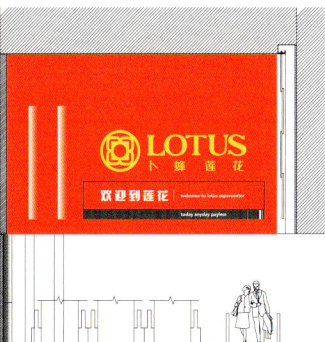

Central World Office Tower and Shopping Complex

Location: Rajdamri Intersection, Bangkok, Thailand
Client: Central World & Central Pattana
Year: 2007

The identity and environmental design for the Central World complex covers extra large, large, medium, small, and extra small graphics. The extra large scale includes graphic applications to the new façade, project names that are visible from a long distance, and exterior signage and its lighting. Large-scale graphics shape the space and theme of rooms and parking system graphic themes and signage. The medium scale covers interior directional, directory, and miscellaneous interior graphics and signage, and street furniture themes inside and outside the mall. Small and extra small items include all graphic details including typography, maps, pictograms and icons, and various identity signs and ornamentation.

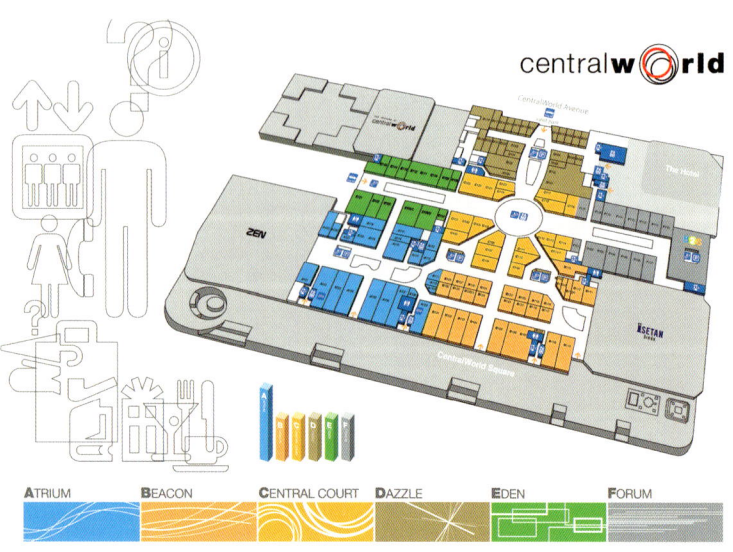

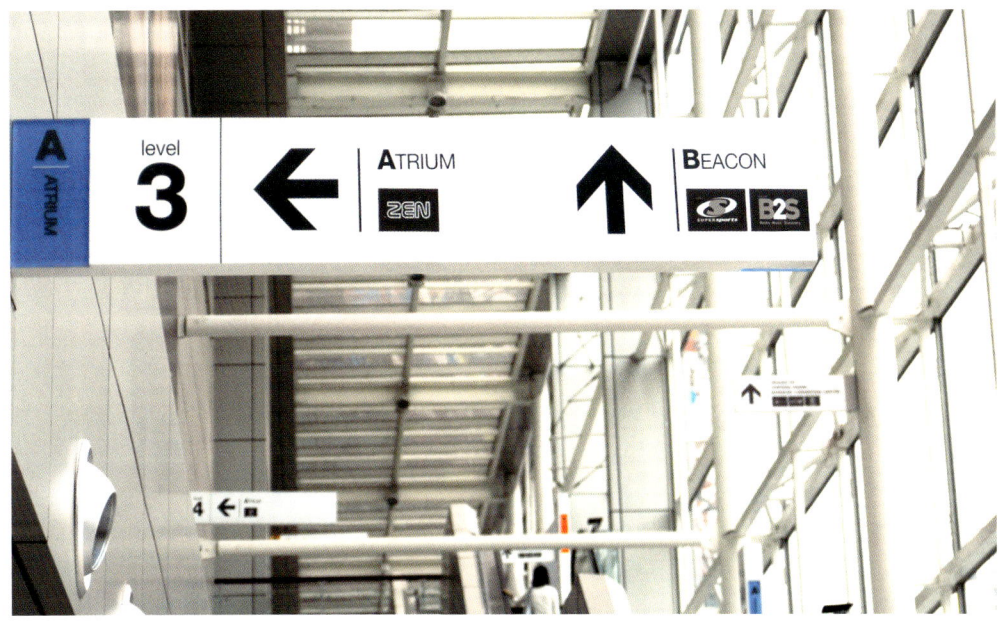

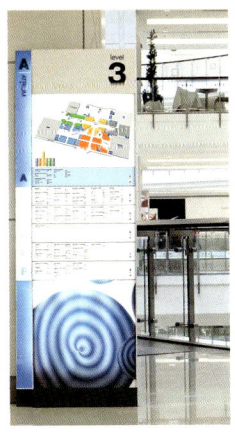

Space planning of this very large place is underpinned by the wayfinding strategy, which was created by G49 at an early stage. Identity systems for each zone/room were created to respond to the environment, with reference to the original logo and the complex's brand, "World," which incorporates the idea of overlapping spheres.

The various zones that make up the complex are identified by unique identity systems that include zonal logotypes, basic colors, and graphic patterns, all created to suit and apply to each zone's architecture, features, and atmosphere.

Despite a low project budget, the key visual graphics and corporate identity have infused into the complex in all possible ways, not only in information and signage design but throughout interior details, paving patterns, decorative walls, and lighting fixtures. It is fun to discover the exhilarating graphic applications which together show visitors the way. The unique identity of the whole complex is generated and complemented by the strong graphical sub-identity.

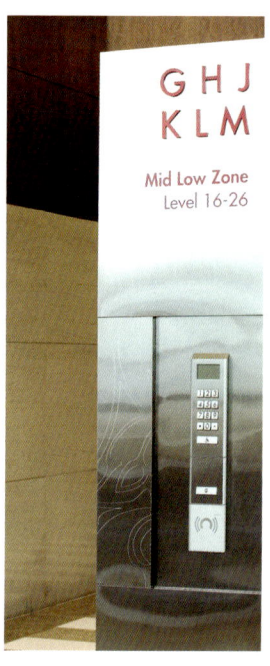

Thailand Creative and Design Center (TCDC)

Location: Emporium Shopping Mall, Bangkok, Thailand
Client: Thailand Creative and Design Center (TCDC)
Year: 2006

The environmental graphics for TCDC were inspired by the flexibility of the center's programs, its complicated circulation, and accessibility of interior spaces. Empty walls clad with unfinished raw steel sheets meant that wayfinding elements were required, but they also provided potential for add-on information. The signage system was designed in puzzle-like modular units that can be placed and removed freely and creatively for both wayfinding and information purposes on any wall.

The sign unit itself represents an innovative design creation. In addition, the chosen material gives depth to the graphics while its toy-like quality imparts a more playful atmosphere to the center.

The project won an honor award from the Society of Environmental Graphics (SEGD), Washington DC, in 2007.

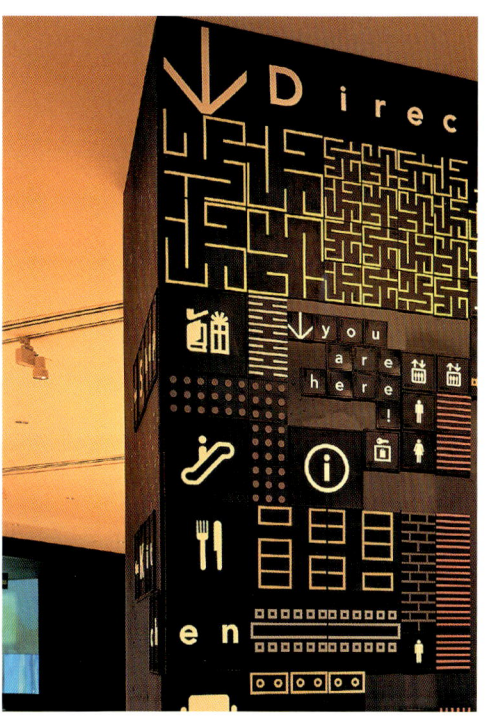

King Power Complex: Headquarters, Duty Free Shops, Joe Louis Puppet Show, Ramayana Restaurants, and Pullman Hotel

Location: Rangnam Road, Bangkok, Thailand
Client: King Power International
Year: 2008

At the King Power complex, wayfinding architectural signage is designed to not interfere with the prominent architecture and interior spaces, but to complement them. With the international modern architectural design of the complex, the role of the graphics is to add a modern Thai flavor to enhance its major business—the duty free mall—which serves mainly tourists and to help promote both local goods and international brands. The main restaurant and new auditorium in the complex serve specialty food and offer shows based on traditional Thai story themes to attract the same visitors.

The graphics and signage design for the complex features a system of deep Thai colors specifically assigned to provide an identity for each building. Also featured are simplified Thai–Hindu god and goddess patterns resembling the woven diamond squares that are usually found at the doors of temples or palaces. It is intended that this pattern be used at the main domed entry hall in an exterior suspended structure designed by the architect.

The original typographic "K" of the complex has also been reinvented and placed inside a circle as the new complex signature; all the information pictograms are treated in a similar way. The signage's final design and housing is very simple and elegant, and cautious in its placement, as was the design of the building. Elaborate refinements are in the typography, patterns, maps, and the design of added information.

Ramayana Restaurants. An epic story originating from India that has had a profound impact on art and culture in the Indian subcontinent and Southeast Asia was chosen to be the main theme of the restaurants. Puppets are used as decoration, to promote the Joe Louis Puppet Show at the adjacent auditorium. The emblem portrays two main traditional characters of the Ramayana—Hanuman and Tossakan—in their defeat over the Himmapan forest by depicting the original style of the Ramayana figure and adding an elaborate, entertainment feel to the custom logotype.

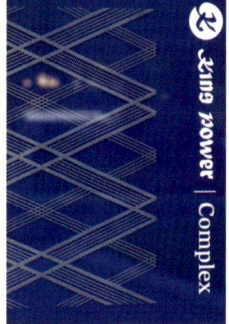 

Joe Louis Puppet Show. An elaborate custom logotype conveys the entertainment aspects of this venue. The puppet in the emblem is similar to that of the Ramayana Restaurant, portraying traditional stories of the Ramayana. Additional puppeteer illustrations in the same style represent the features of the show.

Pullman Hotel. The Pullman Hotel at King Power Complex will be first Pullman Hotel for the Accor Group. The scope of work for G49 is the application and implementation of all exterior and interior graphics and signage programs for the hotel. The aims are to establish the corporate identity as a luxury, trendy brand, and to incorporate wayfinding and branding into the architectural and interior settings. Interior and exterior signage systems for the hotel will be designed and applied together with auxiliary graphics such as glass door stickers and other informational and promotional signs, to complement the hotel's branding and corporate identity.

Pullman Hotel Outlet Identities. In addition to the facilities at the Pullman Hotel are newly created food and beverage outlets. In collaboration with the hotel manager/operator and interior designer, the identity, collateral design, and outlet signage of those new concept restaurants has been designed to fit under the umbrella of the new Pullman brand. Each restaurant has it own lines of food and beverages and unique design atmospheres. The identities of the outlets fulfill the aspects of communication and emphasize the brand's value. All logotypes have been formatted to be consistent with that of the Pullman brand.

Espace: Business center
Winepub: Wine cellar and tapas bar
Glen Bar: Lobby lounge piano bar
@Chann: Modern Thai restaurant and buffet
Cuisine: Western food all-day dining and buffet
Dejavu: Concept restaurant for creation of food by a rotation of world-renowned chefs

LD49

49 Lighting Design Consultants

LD49

49 Lighting Design Consultants complements the 49Group of companies in providing precisely created lighting concepts to all spaces—architectural, interior, or landscape. Lighting is used as a catalyst of spatial perception, to emphasize architectural order, to express material richness, and to challenge the limits of sensory perception.

1

2

Catalyst of spatial perception

The role of lighting is to connect space with human visual perception. People perceive volume, depth, scale, proportion, or even shape and form of space itself, through light in those spaces. Architects are now more likely to integrate interior and exterior space together and light can be the catalyst that makes people perceive relativity and continuity of contiguous space more precisely and easily.

In terms of lighting design, it is preferable to show the existence of adjoining spaces by lighting them in simple but effective ways such as following spatial characteristics to connect them by using the same lighting method inside and out.

In the main atrium of the King Power Complex, the floor plane and ceiling were simply lit to allow the dome-shaped atrium space to be most effectively perceived. The structure that supports the glazing is used as a silhouette to create contrast between the space and its skin.

In the exterior of the VR Residence, balancing exterior and interior lighting while retaining shade in some parts allowed the volume and shape of each space to be perceived more accurately.

1 Main atrium at King Power Complex
2 Light and shade define space in the VR Residence exterior

Emphasis of architectural order

Another component that influences our cognitive process is architectural order. To carefully search for the essence of order and to visualize it creates a particular sense of order. Lighting should employ repetition and rhythm that harmonize with the architectural structure and should avoid adding new elements that will weaken the integrity of the original architectural scheme.

In the main drop-off area of the King Power Complex, floor indicators are allied with the canopy-supported colonnades to visualize a repetition of the architectural order. These indicators also light the colonnade to distinguish it from the main building, allowing the viewer to perceive another architectural layer that is placed behind.

In the Aksara Theater foyer, the order of interior architectural elements is accentuated by gently differentiating light and shade, which gradually reveal the sense of order of the wall and ceiling patterns of the space.

3

4

5

6

Expression of material richness

Light that is too bright or at an inappropriate angle will destroy the ability to differentiate the richness of materials. Restrained and discreet light will always create a comfortable visual environment to stimulate the sense of touch.

In the main atrium of the King Power Complex, horizontal fins are lit up and mirrored on the surface of an adjacent ring-shaped reflecting pool. The glitter of light on the water when ripples spread across encouraged people to sense the water in a more sophisticated way.

In the interior of the VR Residence, the main staircase's travertine wall was smoothly lit to evoke and diversify the material's sense of touch via visual perception.

Beyond the edge of perception

Deductive formulas have always been applied in the design of pure architectural spaces. Challenging the limits of sensory perception could lead us to more refined lighting concepts in which we acknowledge the impact perceptible light has on the sense of space, order, and materials. In this way, maximized perception could be combined with minimized effect to achieve wholeness and unity of architectural space.

3   Repetition of indicators synchronize with architectural order at King Power Complex's main drop-off area

4   Light following the order of elements in the Aksara Theater foyer

5   Reflection of horizontal architectural elements over King Power Complex's main atrium reflecting pool

6   Smoothly lit travertine wall stimulate sense of materials in VR Residence interior

Appendix

Project Chronology
A49

1994

MCOT Operation Building (1)
1994–2001
Rama IX Road, Bangkok, Thailand
Mass Communication Organization of Thailand
1994, contract winning design

1997

Mae Fah Luang University (2)
1997–2002
Doi Ngam, Chiang Rai, Thailand
University Affairs
1997, contract winning design

1998

The Royal Bangkok Sports Club (3)
1998–2002
Henri Dunant Road, Bangkok, Thailand
The Royal Bangkok Sports Club
1998, contract winning design

1999

Faculties of Sociology and Anthropology, Thammasat University (4)
1999–2008
Rangsit, Pathum Thani, Thailand
Thammasat University

Oasis at Mulberry (5)
1999–2004
Singapore
Tan Chong Land
1999, contract winning design

2000

Pine Valley Golf Resort & Country Club (6)
1999–2003
Beijing, China
Pine Valley

Southeast Asian Ceramics Museum (7)
2000–2004
Rangsit, Pathum Thani, Thailand
Bangkok University

Surat Osathanugrah Library (8)
2000–2002
Rangsit, Pathum Thani, Thailand
Bangkok University

The Tubkaak Krabi Boutique Resort (9)
2000–2002
Krabi, Thailand
Teicon

Windsor Park II (10)
2000
Shanghai, China
Multi Field International Holding

2001

Bangkok Bank Head Office Renovation (11)
2001–2003
Silom Road, Bangkok, Thailand
Bangkok Bank

Bank of Thailand Headquarters (12)
2001
Phra Nakhon, Bangkok, Thailand
Bank of Thailand
2001, competition entry

Bhutan International Conference Center (13)
2001
Thimphu, Bhutan
The Royal Government of Bhutan
2001, contract winning design

The Bukit Gita Bayu Garden Villas (14)
2001–2003
Kuala Lumpur, Malaysia
Yee Seng Heights

Pongthip Osathanugrah Communication Arts Complex (15)
2001–2004
Rangsit, Pathum Thani, Thailand
Bangkok University

The French School (16)
2001
Pracha Uthit Road, Bangkok, Thailand
Lycée Français International de Bangkok
2001, competition entry

Mission Hills Phuket Golf Resort & Spa (17)
2001–2003
Phuket, Thailand
Rung Sin Construction

Ocean Newline Headquarters (18)
2001
Rama IV Road, Bangkok, Thailand
Ocean Newline

Panya Ramindra Housing Project (19)
2001–2002
Panya Ramindra Road, Bangkok, Thailand
Panya Property

Saphan Kwai Office (20)
2002–2006
Phahon Yothin 14, Bangkok, Thailand
Kriangsak Issarachaiyos

T.C. Pharmaceutical Office (21)
2001–2004
Prachin Buri, Thailand
T.C. Pharmaceutical Industrial

Thammasat University Academic Resource Center (22)
2000–2002
Rangsit, Pathum Thani, Thailand
Thammasat University

Wat Pah Sunantawanaram (23)
2001–2002
Kanchanaburi, Thailand
Wat Pah Sunantawanaram & Mayakotame Foundation
2004, Citation, ASA Architectural Design Awards

2002

Bangkok Airways Head Office Renovation (24)
2002
Vibhavadi Rangsit Road, Bangkok, Thailand
Bangkok Airways

Bangkok Museum of Contemporary Art (25)
2002
Rama IV Road, Bangkok, Thailand
Petch Osathanugrah

The Bhumirak Dhamachart, The Royal Nature Conservation Center (26)
2002–2004
Nakhon Nayok, Thailand
Old Vajiravudh Student Association

The Bukit Gita Bayu Hill Villas (27)
2002–2004
Kuala Lumpur, Malaysia
Yee Seng Heights

Chiva-Som Health Resort & Spa (28)
2002–2006
Khao Kho, Phetchabun, Thailand
Chiva-som International
2002, contract winning design

The Embassy of the Kingdom of the Netherlands (29)
2003–2005
Pleon Chit Road, Bangkok, Thailand
The Royal Netherlands Embassy, Thailand

Honda Showroom – Ekamai (30)
2002–2005
Sukhumvit Road, Bangkok, Thailand
Sukhumvit Honda Automobile

K1 Computer Center (31)
2002–2005
Bangkok, Thailand

Le Meridien Chiang Sean Resort & Spa (32)
2002
Chiang Rai, Thailand
Chiang Saen Lake Hill

S1 Data Center (33)
2003–2005
Vibhavadi Rangsit Road, Bangkok, Thailand

Siam Winery Trading Plus Office & Warehouse (34)
2002–2006
Pathum Thani, Thailand
Trading Plus

Tourism Authority of Thailand Head Office (35)
2002–2003
New Petchaburi Road, Bangkok, Thailand
Tourism Authority of Thailand
2002, contract winning design

Urbana Sukhumvit 15 (36)
2002–2003
Sukhumvit 15, Bangkok, Thailand
Urbana Estate

Vichai Trading Office (37)
2002–2003
Sukhumvit 63, Bangkok, Thailand
Vichai Trading

2003

The 49 Terrace (38)
2003–2005
Sukhumvit 49, Bangkok, Thailand
The 49 Terrace

Baan Issara Rama IX (39)
2003–2004
Ramkhamhaeng Road, Bangkok, Thailand
Charn Issara Development

Baan Mor Market Development (40)
2003–2007
Phra Nakhon, Bangkok, Thailand
The Heritage of Chao Phraya Dhevej

The Centric Place (41)
2003–2004
Phahon Yathin Road, Bangkok, Thailand
SC Asset Corporation

Chiang Mai International Convention Center (42)
2003
Chiang Mai, Thailand
Tourism Authority of Thailand
2003, competition entry

Cocoon Life Style (43)
2003–2006
Phuket, Thailand
Anupaspirom Resort

Community Organizations Development Institute Office (44)
2003
Bang Kapi, Bangkok, Thailand
Community Organizations Development Institute
2003, competition entry

The Fraser Suites Urbana Sathorn (45)
2003–2007
Sathorn Road, Bangkok, Thailand
Urbana Estate
2008, Citation, ASA Architectural Design Awards

Hilton Krabi Resort & Spa (46)
2003
Krabi, Thailand
Southern Beach

IMAGIMAX (47)
2003–2006
Narathiwas Rajanakarindra Road, Bangkok, Thailand
Saksiri Koshapasharin

MCOT Complex (48)
2003–2007
Rama IX Road, Bangkok, Thailand
MCOT

Panya Ramindra Village (49)
2003
Ramindra Road, Bangkok, Thailand
Panya Properties

Pipattanasin Office Building (50)
2003–2006
Narathiwas Rajanakarindra Road, Bangkok, Thailand
Pipattanasin

Prommitr Production & Moon Beam Equipment Office (51)
2003
Krung Thep Kritha Road, Bangkok, Thailand
Prommitr Production & Moon Beam Equipment

Redevelopment of the Pre-Cadet School site (52)
2003
Wireless Road, Bangkok, Thailand
The Pre-Cadet School
2003, competition entry

Central World (53)
2003–2006
Ratchadamri Road, Bangkok, Thailand
Central Pattana

SK 41 Condominium (54)
2003–2006
Sukhumvit Road, Bangkok, Thailand

Surawong Complex (55)
2003
Surawong Road, Bangkok, Thailand
T.C.C. Commercial Property Management
2003, competition entry

Suvarnabhumi Airport Hotel (56)
2003
Suvarnabhumi Airport, Samut Prakan, Thailand
Suvarnabhumi Airport Hotel
2003, competition entry

Thai Airways International Cargo & Mail Commercial Service Bangkok International Airport No.2 (57)
2003
Suvarnabhumi Airport, Samut Prakan, Thailand
Thai Airways
2003, competition entry

Thai Burner Industrial Heat Office (58)
2003–2005
Praditmanutham Road, Bangkok, Thailand
Thai Burner Industrial Heat

Urbana Langsuan (59)
2003–2004
Sukhumvit Road, Bangkok, Thailand
Urbana Estate

2004

The Athenee Place (60)
2004–2007
Wireless Road, Bangkok, Thailand
TCC Capital Land

Energy Complex (61)
2004–2009
Vibhavadi Rangsit Road, Bangkok, Thailand
Energy Complex Group
2004, contract winning design

The Funama Resort & Spa (62)
2004
Funamaudua Island, North Huvadhoo Atoll, Maldives
Aminath Shafia – M. Park Lane

The Lonudhua Resort & Spa (63)
2004
Lonudhuahuttaa Island, South Huvadhoo Atoll, Maldives
Ahmed Hamza Ma. Kinbi

The Maavela Resort & Spa (64)
2004
Maavelavaru Island, South Miladhunmadulu Atoll, Maldives
Ali Shiyam M. Fenfiyaazuaage

King Power Complex (65)
2004–2007
Rang Nam Road, Bangkok, Thailand
King Power International Group

NIKS (Thailand) Head Office (66)
2004
Rama III Road, Bangkok, Thailand
NIKS (Thailand)

Port Authority of Thailand Urban Development Project (67)
2004
Khlong Toei, Bangkok, Thailand
Port Authority of Thailand

Pullman Bangkok King Power (68)
2004–2007
Rang Nam Road, Bangkok, Thailand
King Power International Group

Raveevan Suite (69)
2004–2007
Sukhumvit 39, Bangkok, Thailand
Suppachot

Royal Cliff Hotel (70)
2004
Rama III, Bangkok, Thailand
Royal Cliff Hotel

Siriraj Toward Medical Excellence in Southeast Asia (71)
2004
Bangkok Noi, Bangkok, Thailand
Faculty of Medicine, Siriraj Hospital, Mahadol University
2004, competition entry

SK6 (72)
2004
Sukhumvit Road, Bangkok, Thailand
Jusmin Creation

WFS-PG Cargo: Air Cargo Terminal Services (73)
2004–2005
Suvarnabhumi Airport, Samut Prakan, Thailand
World Wide Flight Services Bangkok Airways Ground Handling

2005

Bangkok Airways New Office (74)
2005–2007
Suvarnabhumi Airport, Samut Prakan, Thailand
Bangkok Airways

Cementhai Building Products Gallery (75)
2005
Bang Sue, Bangkok, Thailand
Cementhai Building Products
2006, contract winning design

The Clover (76)
2005–2007
Thonglor 18, Bangkok, Thailand
Wanchai Supphayak/Top Line Living

The Emporio (77)
2005–2007
Sukhumvit 24, Bangkok, Thailand
TCC Capital Land

Hua Hin Boulevard (78)
2005–2008
Hua Hin, Prachuap Khiri Khan, Thailand

Hua Hin Resort (79)
2005
Hua Hin, Prachuap Khiri Khan, Thailand
Supachok Angsuvarnsiri

Land & House Urban Development Chiang Mai (80)
2005
Chiang Mai, Thailand
Land & Houses

Land Utilization of Rama IV Crossroad (81)
2005
Rama IV – Ratchadaphisek Road, Bangkok, Thailand
Stock Exchange of Thailand

Marukhathaiyawan Museum (82)
2005
Hua Hin, Prachuap Khiri Khan, Thailand

Maharattanaviharnkot Wat Pra Dhammakaya (83)
2005
Khlong Luang, Pathum Thani, Thailand
Dhammakaya Foundation

Niks Building (84)
2005
Surawong Road, Bangkok, Thailand
NIKS (Thailand)

Poh Teck Tung Foundation (85)
2005
Pom Prap Sattru Phai, Bangkok, Thailand
Poh Teck Tung Foundation
2005, competition entry

The Sofitel Patong (86)
2005
Phuket, Thailand
Boonchai – Pobchai Chivavisitthanon

Subaru 3S Centre (87)
2005–2006
Bueng Kum, Bangkok, Thailand
Motor Image Subaru (Thailand)

The Thai Red Cross Society Museum (88)
2005–2008
Rama IV Road, Bangkok, Thailand
The Thai Red Cross Society

Vajiravudh College Library (89)
2005–2007
Dusit, Bangkok, Thailand
Vajiravudh College

Wanasorn Education Center (90)
2005
Ratchathewi, Bangkok, Thailand
Wanasorn Business
2005, competition entry

2006

Al Yasmeen Islands (91)
2006–2010
Abu Dhabi, United Arab Emirates
Tamouh Investment

Apartment Soi 24 (92)
2006
Sukhumvit 24, Bangkok, Thailand
Pakakeo Bunnag

Assumption College Building (93)
2006
Bang Rak, Bangkok, Thailand
Assumption College

Bangkok University Landmark Complex (94)
2006–2009
Pathum Thani, Thailand
Bangkok University

Cheras Residential Development (95)
2006–2010
Kuala Lampur, Malaysia
Hong Leong Group

The Danet Gateway (96)
2006–2010
Danet, Abu Dhabi, UAE
Tamouh Investment

I.P. Trading (97)
2006–2007
Saphan Sung, Bangkok, Thailand
I.P. Trading

Koh Kood Resort (98)
2006
Koh Kood, Trat, Thailand
Apichart Chulankool

L&H Business Park (99)
2006
Si Nakarindra Road, Bangkok, Thailand
Land & Houses

Library of Her Majesty the Queen (100)
2006–2008
Dusit, Bangkok, Thailand

Mahaviharn Pra Mongkolthepmunee Memorial (101)
2006–2009
Song Phi Nong, Suphan Buri, Thailand
Dhammakaya Foundation

Mahidol University Technology Innovation Center & Main Auditorium (102)
2006–2009
Putthamonthon, Nakhon Pathom, Thailand
Mahidol University
2006, contract winning design

Ocean Point (103)
2006–2008
Ko Samui, Surat Thani, Thailand

Royal Archive (104)
2006–2007
Nakhon Pathom, Thailand
The Office of His Majesty's Principal Private Secretary

Samui Pavilion (105)
2006–2008
Koh Samui, Surat Thani, Thailand
Pollapat Karnnasut

Rajini School (106)
2006–2009
Phra Nakhon, Bangkok, Thailand
Rajini Foundation

Thailand Cultural Center (107)
2006–2009
Huai Khwang, Bangkok, Thailand
Ministry of Culture
2006, contract winning design

Tsunami Memorial & Museum (108)
2006
Phang-Nga, Thailand
Ministry of Culture
2006, competition entry

UD Service Center & Warehouse (109)
2006–2007
Vibhavadi Rangsit Road, Bangkok, Thailand
Y & Associates

W Hotel Bangkok (110)
2006
Sathon Road, Bangkok, Thailand
W Hotel
2006, competition entry

2007

Faculty of Arts, Mahidol University (111)
2007
Putthamonthon, Nakhon Pathom, Thailand
Faculty of Arts, Mahidol University
2007, contract winning design

The Gateway Ekamai (1120
2007
Sukhumvit 42, Bangkok, Thailand
The Thai Red Cross Society
2007, competition entry

I.P. Trading Retail A (113)
2007–2008
Saphan Sung, Bangkok, Thailand
I.P. Trading

Jumeirah Phuket Private Island (114)
2007
Phuket, Thailand
Dilokpol Sundaravej

Ocean Newline Office & Residence (115)
2007–2009
Rama IV Road, Bangkok, Thailand
Ocean Newline

Phuket Renaissance (116)
2007–2009
Phuket, Thailand
Seacon Hotel & Resort

Ploenchit Urban Development (117)
2007–2009
Pathum Wan, Bangkok, Thailand
Pasakornnatee (Oishi Group)
2006, competition entry

SCG Experience (118)
2007–2009
At Narong Road, Bangkok, Thailand
Cementhai Building Products

SET Multipurpose Building (119)
2007–2008
Don Mueang, Bangkok, Thailand
The Stock Exchange of Thailand
2007, contract winning design

Siam Square Commercial Development (120)
2007
Pathum Wan, Bangkok, Thailand
Chulalongkorn University
2007, competition entry

Pagoda of Wat Pah Sunantawanaram (121)
2007–2008
Kanchanaburi, Thailand
Wat Pah Sunantawanaram

Wireless Road Project (122)
2007
Wireless Road, Bangkok, Thailand
Thai Contractor Assets
2007, competition entry

World Peace Valley (123)
2007–2008
Nakorn Rachasima, Thailand
Dhammakaya Foundation

2008

Central Plaza Chiang Rai (124)
2008
Chiang Rai, Thailand
Central Pattana

Central Plaza Khon Kaen (125)
2008
Khon Kaen, Thailand
Central Pattana

Holiday Inn Express (126)
2008
Rama I Road, Bangkok, Thailand
Holiday Inn

Jumeirah Park Apartments (127)
2008
Dubai, United Arab Emirates
Nakheel

Pagoda of Wat Pah Nikhotharam (128)
2008–2009
Udorn Thani
Wat Pah Nikhrotharam

A49 International

2006

Cheras Bangalow (1)
2006
Kuala Lumpur, Malaysia
Hong Leong

Cheras Condominium (2)
2006
Kuala Lumpur, Malaysia
Hong Leong

The Danet Gateway (3)
2006
Abu Dhabi, United Arab Emirates
Tamouh

Al Yasmeen Islands (4)
2006
Abu Dhabi, United Arab Emirates
Tamouh

2007

Bangsar Mixed-Use Development (5)
2007
Kuala Lumpur, Malaysia
Hong Leong

The Emerald (6)
2007
Kuala Lumpur, Malaysia
Hong Leong

Seputeh Garden (7)
2007
Kuala Lumpur, Malaysia
Hong Leong

The Peak (8)
2007
Kuala Lumpur, Malaysia
E&O Property

Lot 89 (9)
2007
Kuala Lumpur, Malaysia
Planet Uno

Jumeirah Park Apartments (10)
2007
Dubai, United Arab Emirates
Nakheel

Dolphin Island (11)
2007
Abu Dhabi, United Arab Emirates
Al Tamouh

Holiday Inn Express Rama I (12)
2007
Bangkok, Thailand
Amburaya Resort

Jumeirah Phuket – Private Island Resort (13)
2007
Phuket, Thailand
TGR Asia

Wireless Road Project (Competition) (14)
2007
Bangkok, Thailand
Thai Contractor Association

2008

Thu Thiem New Urban Area (15)
2008
Thu Thiem Peninsula, Vietnam
Al Tamouh

Upper Bukit Timah (16)
2008
Singapore
Tan Chong

Zhongshan White Stone View (17)
2008
Zhongshan, China
Zhongshan

City of Light (18)
2008
Abu Dhabi, United Arab Emirates
Al Tamouh

A49 Chiang Mai

2005

Bodhimongkol Crematorium (1)
2005–2009
Ta Sala, Chiang Mai
Chiapak Osataphant

Baan Mae Rim (2)
2005–2009
Mae Rim, Chiang Mai
Nithi Sthapitanonda

Baan Ounrak (3)
2005
Mae Rim, Chiang Mai
CJN Realty

TITA Gallery renovation and extension (4)
2005–2006
Mae Rim, Chiang Mai
Thitaya Phiuon

Baan San Kamphaeng (5)
2005–2009
San Kamphaeng, Chiang Mai
Chiapak Osataphant

Baan San Khampaeng Land Development (6)
2005–2009
San Kamphaeng, Chiang Mai
Chiapak Osataphant

2006

Srichawala Building (7)
2006–2009
CM Business Park, Chiang Mai
Archara Srichawala

Chiang Mai Transit System Study (8)
2006
Chiang Mai, Thailand
Engineering Service Center, Chiang Mai University

Boutique Villa Resort (9)
2006–2009
Mae Hia, Chiang Mai
Land & Houses

2007

Advanced Manufacturing Center (10)
2007
Chiang Mai University, Chiang Mai
Faculty of Engineering, Chiang Mai University

Baan Karat Building Renovation (11)
2007–2008
Huay Kaew, Chiang Mai
Chainarong-Sasikarn Rungkagoonnuwat

Renovation of DOH Store Building, CMU (12)
2007
Chiang Mai University, Chiang Mai
Faculty of Engineering, Chiang Mai University

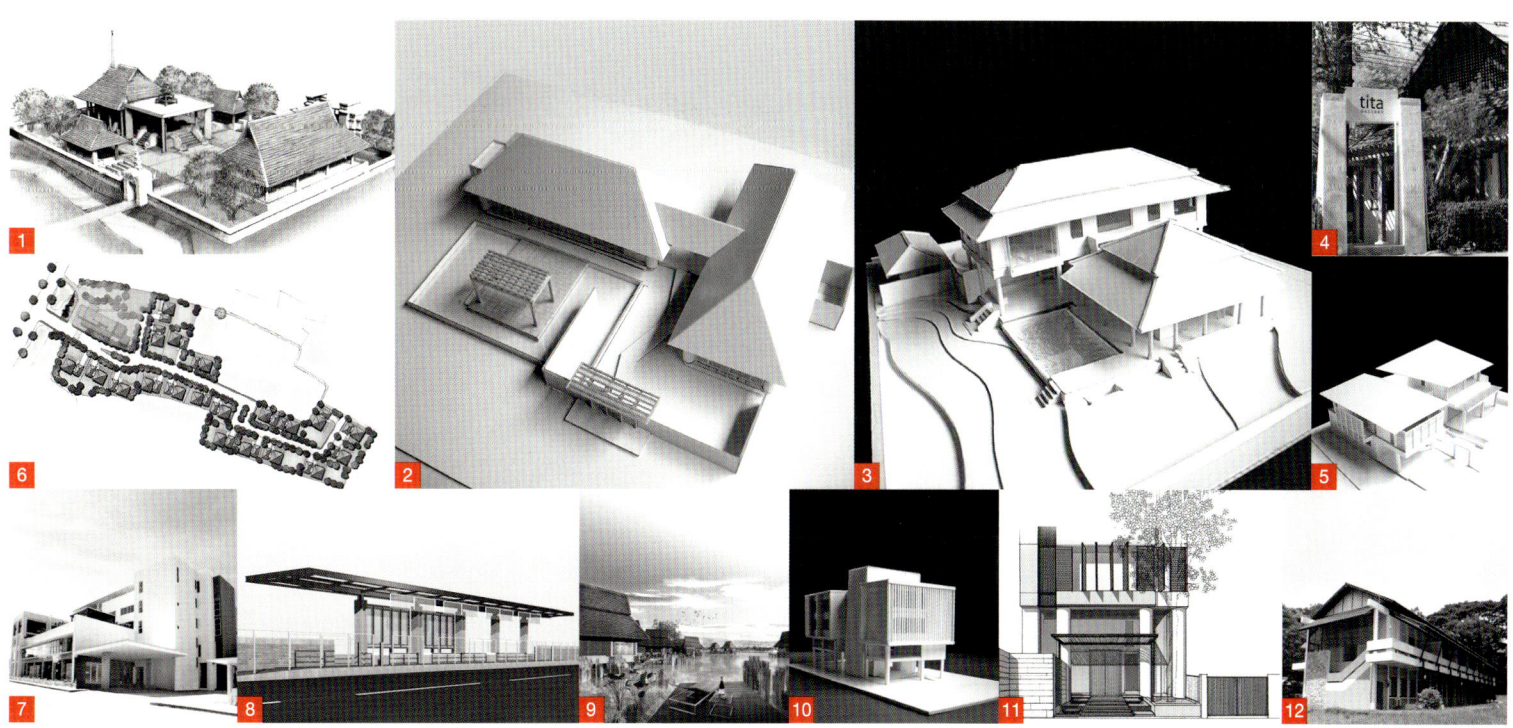

Site Study for Land Development, Rim Kok, Chiang Rai (13)
2007
Chiang Rai
Krerkchai Siripakdi

Vacation House Re-façade (14)
2007
Mae Joe, Chiang Mai
Chumpol Na Lamliang

Housing Project Master Plan (15)
2007
Doisaket, Chiang Mai
Chiang Mai Retreat Development

Nathika Apartment Re-façade (16)
2007
Chiang Mai
Chiang Mai Retreat Development

Mae Rim Housing Project Master Plan (17)
2007
Mae Rim, Chiang Mai
Design Basic

2008

Van Den Berghe Residence (18)
2008–2009
Mae Rim, Chiang Mai
Urai Jenarewong & Dirk Van den Berghe

Land & Houses Condominium (19)
2008
Mae Hia, Chiang Mai
Land & Houses

Wiang Inn – Entrance Renovation (20)
2008
Chiang Rai
Wiang Inn Hotel

Wiang Inn – Study of Banquet Hall (21)
2008
Chiang Rai
Wiang Inn Hotel

Sukniran Renovation & Extension Wing Study (22)
2008
Chiang Rai
Ruangchai Jitsakul

Bluechips Microhouse New Factory (23)
2008–2009
San Khampaeng, Chiang Mai
Bluechips Microhouse

Reisinger Residence (24)
2008–2009
Mae Rim, Chiang Mai
Supaporn Chuenjai

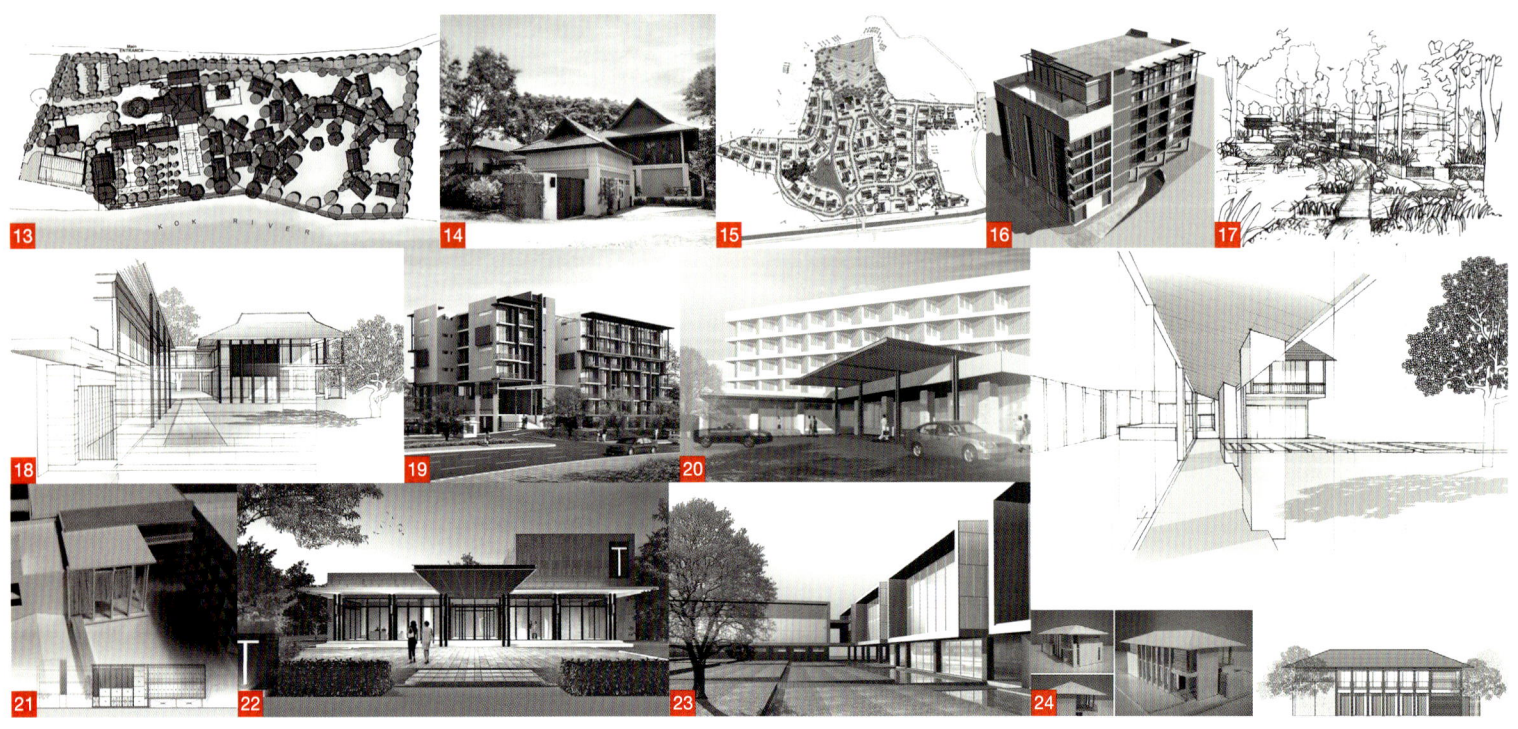

A49 Phuket

2006

Bangkok Hospital Phuket – IPD (1)
2006
Hongsyokuthit Road, Phuket, Thailand
Bangkok Phuket Hospital

Baan Vichit Songkarm (2)
2006
Phuket, Thailand
Tanit Rattanakumchai

Baan Hongsyok (3)
2006
Phuket, Thailand
Boonsri Hongsyok

Ocean Point (4)
2006–2008
Ko Samui, Surat Thani, Thailand

2007

B95 Radio Bulletin Station (5)
2007–2007
Phuket, Thailand
Tanit Rattanakumchai

Phuket Medical Center (6)
2007
Phuket, Thailand

Kalim Beach Resort (7)
2007
Kalim Beach, Phuket, Thailand
Veerachai Ungtrakul

Phulay Beach Resort – Restaurant (8)
2007
Tubkaak Beach, Krabi, Thailand
Piya International

Phuket Memorial Hall & Modern Art Center (9)
2007
Phuket, Thailand
Tanit Rattanakumchai

2008

Phulay Beach Resort – Spa (10)
2008
Tubkaak Beach, Krabi, Thailand
Piya International

La Colline (11)
2008
Layan, Phuket, Thailand
Property 55

Guan-Yin Shrine (12)
2008
Sapan Hin, Phuket, Thailand
Phuket Municipality

Project Data: A49

Architecture by Architects 49 except where otherwise noted.

The 49 Terrace 2003–2005
Location: Sukhumvit 49, Bangkok, Thailand
Client: The 49 Terrace
Area: 1,885 square meters
Cost: 31.25 million baht
System Engineer: M&E Engineering 49
Construction Manager: Consulting & Management 49

Athenee Place, The 2004–2008
Location: Wireless Road, Bangkok, Thailand
Client: TCC Capital Land
Area: 180,000 square meters
Cost: 4,000 million baht
Structural Engineer: PB Asia
System Engineer: PB Asia
Interior Architect: LEO International Design Group
Landscape Architect: Bensley Design Studios
Façade Consultant: BBG-BBGM
Contract Administration: Davis Langdon & Seah

Baan Hua Hin 1999–2005
Location: Hua Hin, Prachuap Khiri Khan, Thailand
Area: 1,800 square meters
Structural Engineer: 49 Engineering Consultants
System Engineer: 49 Engineering Consultants
Interior Architect: Interior Architects 49
Landscape Architect: Landscape Architects 49
Lighting design for entrance: 49 Lighting Design Consultants
Outdoor and interior lighting: Kanokporn Nuchsaeng

Baan Lat Phrao 2000–2001
Location: Lat Phrao, Bangkok, Thailand
Area: 800 square meters
Structural Engineer: 49 Engineering Consultants
System Engineer: 49 Engineering Consultants
Interior Architect: Interior Architects 49

Baan Muang Thong 3 2000–2002
Location: Muang Thong 3 Village, Nonthaburi, Thailand
Area: 1,350 square meters
Structural Engineer: 49 Engineering Consultants
Interior Architect: Interior Architects 49
Landscape Architect: Landscape Architects 49

Baan Sukhumvit 38 2000–2002
Location: Sukhumvit 38, Bangkok, Thailand
Area: 2,000 square meters
Structural Engineer: 49 Engineering Consultants
System Engineer: 49 Engineering Consultants
Interior Architect: Interior Architects 49

Baan Windmill 2001–2004
Location: Bangna-Trat Road, Samut Prakan, Thailand
Area: 1,290 square meters
Structural Engineer: 49 Engineering Consultants
System Engineer: 49 Engineering Consultants
Interior Architect: Interior Architects 49
Landscape Architect: Landscape Architects 49

Bangkok Airways New Office 2005–2007
Location: Suvarnabhumi Airport, Samut Prakan, Thailand
Client: Bangkok Airways
Area: 7,500 square meters
Cost: 117 million baht
Structural Engineer: Architectural Engineering 49
System Engineer: M&E Engineering 49

The Bhumirak Dhamachart, The Royal Nature Conservation Center 2002–2004

Location: Nakhon Nayok, Thailand

Client: Old Vajiravudh Student Association and The Chaipattana Foundation

Area: 2,900 square meters

Cost: 30 million baht

Structural Engineer: 49 Engineering Consultants

System Engineer: 49 Engineering Consultants

Landscape Architect: Landscape Architects 49

The Bukit Gita Bayu 2001–2003

Location: Kuala Lumpur, Malaysia

Client: Yee Seng Heights

Area: 14,680 square meters

Bangkok University Landmark Complex 2006–2009

Location: Rangsit, Pathum Thani, Thailand

Client: Bangkok University

Area: 25,000 square meters

Cost: 600 million baht

Structural Engineer: Architectural Engineering 49

System Engineer: M&E Engineering 49

Interior Architect: Interior Architects 49

Landscape Architect: Landscape Architects 49

Lighting Consultant: 49 Lighting Design Consultants

Ccmcnthai Building Products Gallery 2005

Location: Bang Sue, Bangkok, Thailand

Client: Cementhai Building Products

Area: 48,250 square meters

Cost: 1,100 million baht

Award: 2006, contract winning design

Structural Engineer: Architectural Engineering 49

System Engineer: M&E Engineering 49

Interior Architect: Interior Architects 49

Landscape Architect: Landscape Architects 49

Lighting Consultant: 49 Lighting Design Consultants

Exhibition Consultant: Rightman

Energy Consultant: Pirast Pacharaswate Kamol Keatruangkamala

Central Plaza Khon Kaen 2008

Location: Khon Kaen, Thailand

Client: Central Pattana

Area: 72,500 square meters

Structural Engineer: Architectural Engineering 49

Interior Architect: Interior Architects 49

Central World, The 2003–2006

Location: Ratchadamri Road, Bangkok, Thailand

Client: Central Pattana

Area: 440,000 square meters

Cost: 6,700 million baht

Design Consultant: Altoon + Porter Architects

Structural Engineers: K.C.S & Associates, SSK

System Engineer: Mitr Technical Consultant

Interior Architect: Interior Architects 49

Landscape Architect: Landscape Architects 49

Graphic Designer: Graphic 49

Lighting Consultant: With Light

Construction Manager: Project Planning Services Project Planning Services (North)

Cheras Residential Development 2006–2010

Location: Kuala Lumpur, Malaysia

Client: Hong Leong Properties

Area: 500 square meters per unit

Cost: 60 million baht per unit

Associate Architect: Architects 49 International

Clover, The 2005–2007

Location: Thonglor 18, Bangkok, Thailand

Client: Top Line Living

Area: 42,000 square meters

Cost: 718 million baht

Structural Engineer: Architectural Engineering 49

System Engineer: M&E Engineering 49

Interior Architect: LEO International Design Group

Landscape Architect: Landscape Architects 49

Marketing: Aquarius

Construction Manager: Consulting & Management 49

Cocoon Life Style 2003–2006

Location: Phuket Country Club, Phuket, Thailand
Client: Anupaspirom Resort
Area: 600–800 square meters per unit
Cost: 12–16 million baht per unit
Structural Engineer: Architectural Engineering 49
System Engineer: M&E Engineering 49
Landscape Architect: Landscape Architects 49

The Danet Gateway 2006–2010

Location: Danet, Abu Dhabi, United Arab Emirates
Client: Al Tamouh
Area: 1.15 million square feet
Cost: 180 million USD
Associate Architect: Architect International 49
Landscape Architect: Landscape Architects 49
Graphic Designer: Graphic 49
Lighting Consultant: 49 Lighting Design Consultants

The Embassy of The Kingdom of The Netherlands
2003–2005

Location: Pleon Chit Road, Bangkok, Thailand
Client: The Royal Netherlands Embassy, Thailand
Area: 4,000 square meters
Cost: 116.5 million baht
Associate Architect: Hubert – Henket & Partners Architecten
Structural Engineer: MAA Consultants
System Engineer: MAA Consultants
Landscape Architect: Landscape Architects 49

Emporio, The 2005–2007

Location: Sukhumvit 24, Bangkok, Thailand
Client: TCC Capital Land
Area: 70,125 square meters
Cost: 1,650 million baht
Structural Engineers: Tham & Wong
Qbic Engineers and Architects
System Engineer: M&E Engineering 49
Interior Architect: P Interior & Associates
Landscape Architect: P Landscape
Lighting Consultant: Lightbox Design
Specialist: KPK Quantity Surveyors (Thailand)
Construction Manager: Consulting & Management 49

Energy Complex 2004–2009

Location: Vibhavadi Rangsit Road, Bangkok, Thailand
Client: Energy Complex Group
Area: 177,000 square meters
Cost: 5,430 million baht
Award: 2004, contract winning design
Associate Architect: Design Concept
Structural Engineer: Thai Engineering Consultant
System Engineer: Mitr Technical Consultant
Energy Consultant: Newcomb & Boyd's Consulting Engineering Group
Façade Consultants: Werner Sobek Ingenieure
Ove Arup & Partners Singapore

Faculty of Arts, Mahidol University 2007

Location: Phutthamonthon, Nakhon Pathom, Thailand
Client: Mahidol University
Area: 15,200 square meters
Cost: 279 million baht
Structural Engineer: Architectural Engineering 49
System Engineer: M&E Engineering 49
Interior Architect: Interior Architects 49
Landscape Architect: Landscape Architects 49

Fraser Suites Urbana Sathorn, The 2003–2007

Location: Sathorn Road, Bangkok, Thailand
Client: Urbana Estate
Area: 40,860 square meters
Cost: 720 million baht
Structural Engineer: Architectural Engineering 49
System Engineer: UCC Consultants

The Gateway Ekamai 2008

Location: Sukhumvit 42, Bangkok, Thailand
Client: The Thai Red Cross Society
Area: 113,500 square meters
Cost: 3,200 million baht
Structural Engineer: Architectural Engineering 49
System Engineer: M&E Engineering 49
Lighting Consultant: 49 Lighting Design Consultants
Retail Consultant: RDG Planning & Design Consultants
Traffic Consultant: ANP Consultants

Guan-Yin Shrine 2008–2009
Location: Sapan Hin, Phuket, Thailand
Client: Phuket Municipality
Associate Architect: Architects 49 Phuket

Holiday Inn Express 2008–2010
Location: Rama 1 Road, Bangkok, Thailand
Client: Holiday Inn
Area: 20,160 square meters
Cost: 900 million baht
Structural Engineer: Architectural Engineering 49
Interior Architect: Interior Architects 49
Landscape Architect: Landscape Architects 49
Graphic Designer: Graphic 49
Construction Manager: Consulting & Management 49

Honda Showroom 2002–2005
Location: Ekamai Road, Bangkok, Thailand
Client: Sukhumvit Honda Automobile
Area: 10,000 square meters
Cost: 110 million baht
Structural Engineer: 49 Engineering Consultants
System Engineer: Escon
Interior Architect: Interior Architects 49
Construction Manager: Engineering System Consultants

Hua Hin Boulevard 2005–2008
Location: Hua Hin, Prachuap Khiri Khan, Thailand
Area: 14,000 square meters
Cost: 225 million baht
Structural Engineer: Cubic Design
System Engineer: PU Associates

I.P. Trading 2007–2008
Location: Saphan Sung, Bangkok, Thailand
Client: I.P. Trading
Area: 4,300 square meters
Cost: 80 million baht
Structural Engineer: Architectural Engineering 49
System Engineer: M&E Engineering 49
Interior Architect: Interior Architects 49
Landscape Architect: Group Three Design
Construction Manager: Consulting & Management 49

Imagimax 2003–2006
Location: Narathiwas Rajanakarindra Road, Bangkok, Thailand
Client: Saksiri Koshapasharin
Area: 11,179 square meters
Cost: 170 million baht
Structural Engineer: Architectural Engineering 49
System Engineer: M&E Engineering 49
Interior Architect: Interior Architects 49
Landscape Architect: Landscape Architects 49
Lighting Consultant: 49 Lighting Design Consultants
Construction Manager: Arun-Chaiseri Consulting Engineers

Jumeirah Park Apartments 2007–2009
Location: Dubai, United Arab Emirates
Client: Nakheel
Area: 500,000 square meters
Cost: 303 million USD
Associate Architect: Architects 49 International
Structural Engineer: Architectural Engineering 49
System Engineer: M&E Engineering 49
Landscape Architect: Landscape Architects 49

Jumeirah Phuket Private Island 2007–2009
Location: Phuket, Thailand
Client: Dilokpol Sundaravej
Area: 35,500 square meters
Cost: 1,500 million baht
Structural Engineer: R.K.V. Engineering Consultant
System Engineer: Environmental Engineering Consultants
Interior Architect: Hirsch Bedner Associates
Landscape Architect: Belt Collins
Construction Manager: Bovis Lend Lease (Thailand)

K1 Computer Center 2002–2005
Location: Bangkok, Thailand
Area: 6,105 square meters
Cost: 400 million baht
Structural Engineer: 49 Engineering Consultants
System Engineer: Environmental Engineering Consultants
Interior Architect: Interior Architects 49
Landscape Architect: Landscape Architects 49
Construction Manager: Project Planning Service

King Power Complex 2004–2007

Location: Rangnam Road, Bangkok, Thailand
Client: King Power International Group
Area: 145,000 square meters
Cost: 4,138 million baht
Structural Engineer: Architectural Engineering 49
System Engineer: M&E Engineering 49
Interior Architect: Interior Architects 49
Landscape Architect: Landscape Architects 49
Graphic Designer: Graphic 49
Lighting Consultant: 49 Lighting Design Consultants
Construction Manager: Consulting & Management 49
Curtain wall Consultant: Ove Arup & Partners Singapore
Theatre Design Consultant: Theatre Projects Consultants

Koh Kood Resort 2006

Location: Koh Kood, Trad, Thailand
Client: Summit Auto Seats Industry
Area: 19,212 square meters
Cost: 1,515 million baht
Structural Engineer: Architectural Engineering 49
System Engineer: M&E Engineering 49
Interior Architect: Interior Architects 49
Landscape Architect: Landscape Architects 49
Graphic Designer: Graphic 49
Lighting Consultant: 49 Lighting Design Consultants

Land & Houses Urban Development Chiang Mai
2005–2010

Location: Chiang Mai, Thailand
Client: Land & Houses
Area: 115 hectares
Landscape Architect: Landscape Architects 49

Library of Her Majesty the Queen 2006–2008

Location: Dusit, Bangkok, Thailand
Area: 650 square meters
Cost: 50 million baht
Structural Engineer: Architectural Engineering 49
System Engineer: M&E Engineering 49
Interior Architect: Interior Architects 49
Lighting Consultant: 49 Lighting Design Consultants

Mae Fah Luang University 1997–2002

Location: Doi Ngam, Chiang Rai, Thailand
Client: University Affairs
Area: 180,000 square meters
Cost: 2,500 million baht
Award: 1997, contract winning design
Associate Architects: SJA+3D; Architects 110
Structural Engineers: 49 Engineering Consultants
Infrastructural Engineers: W and Associates Consultants
CEDA
Landscape Architects: Landscape Architects 49
Belt Collins Thailand
Construction Managers: TPFC International

Maharattanaviharnkot Wat Pra Dhammakaya 2005–2007

Location: Khlong Luang, Pathum Thani, Thailand
Client: Dhammakaya Foundation
Area: 1 million square meters
Structural Engineer: ACTEC
System Engineer: PKT Engineering Supply
Construction Manager: K.C.S. & Associates

Mahaviharn Pra Mongkol Thepmunee Memorial
2008–2009

Location: Song Phi Nong, Suphan Buri, Thailand
Client: Dhammakaya Foundation
Area: 4,600 square meters

Mahidol University Technology Innovation Center & Main Auditorium 2006

Location: Phutthamonthon, Nakhon Pathom, Thailand
Client: Mahidol University
Area: 15,000 square meters
Cost: 1,500 million baht
Award: 2006, contract winning design
Structural Engineer: Architectural Engineering 49
System Engineer: M&E Engineering 49
Interior Architect: Interior Architects 49
Landscape Architect: Landscape Architects 49
Lighting Consultant: 49 Lighting Design Consultants
Specialist: Theater Projects Consultants
Professor Dr. Atch Sreshthaputra

Maldives Resort & Spa
The Funama Resort & Spa 2004
Location: Funamaudua Island, North Huvadhoo Atoll, Maldives
Client: Aminath Shafia – M. Park Lane
Area: 16,055 square meters
Interior Architect: Interior Architects 49
Landscape Architect: Landscape Architects 49
Graphic Designer: Graphic 49

The Lonudhua Resort & Spa 2004
Location: Lonudhuahuttaa Island, South Huvadhoo Atoll, Maldives
Client: Ahmed Hamza Ma. Kinbi
Area: 15,248 square meters
Interior Architect: Interior Architects 49
Landscape Architect: Landscape Architects 49
Graphic Designer: Graphic 49

The Maavela Resort & Spa 2004
Location: Maavelavaru Island, South Miladhunmadulu Atoll, Maldives
Client: Ali Shiyam M. Fenfiyaazuaage
Area: 25,639 square meters
Interior Architect: Interior Architects 49
Landscape Architect: Landscape Architects 49
Graphic Designer: Graphic 49

MCOT : Operation Building 1994–2001
Location: Rama IX Road, Bangkok, Thailand
Client: The Mass Communication Organization of Thailand
Area: 32,000 square meters
Cost: 240 million baht
Award: 1994, contracting winning design
Structural Engineer: 49 Engineering Consultants
System Engineer: Environmental Engineering Consultants
Interior Architect: Interior Architects 49
Landscape Architect: Landscape Architects 49

MCOT Complex 2003–2007
Location: Rama IX Road, Bangkok, Thailand
Client: MCOT
Area: 48,814 square meters
Cost: 518 million baht
Structural Engineer: Architectural Engineering 49
System Engineer: M&E Engineering 49
Interior Architect: Interior Architects 49
Landscape Architect: Landscape Architects 49
Graphic Designer: Graphic 49
Construction Manager: Consulting & Management 49

Mission Hills Phuket Golf Resort & Spa 2001–2003
Location: Phuket, Thailand
Client: Rung Sin Construction
Area: 7,500 square meters
Cost: 150 million baht
Structural Engineer: 49 Engineering Consultants
Interior Architect: MLTD & Associates
Landscape Architect: D.S.B. Associates

NIKS (Thailand) Head Office 2004
Location: Rama III Road, Bangkok
Client: NIKS (Thailand)
Area: 12,148 square meters
Cost: 298 million baht
Structural Engineer: Architectural Engineering 49
System Engineer: M&E Engineering 49
Interior Architect: Interior Architects 49

Oasis at Mulberry 1999–2004
Location: Upper Aljunied Road, Singapore
Client: Tan Chong Land
Area: 23,028 square meters
Award: 1999, contract winning design
Associate Architect: A90 Architects International, Singapore
Structural Engineer: Ove Arup & Partners Singapore

Ocean Newline Office & Residence 2007–2009
Location: Rama IV Road, Bangkok, Thailand
Client: Ocean Newline
Area: 9,957 square meters
Cost: 256 million baht
Structural Engineer: Architectural Engineering 49
System Engineer: M&E Engineering 49
Interior Architect: Interior Architects 49

The Peak 2008–2010
Location: Kuala Lumpur, Malaysia
Client: E & O Properties
Area: 1,500 square meters per unit
Cost: 120 million baht per unit
Associate Architect: Architects 49 International

Phuket Renaissance 2007–2009
Location: Phuket, Thailand
Client: Seacon Hotels and Resorts
Area: 22,000 square meters
Cost: 1,100 million baht
Structural Engineer: Architectural Engineering 49
System Engineer: M&E Engineering 49
Interior Architect: Interior Architects 49
Landscape Architect: Landscape Architects 49

Pine Valley Golf Resort & Country Club 1999–2003
Location: Beijing, China
Client: Pine Valley
Area: 9,000 square meters
Cost: 62.8 million baht
Structural Engineer: 49 Engineering Consultants
System Engineer: 49 Engineering Consultants
Interior Architect: Interior Architects 49
Landscape Architect: Bensley Design Studios

Pipattanasin Office Building 2003–2006
Location: Narathiwas Rajanakarindra Road, Bangkok, Thailand
Client: Pipattanasin
Area: 19,000 square meters
Structural Engineer: CEDA
System Engineer: 49 Engineering Consultants

Poh Teck Tung Foundation 2005
Location: Pom Prap Sattru Phai, Bangkok, Thailand
Client: Poh Tek Tung Foundation
Area: 8,632 square meters
Cost: 156 million baht
Structural Engineer: Architectural Engineering 49
System Engineer: M&E Engineering 49

Pongthip Osathanugrah Communication Arts Complex 2001–2004
Location: Rangsit, Pathum Thani, Thailand
Client: Bangkok University
Area: 18,000 square meters
Cost: 350 million baht
Structural Engineer: 49 Engineering Consultants
System Engineer: 49 Engineering Consultants
Interior Architect: Interior Architects 49
Landscape Architect: Landscape Architects 49

Pra Bhothiyanathera Pagoda 1992–1996
Location: Ubon Ratchathani, Thailand
Client: Wat Nong Pah Pong
Area: 300 square meters
Cost: 3.2 million baht

Pullman Bangkok King Power 2004–2007
Location: Rang Nam Road, Bangkok, Thailand
Client: King Power International Group
Area: 41,490 square meters
Cost: 1,455 million baht
Structural Engineer: Architectural Engineering 49
System Engineer: M&E Engineering 49
Interior Architect: Interior Architects 49
Landscape Architect: Landscape Architects 49
Graphic Designer: Graphic 49
Lighting Consultant: 49 Lighting Design Consultants
Construction Manager: Consulting & Management 49
Acoustic Consultant: Maple Solution

Rajini School 2006–2009
Location: Phra Nakhon, Bangkok, Thailand
Client: Rajini Foundation
Area: 10,000 square meters
Cost: 211 million baht
Structural Engineer: Architectural Engineering 49
System Engineer: M&E Engineering 49

Red Mountain 2008–2010
Location: Phuket, Thailand
Client: MBK
Area: 22,000 square meters

Cost: 680 million baht
Structural Engineer: Architectural Engineering 49
System Engineer: M&E Engineering 49
Interior Architect: P Interior & Associates

Royal Archive 2006–2009
Location: Nakhon Pathom, Thailand
Client: The Office Of His Majesty's Principal Private Secretary
Area: 17,653 square meters
Cost: 479 million baht
Structural Engineer: Architectural Engineering 49
System Engineer: M&E Engineering 49
Interior Architect: Interior Architects 49
Construction Manager: Consulting & Management 49

Royal Bangkok Sports Club, The 1998–2002
Location: Henri Dunant Road, Pathum Wan, Bangkok, Thailand
Client: The Royal Bangkok Sports Club
Area: 14,344 square meters
Cost: 340.26 million baht
Award: 1998, contract winning design
Structural Engineer: 49 Engineering Consultants
System Engineer: Environmental Engineering Consultants
Interior Architect: LEO International Design Group

S1 Data Center 2003–2005
Location: Vibhavadi Rangsit Road, Bangkok, Thailand
Client: Stock Exchange of Thailand
Area: 11,600 square meters
Cost: 348.5 million baht
Structural Engineer: 49 Engineering Consultants
System Engineer: Environmental Engineering Consultants
Interior Architect: Interior Architects 49
Landscape Architect: Landscape Architects 49

Samui Pavilion 2006
Location: Samui Island, Surat Thani, Thailand
Client: Nawarat Patanakarn
Area: 450 square meters per unit
Cost: 38 million baht
Structural Engineer: Architectural Engineering 49
System Engineer: M&E Engineering 49
Landscape Architect: Landscape Architects 49

SCG Experience 2007–2009
Location: At Narong Road, Bangkok, Thailand
Client: Cement Building Products
Area: 6,200 square meters
Cost: 312 million baht
Structural Engineer: Architectural Engineering 49
System Engineer: M&E Engineering 49
Interior Architect: Interior Architects 49
Lighting Consultant: 49 Lighting Design Consultants

SET Multipurpose Building 2007–2008
Location: Don Mueang, Bangkok, Thailand
Client: The Stock Exchange of Thailand
Area: 4,800 square meters
Award: 2007, contract winning design
Structural Engineer: Architectural Engineering 49
System Engineer: EEC Engineering Network
Interior Architect: Interior Architects 49
Landscape Architect: Landscape Architects 49

Siam Square Commercial Development 2007
Location: Pathum Wan, Bangkok, Thailand
Client: Chulalongkorn University
Area: 73,196 square meters
Cost: 1,375 million baht
Structural Engineer: Architectural Engineering 49
System Engineer: M&E Engineering 49
Interior Architect: Interior Architects 49
Landscape Architect: Landscape Architects 49
Lighting Consultant: 49 Lighting Design Consultants
Graphic Designer: Graphic 49

Siam Winery Trading Plus Office & Warehouse 2002–2006
Location: Pathum Thani, Thailand
Client: Trading Plus
Area: 8,900 square meters
Cost: 107 million baht
Structural Engineer: 49 Engineering Consultants

SK 41 Condominium 2003–2007
Location: Sukhumvit 41, Bangkok, Thailand
Area: 39,538 square meters
Cost: 700 million baht

Structural Engineer: 49 Engineering Consultants
System Engineer: M&E Engineering 49
Interior Architect: Woods Bagot (Thailand)

Sofitel Patong, The 2005
Location: Patong, Phuket
Client: Phuket Income
Area: 34,000 square meters
Cost: 1,800 million baht
Structural Engineer: Architectural Engineering 49
System Engineer: M&E Engineering 49
Interior Architect: LEO International Design Group
Landscape Architect: Belt Collins International

Southeast Asian Ceramics Museum 2000–2002
Location: Rangsit, Pathum Thani, Thailand
Client: Bangkok University
Area: 1,740 square meters
Cost: 43 million baht
Award: 2008, Gold Medal, ASA Architectural Design Awards
Structural Engineer: 49 Engineering Consultants
Interior Architect: Interior Architects 49
Landscape Architect: Landscape Architects 49
Graphic Designer: Graphic 49
Construction Manager: Consulting & Management 49

Subaru 3S Center 2005–2006
Location: Sukhapiban Road, Bangkok, Thailand
Client: Motor Image Subaru (Thailand)
Area: 4,390 square meters
Cost: 158 million baht
Structural Engineer: Architectural Engineering 49
System Engineer: M&E Engineering 49
Interior Architect: Interior Architects 49
Graphic Designer: Graphic 49
Quantity Sueveyort: KPK Quantity Surveyor (Thailand)
Construction Manager: Consulting & Management 49

Surat Osathanugrah Library 2000–2003
Location: Rangsit, Pathum Thani, Thailand
Client: Bangkok University
Area: 19,410 square meters

Cost: 300 million baht
Award: 2004, Citation, ASA Architectural Design Awards
Structural Engineer: 49 Engineering Consultants
System Engineer: 49 Engineering Consultants
Interior Architect: Interior Architects 49
Landscape Architect: Landscape Architects 49
Construction Manager: Consulting & Management 49

T.C. Pharmaceutical Office 2002–2004
Location: Prachin Buri, Thailand
Client: T.C. Pharmaceutical Industrial
Area: 13,570 square meters
Cost: 205 million baht
Structural Engineer: 49 Engineering Consultants
Interior Architect: Interior Architects 49
Landscape Architect: Landscape Architects 49

The Thai Red Cross Society Museum 2005–2008
Location: Rama IV Road, Bangkok, Thailand
Client: The Thai Red Cross Society
Area: 11,415 square meters
Cost: 239.5 million baht
Structural Engineer: Architectural Engineering 49
System Engineer: M&E Engineering 49

Thailand Cultural Center 2006–2009
Location: Huai Khwang, Bangkok, Thailand
Client: Ministry of Culture
Area: 173,831 square meters
Cost: 3,700 million baht
Award: 2006, contract winning design
Structural Engineer: Architectural Engineering 49
System Engineer: M&E Engineering 49
Interior Architect: Interior Architects 49
Landscape Architect: Landscape Architects 49
Lighting Consultant: 49 Lighting Design Consultants
Specialist: Theater Project Consultants

Thu Thiem New Urban Area 2008–2010
Location: Ho Chi Minh City, Vietnam
Client: Al Tamouh
Associate Architect: Architects 49 International

The Tubkaak Krabi Boutique Resort 2000–2002

Location: Krabi, Thailand
Client: Teicon
Area: 4,800 square meters
Cost: 150 million baht
Award: 2004, Citation, ASA Architectural Design Awards
Structural Engineer: 49 Engineering Consultants
Interior Architect: Interior Architects 49
Landscape Architect: Landscape Architects 49
Graphic Designer: Graphic 49

Urbana Langsuan 2003–2005

Location: Lang Suan Road, Bangkok, Thailand
Client: Urbana Estate
Area: 23,822 square meters
Cost: 600 million baht

Wat Pah Nikhotharam Pagoda 2008–2009

Location: Udon Thani, Thailand
Client: Wat Pah Nikhotharam
Area: 80 square meters
Cost: 1 million baht

Wat Pah Sunantawanaram 2001–2002

Location: Kanchanaburi, Thailand
Client: Wat Pah Sunantawanaram & Mayakotame Foundation
Area: 1,100 square meters
Cost: 1 million baht
Award: 2004, Citation, ASA Architectural Design Awards

Wat Pah Sunantawanaram Pagoda 2007–2009

Location: Kanchanaburi, Thailand
Client: Wat Pah Sunantawanaram
Area: 149 square meters
Cost: 2.5 million baht

Waterfront Development at Khlong Toei 2004

Location: Khlong Toei, Bangkok, Thailand
Area: 3,764,800 square meters
Cost: 800 million baht

Wireless Road Project 2007

Location: Wireless Road, Bangkok, Thailand
Client: Thai Contractor Assets
Area: 34,817 square meters
Cost: 1,540 million baht
Structural Engineer: Architectural Engineering 49
System Engineer: M&E Engineering 49
Interior Architect: Interior Architects 49

World Peace Valley 2007–2008

Location: Khao Yai, Nakorn Ratchasima, Thailand
Client: Dhammakaya Foundation
Area: 10,000 square meters
Cost: 120 million baht
Structural Engineer: Ritta
System Engineer: Ritta

Project Data: IA49

Architecture by Architects 49 and Interior architecture by Interior Architects 49 except where otherwise noted.

Aksra Theater 2005–2007

Location: Rangnam Road, Bangkok, Thailand
Client: King Power International Group
Area: 4,017 square meters
Cost: 139.40 million baht
Structural Engineer: Architectural Engineering 49
System Engineer: M&E Engineering 49
Landscape Architect: Landscape Architects 49
Graphic Designer: Graphic 49
Lighting Consultant: 49 Lighting Design Consultants

Bangkok University Landmark Complex 2007–2009

Location: Rangsit, Pathum Thani, Thailand
Client: Bangkok University
Area: 13,090 square meters
Cost: 105.55 million baht
Structural Engineer: Architectural Engineering 49
System Engineer: M&E Engineering 49
Landscape Architect: Landscape Architects 49
Lighting Consultant: 49 Lighting Design Consultants

Central World 2004–2006

Location: Rajprasong Road, Bangkok, Thailand
Client: Central Pattana
Area: 71,500 square meters
Cost: 400 million baht
Landscape Architect: Landscape Architects 49
Graphic Designer: Graphic 49

Dholhiyadhoo Lagoon Resort and Spa 2006–2008

Location: Dholhiyadhoo, Maldives
Client: AAA Hotel & Resort
Area: 16,500 square meters
Cost: 11 million USD
Architect: KTGY International
Lighting Consultant: 49 Lighting Design Consultant

King Power Headquarters 2005–2007

Location: Rangnam, Bangkok, Thailand
Client: King Power International Group
Area: 17,549 square meters
Cost: 222.77 million baht
Structural Engineer: Architectural Engineering 49
System Engineer: M&E Engineering 49
Landscape Architect: Landscape Architects 49
Graphic Designer: Graphic 49
Lighting Consultant: 49 Lighting Design Consultants

Pullman Bangkok King Power 2005–2007

Location: Rangnam, Bangkok, Thailand
Client: King Power Hotel Management
Area: 27,095 square meters
Cost: 442.40 million baht
Structural Engineer: Architectural Engineering 49
System Engineer: M&E Engineering 49
Landscape Architect: Landscape Architects 49
Graphic Designer: Graphic 49
Lighting Consultant: 49 Lighting Design Consultants

Ramayana Restaurant 2005–2006

Location: Rangnam, Bangkok, Thailand
Client: King Power Hotel Management
Area: 1,630 square meters
Cost: 44.32 million baht
Structural Engineer: Architectural Engineering 49
System Engineer: M&E Engineering 49
Landscape Architect: Landscape Architects 49
Graphic Designer: Graphic 49
Lighting Consultant: 49 Lighting Design Consultants

Seri Tanjung Penang Condominium 2007–2008

Location: Penang, Malaysia
Client: E&O Property Development Berhad
Area: 149,179 square meters
Cost: 112,120–132,270 USD

SO Bangkok 2009

Location: Sathorn Road, Bangkok, Thailand
Client: Oak Tree
Area: 4,560 square meters
Cost: 72 million baht
Associate Interior Architects: PIA Interior/August Design/Deca/IAW
Landscape Architect: Landscape Architects 49

Project Data: L49

Landscape architecture for all projects by Landscape Architects 49.

Baan Sukhumvit Soi 16 2001–2004
Location: Sukhumvit 16, Bangkok, Thailand
Area: 4,170 square meters
Architect: Duangrit Bunnag Architect, KTGY for houses, Landscape Architects 49 for clubhouse kiosk
Structural Engineer: J.E.T. Engineering
System Engineer: J.E.T. Engineering
Interior Architect: Duangrit Bunnag Architect
Construction Manager: Quality Construction

MCOT Operation Building 2003–2005
Location: Rama IX Road, Bangkok, Thailand
Client: Mass Communication Organization of Thailand
Area: 9,775 square meters
Architect: Architects 49
Structural Engineer: 49 Engineering Consultants
System Engineer: Environmental Engineering Consultants
Interior Architect: Interior Architects 49
Construction Manager: Consulting & Management 49

Domus 2004–2007
Location: Sukhumvit 16, Bangkok, Thailand
Client: Gaysorn Property
Area: 4.85 rais
Architect: SCDA Architects
Structural Engineer: K.C.S. & Associates
System Engineer: Mitr Technical Consultants
Interior Architect: Design Worldwide Partnership
Construction Manager: Projects Asia

Pullman Bangkok King Power 2004–2007
Location: Rangnam Road, Bangkok, Thailand
Client: King Power International Group
Area: 48,000 square meters
Architect: Architects 49
Structural Engineer: Architectural Engineering 49
System Engineer: M&E Engineering 49
Interior Architect: Interior Architects 49
Graphic Designer: Graphic 49
Lighting Consultant: 49 Lighting Design Consultants
Construction Manager: Consulting & Management 49

Central World 2005–2007
Location: Rajdamri Road, Bangkok, Thailand
Client: Central Pattana
Area: 96,000 square meters
Architect: Architects 49 for shopping area, Palmer and Turner (Thailand) for office
Structural Engineer: K.C.S. & Associates
System Engineer: Mitr Technical Consultants
Interior Architect: Interior Architects 49
Graphic Designer: Graphic 49
Construction Manager: Project Planning Service

Tala 2007 2007
Location: Rajdamri Road, Bangkok, Thailand
Client: Thai Association of Thailand Architects

Prime Nature Villa 2002–2007
Location: On Nuch Road, Bangkok, Thailand
Client: Prime Nature Villa
Area: 160,000 square meters
Architect: amA Design Studio
Structural Engineer: Wisit Engineering Consultants
System Engineer: Wisit Engineering Consultants
Interior Architects: Prisma Design, Gote Bangkok International
Construction Manager: Integral Engineering Consultants

Prime Nature Villa 2004–2008
Location: Pechkasame Road, Petburi, Thailand
Client: Prime Nature Villa
Area: 163,200 square meters
Architects: AP'stract, amA Design Studio
Structural Engineer: Wisit Engineering Consultants
System Engineer: Wisit Engineering Consultants
Interior Architect: August Design Consultant
Construction Manager: Integral Engineering Consultants

Project Data: G49

Graphic design for all projects by Graphic 49.

Alila 2008
Location: Cha-am, Petchaburi, Thailand
Client: KS Resort & Spa
Architect: Duangrit Bunnag Architects Limited.
System Engineers: EMS Consultants Co., Ltd.
Interior Architect: Duangrit Bunnag Architects Limited.
Construction Manager: Arun Chaiseri Consulting Engineers Co., Ltd.

Bank of Ayudhya 2005
Location: Thailand
Client: Bank of Ayudhya
Contract Winning Design: 2001
Architect: Architects 49 Limited
Structural Engineer: International Project Administration Consultant
System Engineer: Engineering & Environmental Consultant
Interior Architect: P49 Design and Associates
Construction Manager: International Project Administration Consultant

Central World Office Tower and Shopping Complex 2007
Location: Rajdamri Intersection, Bangkok, Thailand
Client: Central World & Central Pattana
Architect: Architects 49
Structural Engineer: Architectural Engineering 49
System Engineer: M&E Engineering 49
Interior Architect: Interior Architects 49
Landscape Architect: Landscape Architects 49
Construction Manager: Project Planning Services

CP Lotus Superstore, Superbrand Mall, Shanghai
2007 (design)
Location: Superbrand Mall, Shanghai, China
Client: CP's Chia Tai Group, China
Architect: The Office of Bangkok Architect (OBA)
Interior Architect: The Office of Bangkok Architect (OBA)
Construction Manager: D Plan, China

Devarana Spa 2004
Location: Dusit Thani Hotel, Bangkok, Thailand
Client: Dusit Thani
Interior Architect: P Interior and Associates Co., Ltd.
Construction Manager: Decho Chiang Hai Furniture

Government Housing Bank 2008
Location: Thailand
Client: Government Housing Bank
Contract Winning Design: 2006
Architect: Architects 49
System Engineer: Engineering & Environmental Consultant
Interior Architect: P49 Design and Associates

King Power Complex; The Headquarters, Duty Free Shops, Joe Louis Puppet Show, Ramayana Restaurants and Pullman Hotel 2008
Location: Rangnam Road, Bangkok, Thailand
Client: King Power International
Architect: Architects 49
Structural Engineer: Architectural Engineering 49
System Engineer: M&E Engineering 49
Interior Architect: Interior Architects 49
Landscape Architect: Landscape Architects 49
Construction Manager: Consulting & Management 49

MCOT Complex 2007

Location: Rama IX Road, Bangkok, Thailand
Client: MCOT
Contract Winning Design: 1994
Architect: Architects 49
Structural Engineer: Architectural Engineering 49
System Engineer: M&E Engineering 49
Interior Architect: Interior Architects 49
Landscape Architect: Landscape Architects 49
Construction Manager: Consulting & Management 49

Savoury Gastrocafe 2006

Location: Siam Paragon Shopping Complex, Bangkok, Thailand
Client: Thippara
System Engineer: Engineering & Environmental Consultant
Interior Architect: P49 Design and Associates

Suvarnabhumi Museum Shop 2006

Location: Suvarnabhumi Airport, Samuth Prakhan, Thailand & King Power Duty Free Mall at King Power Complex, Bangkok, Thailand
Client: King Power Tax Free
System Engineer: Engineering & Environmental Consultant
Interior Architect: P49Deesign and Associates

Thailand Creative and Design Center (TCDC) 2006

Location: Emporium Shopping Mall, Bangkok, Thailand
Client: Thailand Creative and Design Center (TCDC)
Architect: Duangrit Bunnag Architects (DBALP)
Interior Architect: Duangrit Boonnag Architects (DBALP)

TMB Bank 2007

Location: Thailand
Client: TMB Bank Public Co., Ltd.
Contract Winning Design: 2005
Architect: Architects 49
System Engineer: Engineering & Environmental Consultant
Interior Architect: P49 Design and Associates
Construction Manager: SEA Consultant

Honors and Awards

Gold medal awards
(Awarded by The Association of Siamese Architects Under Royal Patronage)

1989 Muang Thai Life Assurance & Phatra Insurance Auditorium, Bangkok, Thailand

1989 Baan Soi Klang, Bangkok, Thailand

1994 Baan Chang Nag, Chiang Mai, Thailand

2002 Baan Rim Tai, Chiang Mai, Thailand

2008 Southeast Asian Ceramics Museum, Bangkok University, Rangsit, Pathum Thani, Thailand

Citations
(Awarded by The Association of Siamese Architects Under Royal Patronage)

1987 Baan Rim Nam, Bangkok, Thailand

1989 Petroleum Authority of Thailand, Head Office, Vibhavadi Rangsit Road, Bangkok, Thailand

1989 Analayo Meditation Pavillion, Phayao, Thailand

1989 Architects 49 Office, Sukhumvit 26, Bangkok, Thailand

1994 Sala Klang Nam, Chiang Mai, Thailand

1994 Natural Park Hill Golf Clubhouse, Chon Buri, Thailand

1996 Krung Thai Training Center, Nakhon Ratchasima, Thailand

2002 Panyavej Hospital, Udon Thani, Thailand

2002 Ministry of Foreign Affairs, Si Ayutthaya Road, Bangkok, Thailand

2002 Baan Osathaphan, Chiang Mai, Thailand

2002 Genco Hazardous Waste Disposal Facility, Rayong, Thailand

2004 Surat Osathanugrah Library, Bangkok University, Rangsit, Pathum Thani, Thailand

2004 Wat Pah Sunantawanaram, Kanchanaburi, Thailand

2004 The Tubkaak Krabi Boutique Resort, Krabi, Thailand

2008 Baan Patong, Phuket, Thailand

2008 The Fraser Suites Urbana Sathorn, Sathorn Road, Bangkok, Thailand

Contract-winning designs—government sector

1992 Ministry of Foreign Affairs, Si Ayutthaya Road, Bangkok, Thailand

1993 Krung Thai Training Center, Nakhon Ratchasima, Thailand

1994 MCOT: Operation Building, Rame IX Road, Bangkok, Thailand

1994 Thailand Export Mart, Ratchadaphisek Road, Bangkok, Thailand

1996 Thammasat University Academic Resource Center & International Conference, Rangsit, Pathum Thani, Thailand

1997 Mae Fah Luang University, Chiang Rai, Thailand

1997 Tourism Authority of Thailand Convention Center, Chon Buri, Thailand

2001 International Conference Center, Thimpu, Bhutan

2002 Tourism Authority of Thailand Head Office, New Petchaburi Road, Bangkok, Thailand

2004 Energy Complex, Vibhavadi Rangsit Road, Bangkok, Thailand

2006 Thailand Cultural Center, Huai Khwang, Bangkok, Thailand

2006 Mahidol University Technology Innovation Center & Main Auditorium, Putthamonthon, Nakhon Pathom, Thailand

2007 Faculty of Arts, Mahidol University, Putthamonthon, Nakhon Pathom, Thailand

Contract-winning designs—private sector

1984 Petroleum Authority of Thailand, Head Office, Vibhavadi Rangsit Road, Bangkok, Thailand

1985 Muang Thai Life Assurance & Phatra Insurance Auditorium, Bangkok, Thailand

1994 Holiday Inn Saigon Hotel, Ho Chi Minh City, Vietnam

1995 Bangkok Bank of Commerce Tower, Sathon Road, Bangkok, Thailand

1995 Osothsapha Corporate Headquarters, Ramkhamhang Road, Bangkok, Thailand

1995 Shell Company of Thailand, Retail And Training Center, Chon Buri, Thailand

1998 The Bangchak Petroleum Head Office, Si Nakarindra Road, Bangkok, Thailand

1998 The Royal Bangkok Sports Club, Henri Dunant Road, Bangkok, Thailand

1999 Oasis at Mulbery, Singapore

2002 Chiva-Som Health Resort & Spa, Petchabun, Thailand

2006 Cementhai Building Products Gallery, Bang Sue, Bangkok, Thailand

2007 SET Multipurpose Building, Don Mueang, Bangkok, Thailand

Bibliography

1989

Sthapitanonda, Nithi, *Renderings in Ink and Perspectives 1969–1989*, Asia Books

1991

Sthapitanonda, Nithi, *Moment in Architectural Drawing*, 49 Graphic and Publications

1993

Architects 49, *Architecture of Asia*, The Images Publishing Group

Powell, Robert, *The Asian House: Contemporary Houses of Southeast Asia*, Select Books (Baan Soi Klang, Baan Rim Nam)

1995

Fuchigami, Masayuki, *581 Architects in the World,* Toto Shuppan

1996

Tettoni, Luca Invernizzi and William Warren*, Thai Garden Style,* Asia Books (Suchin and Rujiraporn Wanglee's House, Nithi Sthapitanonda's House)

Beng, Tan Hock, *Tropical Retreats: the Poetics of Place,* Page one

Powell, Robert, *The Tropical Asian House*, Select Books (Baan Chang Nag)

International Architecture Yearbook Vol. 1 Book 2, The Images Publishing Group (Panya Hill Golf Clubhouse, Sala Klang Nam)

1997

Residential Spaces of the World Vol. 2, The Images Publishing Group (Mr Eaton's Residence)

Water Spaces of the World Vol. 2, The Images Publishing Group (Bubhajit Office Building, The Seri Center, Tipco Headquarters, Lake Rajada Office)

Residential Spaces of the World Vol. 3, The Images Publishing Group (Baan Poonsiriwongse, Baan Jiramaneekul, Baan Kuantrakul, Rotanda House, Baan Techapiboon)

Lutfy, Carol, "A Thai Landscape—A Bangkok Architect's Rustic Retreat Near Chiang Mai," *Architectural Digest*, January, pp. 84–95 (Baan Chang Nag)

International Architecture Yearbook No.2, The Images Publishing Group (Rotunda House, Future Park Plaza)

International Architecture Yearbook No.3, The Images Publishing Group (Krung Thai Training Center, Noble Park Clubhouse)

Sthapitanonda, Nithi, *Nithi Architectural Leisure Drawings*, Corporation 4d

House Design by Architects 49, The Images Publishing Group

1998

Experimental Architects 49: 1991–1997, by Architects 49, Corporation 4d

Architecture of the New Millennium, The Images Publishing Group

Warren, William, "The Glory of Thai Gardens," *Sawasdee* (Thai Airways magazine), May

"Fusion of an Ancient Civilization with Modern Technology: New Hospital Opens in Udon Thani," *Asian Hospital*, March

Lim, William S.W., *Contemporary Vernacular,* Select Books, (Wat Pa Sunantawanaram)

Sthapitanonda, Nithi, "Thai Architects Working Abroad," *ASA Magazine*, November, pp. 40–45

Sthapitanonda, Nithi, "Architectural Profession Situation in Worst Financial Crisis," *ASA Magazine*, November, pp. 62–63

1999

Details in Architecture 3, The Images Publishing Group

2000

Architects of the New Millennium, The Images Publishing Group

Amranand, Ping and William Warren, "An Architect's Rustic Retreat," *Lanna Style*

Feng Shui Today, The Images Publishing Group (Rotunda House, Mr Eaton's Residence)

100 of the World's Best Houses, The Images Publishing Group

Sthapitanonda, Nithi, "The Impact of Various Changes to Studio Teaching and Learning," *ASA Magazine*, February, pp. 30–35

2001

Sthapitanonda, Nithi, "Talk about Council of Thai Architects with Secretariat of Council Thai Architects", *ASA Magazine*, January, pp. 86–87

"Prime Thai," *d+a Design and Architecture*, February

Details in Architecture 3, "Canopy and Sunscreens", The Images Publishing Group

2002

Master Architect Series V: Architects 49, The Images Publishing Group

2003

Boschetti, Joe (ed), *Details in Architecture Vol. 5*, The Images Publishing Group

"On the Right Track-Art: Architect and Carpenter Bring Back to Life Old Timbers in a Joint Show," *Bangkok Post*, August 23

Sthapitanonda, Nithi, "The Development of Contemporary Architecture in Thailand and the Work of Nithi Sthapitanonda," Lecture at Hara Museum

2004

"Ideal House: Baan Suan Sangob," *Architecture Asia*, December

"I, technology: Surat Library," *Architecture Asia,* September

1000 Architects, The Images Publishing Group

Interior Architects 49, *Space Colours & Light: Interior Architectural Renderings*, Corporation 4d

2005

"New Waves from South east Asia," *A+U*, December, pp. 82–87 (Baan Patong)

"Inside Outside," *art4D,* October, (Nithi Sthapatanonda's Residence)

"Future Shapes of China and Southeast Asia", *Architecture 07*, BCI Asia, (Athenee Residence)

Yasuda, Masako, *Sustainable Architecture in Asia*, The Japan Institute of Architects

Sthapitanonda, Nithi and Brian Mertens, *The Architecture of Thailand*, Editions Didier Millet

2006

Freeman, Michael, *The New Oriental Style*, Asia Books

Bose, Apurva, "Global Practices," *a+d,* September, pp. 80–89 (Communication Arts Complex), pp. 90–94 (Honda Showroom)

50+ Vacation Homes, The Images Publishing Group

"Baan Suan Sangob", *12th Asian Congress of Architects,* pp. 90–93

Sthapitanonda, Nithi, *Our House, Architect's House*, Li-Zenn Publishing

2007

Retail Therapy, The Images Publishing Group, pp. 168–169 (The 49 Terrace)

"Up-and-Down Horizon," *id+c Interior Design + Construction*, May, pp. 72–77 (Surat Osathanugrah, Southeast Asian Ceramics Museum)

Mertens, Brian, *Bangkok Design: Thai Ideas in Textiles and Furniture*, "The Master Builder"

Sthapitanonda, Nithi, *Nithi Architectural Sketch Books 1971–2007*, Li-Zenn Publishing

Architects49 Experimental Design 1998–2006, Li-Zenn Publishing

DETAIL: Single Family Houses: Stairs & Railings, Li-Zenn Publishing

Thai Architecture Elements Series: Doors & Windows, Li-Zenn Publishing

Thai Architecture Elements Series: Surfaces, Li-Zenn Publishing

2008

"Mahidol University Technology Innovation Center & Main Auditorium," *FuturArc*, 1st Quarter, pp. 54–57

"Modern Urban Icons," *Architecture+Design*, February, pp. 76–82 (King Power Complex, Bangkok)

"The Golden Architect Award–India," *Architecture+Design*, April, pp. 42–43

"Architecture+Design & Spectrum Foundation Architecture Award 2007," *Architecture+Design*, May, pp. 34–36

"Golden Acclaim," by Krissana Parnsoonthorn, *Bangkok Post*, June 2008, "Pacific Star to Lure More Foreign Funds to Thailand", p. B10

Competition: A49, Li-Zenn Publishing

250 Record Houses: Architects 49, Li-Zenn Publishing

DETAIL Volume 2: Public Buildings: Façade/Canopy/Atrium, Li-Zenn Publishing

DETAIL Volume 3: Single Family Houses: Pool & Swimming Pool, Li-Zenn Publishing

DETAIL Volume 4: Single Family Houses: Façade, Li-Zenn Publishing

Thai Architecture Elements Series: Colors, Li-Zenn Publishing

Thai Architecture Elements Series: Stairs & Railings, Li-Zenn Publishing

Thai Architecture Elements Series: Statuary, Li-Zenn Publishing

Thai Architecture Elements Series: Roofs, Li-Zenn Publishing

Thai Architecture Elements Series: Gateways, Li-Zenn Publishing

Houses by Architects 49 Vol. 2, Li-Zenn Publishing

Company background and guiding principles

Architects 49 was established in 1983 with the goal of setting a new standard for truly professional work and for comprehensive architectural services. A49's services encompass urban planning, master plan preparation, architectural design, and construction management. The company also consults on project feasibility and viability, as well as project development and management. Our range of services extends from the development of a project to its successful completion.

Our watchword since the founding of the company has been, and remains, "teamwork." In 1991, we codified this practice by implementing a "studio approach" that assigns a small, focused studio of designers to take responsibility for each stage of a project from concept through preliminary and detailed design, to working plans and drawings. The studio team follows through with project management and construction supervision until completion to the client's satisfaction.

Each studio team reports directly to our President and Executive Committee who share responsibility for ensuring the high quality of the work. Project directors meet regularly to review their activities, exchange views, and discuss problems of joint concern. This process and these procedures ensure each project receives individual attention and benefits from the collective experience and resources of Architects 49.

Design philosophy

Architects 49's design philosophy is to create aesthetically pleasing buildings, with clean, simple, yet elegant lines, that are attractive and inviting to both daily users and occasional visitors. The design of the internal layout must be functional and practical to maximize the use of space while making maintenance simple and economical.

All of the projects, from large commercial buildings to private residences, show careful attention to detail in all aspects from conception to the selection of materials. Careful deliberation is given to the short- and long-term impact on the residents, the community, and the environment. These structures must assimilate gracefully into their surroundings and become an integral part of the context, while preserving their distinctive artistic appeal.

Inspired by this philosophy, Architects 49 works with a commitment to constantly achieve the highest standards of design and production. We regard our work as a labor of love through which we forge lasting ties among designers, clients, users, and the community.

Architects 49
Principals' Biographies

NITHI STHAPITANONDA
Chairman

Nithi Sthapitanonda is recognized for pioneering a contemporary Thai architecture that enhances international modernism with appropriate adaptations from local tradition. In works ranging from houses and resorts to high-rises and museums, his efforts show sensitivity to nature, climate, and culture as well as user needs.

Nithi received a Bachelor of Architecture degree from Chulalongkorn University in 1971, and a Master of Architecture degree from the University of Illinois at Urbana-Champaign in 1973. While at graduate school he received the highest award from the International Symposium on Housing in the Housing for Older Adults Competition. Nithi was also granted a fellowship for research in India.

He began his professional practice in 1973 in Washington, D.C., at Metcalf and Associates. Returning to Thailand in 1974, Nithi worked at Design 103 Ltd. for nine years before leaving to establish his own practice. He founded Architects 49 in 1983, and led the firm to win several gold medals for best architectural design from the Association of Siamese Architects.

Beyond leading as a practitioner, Nithi has also played an important role as president of the Association of Siamese Architects from 1992 to 1994, and as secretary general and board member of the Architect Council of Thailand from 2000 to 2003. His contribution to these organizations helped establish new standards and regulations that have strengthened the architectural profession in Thailand.

In 1995, the Japan Institute of Architects selected him as an Honorary Fellow (Hon. FJIA). Thailand's Ministry of Culture named him a National Artist in Contemporary Architecture in 2002. In 2007, he won the Golden Award for Excellence in Architecture from India's *Architecture + Design* journal and Spectrum Foundation. The American Institute of Architects named him an Honorary Fellow (Hon. FAIA) in 2008.

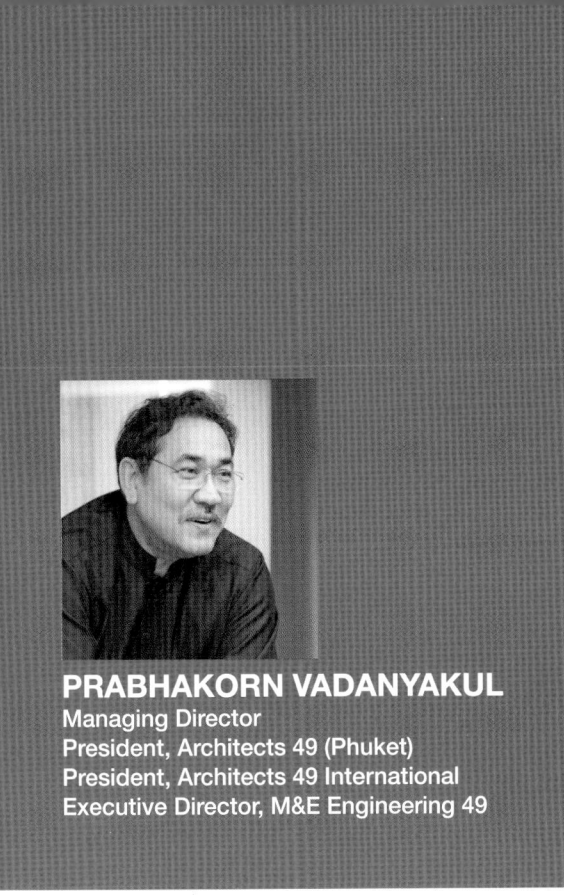

PRABHAKORN VADANYAKUL
Managing Director
President, Architects 49 (Phuket)
President, Architects 49 International
Executive Director, M&E Engineering 49

SUWAT VASAPINYOKUL
Deputy Managing Director
President, Interior Architects 49

Prabhakorn Vadanyakul's chief role at Architects 49 has been to develop its major policies, design concepts, and strategic planning. Since joining Architects 49 in 1985, he has been responsible for projects ranging from mega-complexes and high-rises to private houses and hotels. Most are located in Thailand, while others have been built in China, Malaysia, Singapore, Vietnam, and elsewhere in Asia, adding geographic breadth to A49's portfolio of work. He was appointed president of Architects 49 (Phuket) in 2005, and of Architects 49 International in 2006.

Prabhakorn received a Bachelor of Architecture degree from Chulalongkorn University in 1980, and in 1984 obtained a Master of Architecture degree from The Catholic University of America in Washington, D.C. He then joined the office of Robert Schwinn & Associates in Maryland in 1985.

Prabhakorn served as president of the Association of Siamese Architects from 2002 to 2004. He was the association's vice president of foreign affairs from 1995 to 1997, and its head of public relations from 1992 to 1994. He has actively participated in many subcommittees at both the Architect Council of Thailand and ASA. He is now chairman of the Council's subcommittee for reviewing and granting professional licenses to architects.

Since joining Architects 49 in 1983 as a founding member, Suwat Vasapinyokul has been responsible for architectural works ranging from private residences and apartment buildings to large office buildings and shopping complexes. With training in both management and design, Suwat plays a role at A49 as both a practitioner and key executive.

Suwat joined the firm upon graduating from Chulalongkorn University with a Bachelor of Architecture degree. While working at A49, he pursued postgraduate studies in business at Chulalongkorn, obtaining a Master of Business Administration degree in 1992. He became a director of A49 in 1990 and vice president in 1992.

In 1998, Suwat was appointed managing director of Interior Architects 49, the 49 Group's interior design affiliate. From 1998 through 2008 that position continued to be his main responsibility, but he also took on board management duties at A49. In 2008, he became president of IA49 and a deputy managing director of A49. Suwat has since overseen A49's business development activities and management policies.

Suwat served on the executive committee of the Association of Siamese Architects (ASA) from 1992 to 1994 and as secretary general from 2002 to 2004. He has participated in several subcommittees at both the ASA and Architect Council of Thailand.

PICHAI WONGWAISAYAWAN
Deputy Managing Director
Managing Director, Architects 49 International
Executive Director, Architectural Engineering 49

KIATTISAK VETEEWOOTACHARN
Deputy Managing Director
Executive Director, 49 Lighting Design Consultants

Pichai Wongwaisayawan has been instrumental in most of the international projects undertaken by Architects 49. Having led efforts to serve clients abroad, in 2006 he was named managing director of Architects 49 International, the firm's new affiliate established the same year, taking charge of all overseas projects in locations including Southeast Asia, China, and the Middle East.

Pichai received his Bachelor of Architecture degree from Chulalongkorn University in 1985, the year he joined A49. In 1989, he earned a master's degree from the University of Michigan, graduating with distinction. Pichai then worked at Hobbs & Black Associates in Ann Arbor, Michigan. He later moved to New York City, where he worked for two years as a designer at Hellmuth, Obata + Kassabaum (HOK).

Pichai rejoined A49 in 1992, taking responsibility for large corporate projects. He became executive director in 1995 and deputy managing director in 2001.

Pichai is an active member of the Association of Siamese Architects (ASA), where he was vice president from 1999 to 2001, and was responsible for the Professional Practice Committee. He has participated in many subcommittees at both the Architect Council of Thailand and ASA.

With more than 20 years of experience, Kiattisak Veteewootacharn leads an Architects 49 studio focused on private residences all over Thailand. In addition, he has represented the office on projects of every scale, including Bangkok's Future Park Rangsit, one of the largest shopping malls in Asia. He is also executive director of 49 Lighting Design Consultants, the affiliate established in 2003.

Kiattisak received his Bachelor of Architecture degree with honors from Chulalongkorn University in 1987, when he joined A49. He was appointed as an executive director in 2001, and as deputy managing director in 2006.

He was selected as an outstanding alumnus of Chulalongkorn University's Faculty of Architecture during its 72nd-year anniversary celebrations.

PAKAKEO BUNNAG
Executive Director/Office Manager

In her capacity as executive director, Pakakeo Bunnag is responsible for Architects 49's accounting and administration departments. She joined A49 as a general manager in 1989, becoming a partner in 1995.

Pakakeo graduated from Chulalongkorn University's Faculty of Commerce and Accountancy in 1970, and in 1972 obtained a secretarial course diploma from California's MTI Business College. She began her career in 1973 as executive secretary to the chairman and regional manager of ITT Asia Pacific (Thailand) Limited. In 1984, she became manager of the Special Project Division of Phaibul Sombat Company Limited.

KRISADA TEERAPONGPRACHAYA
Executive Director

Krisada Teerapongprachaya leads an Architects 49 studio focused on large-scale and government projects. Since joining the firm in 1989, he has worked on many large-scale commercial projects, including the King Power Complex, a hotel, entertainment, and shopping center completed in Bangkok in 2007.

Krisada received a Bachelor of Architecture degree from Silpakorn University in 1989. He began his career at Nondha-Truengjai Architects and Planners before joining A49. He was promoted to associate in 1995 while serving as project manager on several government projects. In 2000 he became an associate partner, then executive director, and was appointed partner the following year.

Partners and Associates

Partners
Nithi Sthapitanonda
Prabhakorn Vadanyakul
Suwat Vasapinyokul
Pichai Wongwaisayawan
Kiattisak Veteewootacharn
Pakakeo Bunnag
Krisada Teerapongprachaya
Unnop Veeravutthiphol
Karnchit Punyakanok
Chana Sumpalung
Rattawut Chansritrakul

Associate Partner
Suluck Visavapattamawon

Senior Associates
Prasert Yangthara
Patikorn Na Songkhla
Adul Leesawat
Dhanes Wongtun-yakorn

Associates
Auttawut Kaewsuttipon
Wichai Sriurairatana
Anuchit Sukontasub

Junior Associates
Donrudee Tantiyapinant
Watchara Chirasatit
Worawodth Wongsakda
Krisada Boonchaleow
Chalida Jeerawatana

49Group

The 49Group is a multi-disciplined firm of design professionals and consultants with a combined staff of more than 350. The group represents an affiliation of specialized consulting companies, each supported by a staff of experts. Many of the companies are housed under the same roof, the others are located nearby. The group is organized to work side by side so that the client may be assured of quick, efficient, and thorough service.

The 49Group operates on a teamwork basis, with an emphasis on sharing experiences and mutual collaboration. At the beginning of each project, the affiliated companies establish a working team of experienced personnel. The interdisciplinary team is led by a principal. Project managers of each discipline guide their teams to work in coordination with one another on the project.

The following affiliated companies constitute the 49Group:

Architects 49 Limited (A49)

Architects 49 International Limited (A49 International)

Architects 49 (Chiang Mai) Limited (A49 Chiang Mai)

Architects 49 (Phuket) Limited (A49 Phuket)

Architect 49 Limited Abu Dhabi (A49 Abu Dhabi)

Interior Architects 49 Limited (IA49)

Consulting & Management 49 Limited (CM49)

Landscape Architects 49 Limited (L49)

Graphic 49 Limited (G49)

Architectural Engineering 49 Limited (AE49)

M&E Engineering 49 Limited (ME49)

49 Lighting Design Consultants Limited (LD49)

This methodology pools the company's resources and ideas to find the best solution whether it involves designing, engineering, construction management, project development, or the utilization of a building and its long-term maintenance. The decisions reached collectively often save time and lead to prompt and effective solutions to difficult and otherwise time-consuming problems.

The 49Group is determined to do all it can to ensure that the results are high quality and the client is satisfied.

Architects 49

Services:
Master planning
Architectural design
Feasibility studies
Renovation and rehabilitation

Contacts:
Prabhakorn Vadanyakul
Suwat Vasapinyokul

Address:
81 Sukhumvit 26
Bangkok 10110
Thailand

Tel: +66 (0) 2260 4370
Fax: +66 (0) 2259 3872
Email: a49@a49.com
www.a49.com

Interior Architects 49

Services:
Interior design
Interior architecture
Interior renovation

Contacts:
Theeranuj Karnasuta Wongwaisayawan
Archanart Kespayak

Address:
81 Sukhumvit 26
Bangkok 10110
Thailand

Tel: +66 (0) 2259 3533
Fax: +66 (0) 2661 2186
Email: ia49@ia49.com
www.ia49.com

Branch Offices

Architects 49 International

Contacts:
Pichai Wongwaisayawan
Somkiat Lochindapong

Address:
81 Sukhumvit 26
Bangkok 10110
Thailand

Tel: +66 (0) 2260 9445
Fax: +66 (0) 2259 9448
Email: a49international@a49.com
www.a49.com

Architects 49 (Abu Dhabi)

Contacts:
Pichai Wongwaisayawan
Maythin Chantra-ou-rai

Address:
P.O. Box 128178
Abu Dhabi
United Arab Emirates

Tel: +971 (2) 6768292
Fax: +971 (2) 6768115
Email: a49international@a49.com
www.a49.com

Landscape Architects 49

Services:
Landscape architecture
Site planning
Urban design

Contacts:
Predapond Bandityanond
Arrak Ouiyamaphan

Address:
81 Sukhumvit 26
Bangkok 10110
Thailand

Tel: +66 (0) 2661 2618, +66 (0) 2661 4947
Fax: +66 (0) 2661 1422
Email: L49@49group.com
www.49group.com

Architects 49 (Chiang Mai)

Contacts:
Karnchit Punyakanok
Viyada Charoensook Wongwigkarn

Address:
49/19 Huay Kaew Road
Changpuek, Muang District
Chiang Mai 50300
Thailand

Tel: + 66 (0) 5322 0158
Fax: + 66 (0) 5322 0157
Email: a49chiangmai@a49.com
www.a49.com

Architects 49 (Phuket)

Contacts:
Chana Sumpalung
Nitis Sthapitanonda

Address:
77 Deebuk Road,
Taladnua, Muang District,
Phuket 83000
Thailand

Tel: +66 (0) 7621 3949
Fax: +66 (0) 7621 3804
Email: a49phuket@a49.com
www.a49.com

Graphic 49

Services:
Environmental graphic design
Corporate identity design
Printing design

Contacts:
Krissana Tanatanit
Nattaya Chaiwanakupt

Address:
81 Sukhumvit 26
Bangkok 10110
Thailand

Tel: +66 (0) 2259 3863, +66 (0) 2259 7707
Fax +66 (0) 2259 3872
Email: g49@49group.com
www.49group.com

49 Lighting Design Consultants

Services:
Architectural lighting design
Interior lighting design
Landscape and environmental lighting design

Contact:
Kris Manopimok

Address:
4th Floor, Richmond Tower
75/9 Sukhumvit 26
Bangkok 10110
Thailand

Tel: +66 (0) 2261 0510
Fax +66 (0) 2261 0511
Email: LD49@49group.com
www.49group.com

Consulting & Management 49

Services:
Project management
Construction management
Quantity surveyor

Contacts:
Thanee Vattanasook
Chaicharn Ungsriwong
Kanit Poncheewin

Address:
10th Floor, Richmond Tower
75/20 Sukhumvit 26
Bangkok 10110
Thailand

Tel: +66 (0) 2261 8263-8
Fax: +66 (0) 2261 8269
Email: cm49@cm49.com
www.cm49.com

Architectural Engineering 49

Services:
Structural engineering
Civil engineering
Foundation engineering

Contacts:
Sayan Phalittagram
Tarn Buranasiri

Address:
8th Floor, Athakravi Building
102 Sukhumvit 26
Bangkok 10110
Thailand

Tel: +66 (0) 2661 4030-1
Fax +66 (0) 2204 1848
Email: ae49@49group.com
www.49group.com

M&E Engineering 49

Services:
Electrical and communication engineering
Mechanical and HVAC engineering
Sanitary engineering
Fire protection

Contacts:
Thana Chatavaraha
Pittaya Vichiraprasirt

Address:
4th Floor, Athakravi Building
102 Sukhumvit 26
Bangkok 10110
Thailand

Tel: +66 (0) 2261 4449
Fax +66 (0) 2261 4447
Email: me49@49group.com
www.49group.com

Architects 49 International

PICHAI WONGWAISAYAWAN
Managing Director

SOMKIAT LOCHINDAPONG
Deputy Managing Director

MAYTHIN CHANTRA-OU-RAI
Director

Somkiat Lochindapong received a bachelor's degree from Silpakorn University in 1986 and, in 1989, a master's degree from the University of California, Los Angeles (UCLA). Somkiat practiced in Los Angeles, with Charles Moore at the Urban Innovations Group, and at K.Y. Cheung Design Associates. Returning to Thailand, he worked as a senior architect at Design i Develop from 1992 to 1995 and at Palmer & Turner from 1995 to 1996. After practicing independently for seven years, Somkiat joined Architects 49 as senior architect. He was later promoted to director at Architects 49 International.

Somkiat has extensive experience in office and residential buildings. At A49, he worked on major projects such as the Cementhai Building Product Center, Tsunami Memorial, and high-end residential buildings. At Architects 49 International, Somkiat is responsible for all overseas projects from Abu Dhabi and Dubai to Kuala Lumpur. Somkiat taught at Silpakorn University from 1996 to 2003, and served as a member of the board of the Silpakorn University Alumni Association during 1999 and 2000.

Maythin Chantra-ou-rai joined Architects 49 in 2005 and was appointed director of Architects 49 International in 2008. He plays a key role as a board member responsible for international and local projects in the residential, commercial, and hospitality sectors. He brings to the business a full understanding of design, contract procurement, and commercial factors. His efforts have helped the practice to expand while also attaining both strong financial results and design excellence.

Maythin's recent work has included commercial high-rise, mixed-use projects in Abu Dhabi, Singapore, Malaysia, Singapore, Vietnam, and Thailand. Prior to his career in Thailand, Maythin pursued studies in the United Kingdom, starting in 1992. He graduated from the University of Huddersfield, School of Architecture (RIBA Dip Arch) in 2001, when *Building Design Magazine* chose him as one of 100 top architectural students. He joined HLM Architects the same year and became an associate in 2004, leading HLM's London office in work on residential, commercial, office, and public buildings.

Architects 49 (Phuket)

CHANA SUMPALUNG
Managing Director

NITIS STHAPITANONDA
Deputy Managing Director

Chana Sumpalung began his studies at Chulalongkorn University's Faculty of Architecture in 1986 in order to pursue his passion for architectural rendering. He started practicing before his graduation in 1991, receiving a Bachelor of Architecture degree with Second Class Honors and joined Architects 49 in the same year. In 1996, the firm supported his continuation of study in the United States. He earned a Master of Architectural Design degree at the University of Florida in 1998, when he was named an Outstanding International Student of the Year. Chana then joined the San Francisco office of Skidmore, Owings & Merrill. He returned to Bangkok in 2000 and rejoined A49. He was promoted to senior architect, and two years later became a partner of A49 as well as managing director of Architects 49 (Phuket).

Nitis received his Bachelor of Design degree from the University of Florida in 1999 and a Master of Architecture degree from Columbia University in 2002. He was awarded the William Kinne Fellows Memorial Traveling Prize to study and travel abroad. Nitis worked at the San Francisco office of Skidmore, Owings & Merrill LLP before joining Architects 49 in 2003. Since that time, Nitis has worked on a variety of projects, ranging from private houses and a high-rise condominium to several resorts and a university auditorium.

Nitis was promoted to deputy managing director of Architects 49 (Phuket) in 2006 and associate director of Architects 49 International in 2007. He has also served on the Foreign Affairs Committee of the Association of Siamese Architects since 2004.

Architects 49 (Chiang Mai)

KARNCHIT PUNYAKANOK
Managing Director

RATTAWUT CHANSRITRAKUL
Deputy Managing Director

Karnchit Punyakanok received a Bachelor of Architecture degree with first class honors from Chulalongkorn University in 1990. He continued his education at the University of Illinois at Urbana-Champaign, receiving a Master of Architecture and Master of Sciences in Civil Engineering (Construction Management) in 1993. Upon graduation, Karnchit joined Architects 49 as a designer, working on projects of various scales and types including private residences, Panyavej Hospital, the Mercy Centre hospice, and Central World shopping complex. He was promoted to associate in 2000 and to partner in 2006.

Karnchit has served the Association of Siamese Architects in various roles, including its subcommittee for the Architect Exposition, in 1995, 1996, 2001, 2002, and 2006.

Karnchit has been managing director of Architects 49 (Chiang Mai) since its founding in 2005.

Rattawut received a Bachelor of Architecture with honours from Chulalongkorn University in 1993. After graduation, he joined Architects 49 as a junior architect, working for four years on projects ranging from residences to large-scale commercial buildings. Rattawut continued his education at the University of Michigan, Ann Arbor, where he received a Master of Science in Architecture (Building and Environmental Technology) degree in 1998. On returning to Thailand, he taught at Chulalongkorn University's Faculty of Architecture for three years. Rattawut then rejoined A49 as a senior architect, later becoming an associate partner.

Rattawut became deputy managing director of Architects 49 (Chiang Mai) in 2005. He also works in the private residence studio at the Bangkok office of A49 and lectures as a visiting professor at Chulalongkorn University.

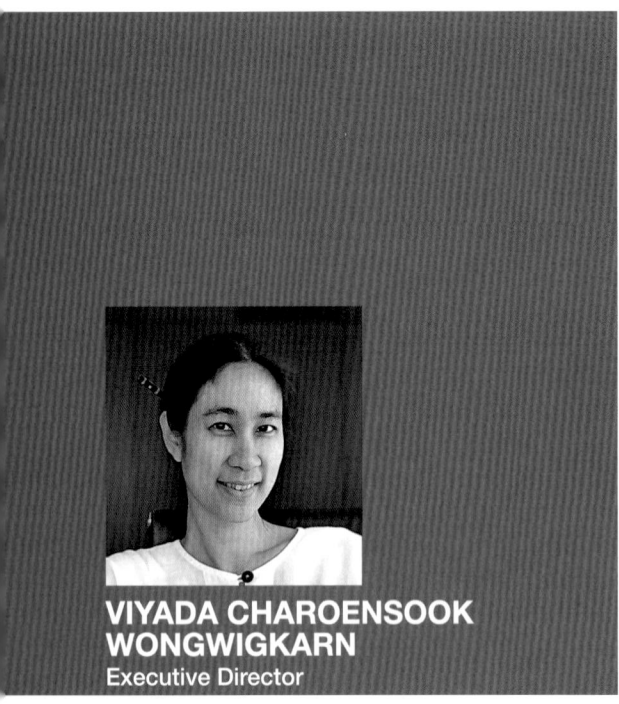

VIYADA CHAROENSOOK WONGWIGKARN
Executive Director

SAWAPAT CHAIYARERK
Executive Director

Viyada Charoensook Wongwigkarn received a Bachelor of Architecture with honors from Chulalongkorn University in 1988. She joined Architects 49 in the same year. Continuing her education in the United States, she received a Master of Architecture degree from the University of Colorado, Denver in 1991. Upon graduation, Viyada worked as a trainee at Bennett Wagner and Grody in Denver. When she returned to Bangkok, she joined Wave Development, a leading property firm. She later became design director and partner at Axis Graphic Limited, where she worked for seven years. She won an award in an emblem design competition for the 50th anniversary celebrations of H.M. King Bhumibol's accession to the throne.

Viyada moved to Chiang Mai in 1999, becoming a lecturer at Chiang Mai University's Faculty of Architecture and head of its undergraduate program. She joined Architects 49 (Chiang Mai) as a founding member in 2005.

Sawapat Chaiyarerk received a Bachelor of Architecture degree from Chulalongkorn University in 1993. After graduation, she worked as a project coordinator on the Sin Sathorn Tower. In 1995, she joined Architects 49, leaving two years later to move to Chiang Mai, where she worked as a freelancer. She was an art director, location manager for many production houses, and a project coordinator for Chiang Mai's Oriental Dhara Dhevi Hotel. In 2005, Sawapat joined Architects 49 (Chiang Mai) as executive director

Interior Architects 49

THEERANUJ KARNASUTA WONGWAISAYAWAN
Managing Director

ARCHANART KESPAYAK
Deputy Managing Director

Theeranuj Karnasuta Wongwaisayawan completed the undergraduate program in interior design at Chulalongkorn University's School of Architecture in 1986. She continued her studies at the University of Michigan's School of Art, where she won the William T. Carter Award as an outstanding interior design student. While at graduate school she worked with Hobbs & Black Associates in Ann Arbor.

After receiving her master's degree and moving to New York City in 1989, Theeranuj joined Mancini Duffy as a designer, working on international projects such as the National Yokohama Conference Hall, the World Trade Center in Osaka, as well as projects in Manhattan that included the Calvin Klein head office and National Westminster Bank. She returned to Bangkok in 1992 to join Architects 49, leading the Interior Space Planning Department, which in 1998 became Interior Architects 49. She was appointed as deputy managing director in charge of design and today leads the firm as its managing director.

Theeranuj served on the executive committee of the Association of Siamese Architects from 1994 to 1996 and on several subcommittees in later years. She is a thesis advisor for the School of Fine and Applied Art, Bangkok University and a thesis juror and lecturer at the School of Architecture, Chulalongkorn University. She is a licensed interior architect under Architect Council of Thailand as well as a member of the Thailand Interior Designers' Association (TIDA).

Archanart Kespayak received her Bachelor of Architecture degree from King Mongkut's Institute of Technology in 1989 and after graduation worked as an architect at Design 103. She moved to New York to continue her studies at the Pratt Institute, earning a Master of Science degree in Interior Design in 1991. She worked in New York as project architect at Peter F. Poon Architect P.C., and was involved in projects around the metropolitan area including the Christian Church in Long Island, the NBC office relocation, and the New York City branch of the Bank of China. In 1993 she joined Architects 49 as a senior interior architect. She has served as a member of the Association of Siamese Architects and a licensed interior architect under the Architect Council of Thailand as well as a member of the Thailand Interior Designers' Association (TIDA). Archanart now leads Interior Architects 49 as deputy managing director.

Landscape Architects 49

PREDAPOND BANDITYANOND
Managing Director

ARRAK OUIYAMAPHAN
Deputy Managing Director

Predapond Bandityanond received his Bachelor of Landscape Architecture degree with first class honors from Chulalongkorn University in 1985, and a master's degree from Harvard University in 1987. During graduate school, he interned with Edaw Inc. in San Francisco. In 1987 he moved to Florida as designer in the office of the SWA Group. He joined Landscape Architects 49 as managing director in 1989.

Predapond has been a visiting lecturer at Chulalongkorn University since 1989. He served on the Executive Committee of the Thailand Association of Landscape Architects for two years. He won an award from The Association of Siamese Architects for "Home II" in 1992.

Arrak Ouiyamaphan received his Bachelor of Landscape Architecture degree from Chulalongkorn University in 1986, and a master's degree from Ohio State University in 1989. While at Ohio State, Arrak was awarded a certificate of honor for excellence by the American Society of Landscape Architects.

Prior to graduate school, he worked with Group Three Design in Bangkok from 1986 to 1987. Arrak worked in Florida with Edward Stone & Associates before returning to Thailand in 1990, when he joined Landscape Architects 49 as deputy managing director.

Graphic 49

KRISSANA TANATANIT
Managing Director

NATTAYA CHAIWANAKUPT
Deputy Managing Director

Krissana Tanatanit received a Bachelor of Industrial Design degree from Chulalongkorn University in 1987. In 1989, he co-founded 49 Graphic & Publication, which was later renamed Graphic 49. Krissana's expertise covers graphic design, corporate identity, and collateral and printed material design. He created *Thai Design Magazine* and *art4d* and was also involved with art direction and corporate re-branding for the Bank of Ayudhya.

Krissana has served on the thesis jury of Chulalongkorn University's Department of Industrial Design since 1995. He has also been a visiting lecturer for various faculties of art, architecture, and communications at Assumption University, Chulalongkorn University, Kasetsart University, Rangsit University, and Silpakorn University. Since 2004, he has been secretary general of the Alumni Association of the Faculty of Architecture of Chulalongkorn University. Krissana served as vice president of the Architectural Exposition 2008 of the Association of Siamese Architects. He is a member of the Industrial Designers Society of Thailand.

Nattaya Chaiwanakupt received a Bachelor of Architecture degree from Chulalongkorn University in 1993, and joined Architects 49 in that year. In 1997, she earned a Master of Architecture degree with high distinction from the University of Michigan for her major in environmental design. During her master's degree studies, she also attended the University of Copenhagen in Denmark, where she completed studies in urban architecture and interior and product design and won an award for her academic performance and design work.

Nattaya has many years of experience working in the USA on a variety of projects, beginning in Chicago with SOM and Teng and Associates. She received her US license to practice architecture before she returned to Bangkok to join Graphic 49 in 2004. She has led G49 to expand into environmental graphic design using her multidisciplinary work experience, helping the team to win an award from the Society for Environmental Graphic Design, Washington, DC in 2007.

Nattaya has frequently served both the architectural and architectural graphic design professions. She belongs to the Association of Siamese Architects organizing committee, and has helped with the Architect Council of Thailand. She has participated in design workshops and award competitions, and has long served as a lecturer for such institutions as Chulalongkorn University, Silpakorn University, and King Mongkut's Institute of Technology.

49 Lighting Design Consultants

Consulting & Management 49

KRIS MANOPIMOK
Managing Director

THANEE VATTANASOOK
Managing Director

Born in Tokyo, Kris Manopimok received a Bachelor of Architecture degree with honors from Chulalongkorn University in 1998. He later completed a master's degree and PhD coursework in architecture at Yokohama National University, with a Japanese government scholarship.

While in Tokyo, Kris joined Lighting Planners Associates as lighting planner in 2001, before returning to Bangkok to join 49 Lighting Design Consultants in 2004. He has served on the Foreign Affairs Committee of the Association of Siamese Architects since 2006. Kris is a visiting lecturer at Chulalongkorn University, King Mongkut's University of Technology Thonburi, and Mahidol University.

Thanee Vattanasook graduated from Chulalongkorn University in 1975 and became an engineer at the National Housing Authority. Starting as a project engineer, he became chief engineer of the engineering laboratory and later project director. He was awarded scholarships from the governments of Japan and France to continue his studies in the field of building and engineering. During his time at the National Housing Authority, he participated in training in housing and infrastructure in India and other parts of Asia. Thanee also worked on several freelance engineering projects as a structural designer and as a construction management planner for high-rise and factory buildings. After obtaining his Master of Business Administration from the National Institute of Development Administration, Thanee joined Consulting & Management 49 in 1994.

CHAICHARN UNGSRIWONG
Deputy Managing Director

KANIT PONCHEEWIN
Deputy Managing Director

Chaicharn Ungsriwong graduated from Chulalongkorn University in 1975 and began his career in 1976 at B. Grimm & Co., where he was a mechanical engineer responsible for cost estimation and installation of mechanical facilities in many types of buildings.

In 1983, he launched the plumbing and fire protection business at A.P. Marketing Co. as department manager. The firm successfully finished M&E works for several major projects including Bai Yoke Tower and Bangkok's Don Mueang International Airport.

Chaicharn joined General Engineering Ltd. in 1988 as sales manager in the concrete products department, responsible for pre-stressed concrete piles. He was promoted to marketing manager in 1989. In 1991, he joined Consulting & Management 49 as deputy managing director.

Chaicharn was elected to serve as president of the Thai Mechanical and Electrical Design and Consulting Engineer Association from 2002 to 2004. He also serves as an arbitrator for the Office of the Judiciary, Ministry of Justice.

Kanit Poncheewin graduated from Chulalongkorn University in 1980 and started his career in 1981 with the Town and Country Planning Division of the Ministry of Interior. In 1982, he joined IT & Associates Co., where he was responsible for architectural design, construction management, and supervision. He later became project coordinator for the head office building of The Union Bank of Bangkok.

Kanit joined Architects 49 in 1985, handling architectural design and office management. One of his responsibilities in that position included project coordination for the headquarters complex of the Petroleum Authority of Thailand.

In 1987, he became office manager and associate partner of Architects 49. Kanit is currently deputy managing director of Consulting & Management 49.

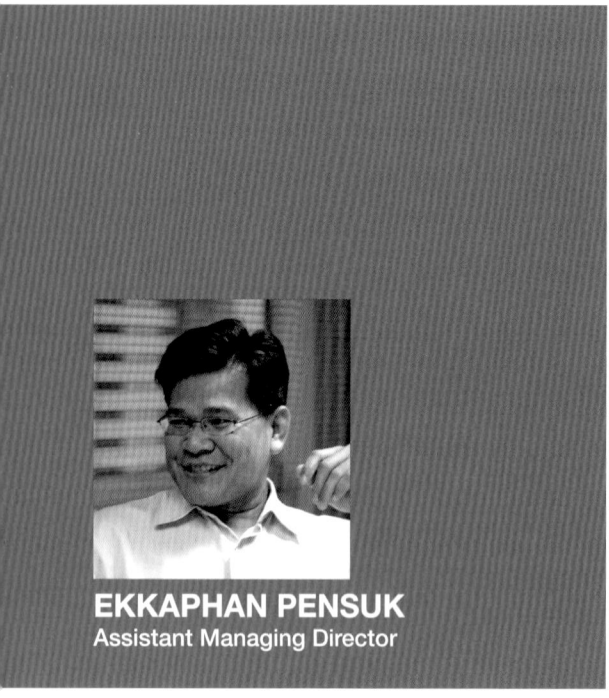

EKKAPHAN PENSUK
Assistant Managing Director

AUNGKOOL VONGPAKDEE
Assistant Managing Director

Ekkaphan Pensuk received his Bachelor of Engineering degree from King Mongkut's Institute of Technology North Bangkok in 1989. He earned a Master of Business Administration degree at Kasetsart University in 2008. Ekkaphan began his career in 1990 as an installation and maintenance engineer for the Hitachi Seiki Division of Saha Mitr Machinery (Public) Co.

Ekkaphan joined Consulting & Management 49 in 1991 as a mechanical engineer in construction management and supervision, continuing through 1996. From 1997 to 2003, he worked for the firm as project manager on the headquarters complex of the Ministry of Foreign Affairs on Sri Ayutthaya Road, responsible for mechanical system design. In 2004 he became a partner of Consulting & Management 49.

A visiting lecturer at Silpakorn University, Ekkaphan has served on the mechanical division subcommittee of the Council of Thai Engineers. He is currently assistant managing director of Consulting & Management 49.

Aungkool Vongpakdee received both his Bachelor of Electrical Engineering degree, in 1987, and his Master of Electrical Engineering degree, in 1992, from Chulalongkorn University. He began his career as an electrical engineer in 1987. Before joining the 49 Group, he held engineering positions at several consulting services, and worked on projects including a telecommunication network, factory, cement plant, and a hypermarket.

Aungkool joined Consulting & Management 49 in 1999 as project engineer, becoming assistant managing director in 2005.

Architectural Engineering 49

SAYAN PHALITTAGRAM
Managing Director

TARN BURANASIRI
Deputy Managing Director

Sayan Phalittagram received a Bachelor of Engineering degree from Chulalongkorn University in 1984 and began his career with Arun Chaiseri Consulting Engineers Co. During his nine years at Arun Chaiseri, he was project engineer, supervising major projects for both private and government clients, and eventually became a director of the firm. He continued his studies at Chulalongkorn, earning a master's degree in 1990. In 1993 he joined Forum Land Development Co. as assistant managing director and later worked as design manager at Unique Engineering and Construction Co. Sayan joined the 49 Group as a founding staff member of Architectural Engineering 49 in 2003.

Tarn Buranasiri received his Bachelor of Engineering degree from Chulalongkorn University in 1995 before beginning a four-year stint as designer at Sindhu Pulsirivong Consultants Co. He furthered his studies at Asian Institute of Technology, attaining a Master of Structural Engineering degree in 2000. He then joined 49 Engineering Consultants, where he worked as a structural designer for three years. During that time, he was assigned to work as principal designer on many projects. In 2003, Tarn joined Architectural Engineering 49 as a founding staff member. He focuses on large-scale projects both in Thailand and overseas.

M&E Engineering 49

THANA CHATAVARAHA
Managing Director

PITTIYA VICHIRAPRASIRT
Deputy Managing Director

Thana Chatavaraha received a Bachelor of Engineering (Electrical) degree from King Mongkut's Institute of Technology Ladkrabang in 1983. From 1983 to 1988 he worked as an electrical engineer at a contracting firm and construction management firm. He continued his studies at Chulalongkorn University, earning a Master of Engineering (Electrical) degree in 1989. Thana worked with Engineering System Consultant Co. in 1988 as a manager of the electrical division, designing and supervising a variety of projects. In 1990, he joined 49 Engineering Consultants as executive director; his main responsibilities included electrical system and M&E system design concepts. In 2003 he joined M&E Engineering 49 as managing director.

Thana served on the Committee for Emergency Light and Exit Sign Standards at the Engineering Institute of Thailand (EIT) in 2001. At the Thai Mechanical and Electrical Design and Consulting Engineering Association, he served on the Electrical Committee from 2005 to 2006. He is licensed as a Senior Professional Engineer.

Pittiya Vichiraprasirth graduated from Chulalongkorn University in 1992 with a Bachelor of Engineering (Mechanical) degree. From 1992 to 1993, he worked as a plumbing engineer at Engineering System Consultant Co. In 1993, he continued his studies at Polytechnic University, New York, attaining a Master of Science in Mechanical Engineering degree in 1995.

After graduation, Pittiya joined the 49 Group as a plumbing and fire protection engineer at 49 Engineering Consultants. In 2003, he became deputy managing director and sanitary section manager at M&E Engineering 49. Pittiya has attended several seminars organized by the National Fire Protection Association (NFPA) and passed the fire protection engineering course at the Engineering Institute of Thailand (EIT).

BUNDIT PLUBNIL
Executive Director

Bundit Plubnil graduated from Kasetsart University with a Bachelor of Engineering (Electrical) degree in 1994. He worked as electrical engineer from 1994 to 2002 and project manager from 2002 to 2004 at Environmental Engineering Consultants Co. During that time he studied at Kasetsart University, earning a Master of Business Economics (Project Management) degree in 2002. In 2004, he joined M&E Engineering 49 Limited as director and electrical section manager. His main responsibilities are to conduct conceptual, preliminary, and detailed design including the preparation of technical documents for tender. He coordinates with other related design teams, including architectural and structural engineering. He also supervises detailed design and construction. Bundit is licensed as a Professional Engineer.

Photography Credits

Except otherwise noted, all photos, renderings, and drawings by Architects 49, Landscape Architects 49, Interior Architects 49

Architects 49

Honda Showroom Ekamai Theerawat Winyarak
The 49 Terrace Wison Tungthanya
Subaru 3S Center Wison Tungthanya
Central World Pirak Anurakyawachon
IMAGIMAX Pirak Anurakyawachon
T.C. Pharmaceutical office Kiattisak Veteewootacharn
Siam Winery Trading Plus Office & Warehouse Pirak Anurakyawachon
K1 Computer Center Pirak Anurakyawachon
S1 Data Center Pirak Anurakyawachon
Bangkok Airways New Office Wison Tungthanya
The Embassy of the Kingdom of The Netherlands Pirak Anurakyawachon
MCOT Operation Building Theerawat Winyarak
MCOT Complex Pruek Dejkhamhaeng
Pipattanasin Office Building Pirak Anurakyawachon
Mae Fah Luang University Pruek Dejkhamhaeng
The Bhumirak Dhamachart, The Royal Nature Conservation Center Kiattisak Veteewootacharn
Surat Osathanugrah Library Skyline Studio
Southeast Asian Ceramics Museum Theerawat Winyarak
Pongthip Osathanugrah Communication Arts Complex Theerawat Winyarak
The Royal Bangkok Sports Club Theerawat Winyarak
The Tubkaak Krabi Boutique Resort Pruek Dejkhamhaeng
Mission Hills Phuket Golf Resort & Spa Chana Sumpalung
Pullman Bangkok King Power Wison Tungthanya
Cocoon Lifestyle Pirak Anurakyawachon
Urbana Langsuan Theerawat Winyarak
The Fraser Suites Urbana Sathon Jaroonrat Withoosuawan
SK 41 Condominium Pirak Anurakyawachon
Athenee Place Pruek Dejkhamhaeng
King Power Complex Wison Tungthanya
Wat Pah Sunantawanaram Skyline Studio
Maharattanaviharnkot Wat Pra Dhammakaya Dhammakaya Foundation
World Peace Valley Pirak Anurakyawachon
Baan Sukhumvit 38 Theerawat Winyarak
Baan Lat Phrao Skyline Studio
Baan Muang Thong 3 Theerawat Winyarak
Baan Windmill Wison Tungthanya
Baan Hua Hin Wison Tungthanya

Interior Architects 49

Central World Space Shift
Ramayana Restaurant Wison Tungthanya
King Power Headquarters Wison Tungthanya
Pullman Bangkok King Power Hotel Pruek Dejkhamhaeng
Aksra Theater Pruek Dejkhamhaeng
House Design Wison Tungthanya (1, 2, 3, 7), Art4d (4, 5, 6), Theerawat Winyarak (10, 11)

Landscape Architects 49

Central World Pirak Anurakyawachon
King Power Complex Pirak Anurakyawachon
Domus Pirak Anurakyawachon
MCOT Complex Pirak Anurakyawachon
Garden Design for Private Residences Pirak Anurakyawachon

Graphic 49

Suvarnabhumi Museum Shop Theerawat Winyarak
Savoury Gastrocafe Krissana Tanatanit, Minchaya Chayosumrit, Choochart Nitijessadawong
Bank of Ayudhya Theerawat Winyarak, Somkid Paimpiyachat
TMB Bank Public Company Limited Weerapon Singnoi
Government Housing Bank Weerapon Singnoi
MCOT Complex Weerapon Singnoi
Central World Office Tower and Shopping Complex Weerapon Singnoi, Theerawat Winyarak, Minchaya Chayosumrit
Thailand Creative and Design Center (TCDC) Wison Tungthanya
King Power Complex Weerapon Singnoi

49 Lighting Design Consultants (LD49)

Wison Tungthanya (1, 3, 5), Theerawat Winyarak (2, 6), Pruek Dejkhamhaeng (4)

Acknowledgments

Editorial Board

Nithi Sthapitanonda
Prabhakorn Vadanyakul
Suwat Vasapinyokul
Pichai Wongwaisayawan
Kiattisak Veteewootacharn
Krisada Teerapongprachaya
Somkiat Lochindapong
Theeranuj Karnasuta Wongwaisayawan
Archanart Kespayak
Predapond Bandityanond
Arrak Ouiyamaphan
Kris Manopimok
Krissana Tanatanit
Nattaya Chaiwanakupt
Karnchit Punyakanok
Chana Sumpalung

Graphic Design Consultant

Graphic 49 Limited

Content Editors

Suluck Visavapattamawon
Natcha Nantakarn
Ruechimon Thanaboonsombut
Panompon Patipannavat

Text Editors

Salyawate Prasertwitayakarn
M.L. Piyalada D. Thaveeprungsriporn

Illustration Editor

Phaithaya Banchakitikun

Drawing Editors

Watchara Chirasatit
Worawodth Wongsakda
Krisada Boonchaleow

Editorial Secretary

Suwanna Punkruawan

Every effort has been made to trace the original source of copyright material contained in this book. The publishers would be pleased to hear from copyright holders to rectify any errors or omissions.

The information and illustrations in this publication have been prepared and supplied by Architects 49. While all reasonable efforts have been made to ensure accuracy, the publishers do not, under any circumstances, accept responsibility for errors, omissions and representations express or implied.

Index

Aksra Theater 284
Alilia 339
Athenee Place 200

Baan Hua Hin 260
Baan Lat Phrao 248
Baan Muang Thong 3 252
Baan Sukhumvit 38 244
Baan Windmill 256
Bangkok Airways New Office 56
Bangkok University Landmark Complex 124, 274
Bank of Ayudhya 340
Bukit Gita Bayu 180

Cementhai Building Products Gallery 98
Central Plaza Khon Kaen 38
Central World Office Tower and Shopping Complex 32, 266, 292, 348
Cheras Residential Development 186
Clover, The 190
Cocoon Life Style 184
CP Lotus Superstore, Super Brand Mall, Shanghai 347

Danet Gateway, The 226
Devarana Spa 336
Dholhiyadhoo Resort & Spa 276
Domus 308

Embassy of The Kingdom of The Netherlands, The 58
Emporio, The 202
Energy Complex 86

Faculty of Arts, Mahidol University 134
Fraser Suites Urbana Sathorn, The 196
Funama Resort & Spa, The 153

Garden Design for Private Residences 322
Gateway Ekamai, The 40
Government Housing Bank 344
Guan Yin Shrine 238

Holiday Inn Express 172
Honda Showroom 18
House Design 286
Hua Hin Boulevard 30

I.P. Trading 76
IMAGIMAX 42

Jumeirah Park Apartments 192
Jumeirah Phuket Private Island 162

K1 Computer Center 52
King Power Complex 208, 296, 354
King Power Headquarters 272
Koh Kood Resort 156

Land & Houses Urban Development at Chiang Mai 224
Logo Design 334
Lonudhua Resort & Spa, The 154

Maavela Resort & Spa, The 155
Mae Fah Luang University 104
Maharattanaviharnkot Wat Pra Dhammakaya 234
Mahavihard Pramongkol Thepmunee Memorial 241
Mahidol University Technology Innovation Center & Main Auditorium 128
Maldives Resort & Spa 152
Master Planning 328
MCOT Complex 64, 300, 346
MCOT Operation Building 62
Mission Hills Phuket Golf Resort & Spa 146

NIKS (Thailand) Head Office 71

Oasis at Mulberry 178
Ocean Newline Office & Residence 74

Peak, The 188
Phuket Renaissance 158
Pine Valley Golf Resort & Country Club 136
Pipattanasin Office Building 82
Poh Teck Tung Foundation 72
Pongthip Osathanugrah Communication Arts Complex 118
Pra Bhothiyanathera Pagoda 240
Prime Nature Villa Hua Hin 312
Prime Nature Villa On Nuch 316
Pullman Bangkok King Power Hotel 278
Pullman Bangkok King Power 166

Rajini School 122
Ramayana Restaurant 270
Red Mountain 174
Residential Compound at Sukumvit 16 318
Royal Archive 80
Royal Bangkok Sports Club, The 138

S1 Data Center 54
Samui Pavilion 182
Savoury Gastrocafe 338
SCG Experience 102
Seri Tanjung Penang Condominium 282
SET Multipurpose Building 78
Siam Square Commercial Development 220
Siam Winery Trading Plus Office & Warehouse 50
SK41 Condominium 198
So Bangkok 280
Sofitel Patong 150
Southeast Asian Ceramics Museum 114
Subaru 3S Center 26
Surat Osathanugrah Library 110
Suvarnabhumi Museum Shop 337

T.C. Pharmaceutical Office 44
TALA 2007 302
Thai Red Cross Society Museum, The 92
Thailand Creative and Design Center (TCDC) 352
Thailand Cultural Center 94
The 49 Terrace 22
The Bhumirak Dhamachart, The Royal Nature Conservation Center 108
Thu Thiem New Urban Area 230
TMB Bank 342
Tubkaak Krabi Boutique Resort, The 140, 304

Urbana Langsuan 194

Wat Pa Sunantawanaram Pagoda 240
Wat Pa Sunantawanaram 232
Wat Pah Nikhotharam Pagoda 241
Waterfront Development at Khlong Toei 222
Wireless Road Project 204
World Peace Valley 236